DAIRY SCIENCE AND TECHNOLOGY

Ajay Kapoor

Vishvabharti Publications

NEW DELHI - 110 002

First Edition 2005

ISBN 81-89000-46-2

Published by:
Vishvabharti Publications
4378/4B Ansari Road, Daryaganj,
New Delhi-110 002
Ph.: 011 - 23285119

Laser Typeset by:
Graphic Era, Delhi-92

Printed at:
Tarun Offset Printers,
Maujpur, Shahdara,
Delhi - 110 053

PREFACE

In many countries a dairy is a facility for the extraction and processing of animal milk (mostly from cows, sometimes from buffaloes or goats) for human consumption. The end product of such processes are known as dairy products. A dairy farm produces milk and a dairy factory processes it.

People milked cows by hand, in some countries small numbers of cows are still milked by hand. Hand-milking is accomplished by grasping the teats (tits) in the hand and expressing milk by either squeezing the fingers, progressively, from the udder end to the tip or by squeezing the teat between thumb and index finger then moving the hand downward from udder towards the end of the teat.

In early times the cow, or cows, would stand in the field or paddock while being milked. Young stock, heifers, would have to be trained to remain still to be milked. In many countries the cows were tethered to a post and milked. The problem with this method is that it still relies on quiet animals because the milking end of the cow is not restrained.

When it became necessary to milk larger numbers of cows especially in such as New Zealand and Australia where the cows are out in the open all year round the cows would be brought to a shed or barn that was set up with bails where the cows could be held from moving about while they were milked. One person could milk more cows this way, as many as 20 for a good milker. It makes no difference whether one milks 10 or 1000 cows, the milking time should not exceed a total of about three hours each day for any cow.

As herd sizes increased, or as machine-milking became more common and larger herd sizes were possible, there was more need to have efficient milking machines, milking sheds, milk-storage facilities (vats), shed cleaning capabilities and the means of getting cows from paddock to shed and back. Farmers, early, found that cows would abandon their grazing area and walk towards the milking area when the time came for milking. This is not surprising really as, in the flush of the milking season, cows must get very uncomfortable with udders full of milk and the place of relief for them is the milking shed.

While preparing the text of this book, I received active cooperation, moral support and miscellaneous assistance from various quarters. My colleagues, friends and well wishers deserve all appreciation for motivating me to undertake this projec. I owe a deep sense of gratitude to all of them. Any suggestions for the improvement of the book are welcome and subsequently added in the revised edition.

Ajay Kapoor

Contents

1

DAIRY PROCESSING

When it became necessary to milk larger numbers of cows ,the cows would be brought to a shed or barn that was set up with bails (stalls) where the cows could be held from moving about while they were milked. One person could milk more cows this way, as many as 20 for a good milker. But having cows standing about in yard and shed waiting to be milked is not good for the cow as she needs as much time in the paddock, grazing, as is possible. It is usual to restrict the twice-daily milking to a maximum of an hour and a half each time. It makes no difference whether one milks 10 or 1000 cows, the milking time should not exceed a total of about three hours each day for any cow.

As herd sizes increased, or as machine-milking became more common and larger herd sizes were possible, there was more need to have efficient milking machines, milking sheds, milk-storage facilities (vats), shed cleaning capabilities and the means of getting cows from paddock to shed and back. Farmers, early, found that cows would abandon their grazing area and walk towards the milking area when the time came for milking. This is not surprising really as, in the flush of the milking season, cows must get very uncomfortable with udders full of milk and the place of relief for them is the milking shed.

As herd numbers increased so did the problems of animal health. The first was improved veterinary medicines that the farmer could use (and the government regulation of the medicines). The second was the generation of veterinary clubs where groups of farmers would employ a veterinarian full-time and share those services throughout the year. It was in the veterinarian's interest to keep the animals healthy and reduce the number of calls from farmers, rather than to ensure that the farmer needed to call for service and pay regularly.

One of the concerns for dairy farmers is the need to milk cows with absolute regularity twice a day. This twice-a-day milking goes on for about 300 to 320 days per year that the cow stays in milk. Some small herds are milked once a day for about the last 20 days of the production cycle but this is not usual for large herds. If a cow is left unmilked just once she is likely to reduce milk-production almost immediately and the rest of the season may see her dried off (giving no milk) and still consuming feed for no production.

Farmers who are contracted to supply whole milk for human consumption often have to manage their herd so that the contracted number of cows are in milk the year round, or the required minimum milk output is maintained. This is done by mating cows outside their natural mating time so that the period when each cow in the herd is giving maximum production is in rotation throughout the year. Northern hemisphere farmers who keep cows in barns almost all the year usually manage their herds to give continuous production of milk so that they get paid all year round. In the southern hemisphere the cooperative dairying systems allow for two months on no productivity because their systems are designed to take advantage of maximum milk production in the spring and because the milk processing plants pay bonuses in the dry season to carry the farmers through the mid-winter. Some year-round milk farms are penalised financially for over-production at any time in the year. Artificial insemination is common in all high-production herds.

Simple dairying

When few cows were kept, up to about the beginning of the 20th century, the milk was usually consumed by the family keeping the cow(s). When people wanted cream, or butter, they would place the milk in a shallow pan in a cool part of their house-the "dairy"-and allow the butterfat portion of the milk to rise to the surface. After a day or so, usually in the cool of the morning the surface of the milk was skimmed to remove the cream. The cream could then be churned so that the particles of butterfat would coagulate in the form of butter, leaving buttermilk. Butter is used as a spread on bread, as a cooking fat, as an addition to baked food such as cakes, as a shortning agent for pastries and a thickening in sauces and rues. It can also be purified and used as a heating and lighting oil.

When cheese is to be made the milk it is bought to the right temperature in a vat and then some form of "starter" (rennet, acid or bacteria, see skim milk below) is added to make curds set. The curds are removed and set in moulds or trays (depending on the cheese) and the excess whey is drained. The cheese may be compressed and the exterior may be treated with a variety of preparations to hasten curing or to form a rind. After the required storage and processing the cheese is usually sold, or consumed by the family.

In some countries this sort of family production is still the norm and the products made from milk vary widely depending on the animal that is milked and the traditional ways of consuming the products made from the milk. For example, today, butter is made in Tibet mainly for candles in monastries. Desert people still process camel milk in goat-skin bags hung off the side of the camel and using the gait of the beast to process the milk.

INDUSTRIAL PRODUCTION

Cream and butter

Today, industrially, milk is separated by large machines in bulk. The cream is processed and reduced variously to produce consumer products with varying names depending on the thickness of the cream and its suitability for uses in the kitchen in various countries. Some cream is dried and powdered, some is condensed (by evaporation) and mixed with varying amounts of sugar and canned. Most cream from New Zealand and Australian factories is made into butter. This is done by churning the cream until the fat globules coagulate and form a monolithic mass. The butter mass is washed and, sometimes, salted to improve keeping qualities. The residual buttermilk goes on to further processing. The butter is packaged (25 to 50 kg boxes) and chilled for storage and sale. At a later stage these packages are broken down into home-consumption sized packs. Butter sells for about US$2200 a tonne on the international market.

Milk

Milk most often means the nutrient fluid produced by the mammary glands of female mammals. It provides the primary source of nutrition for newborns, before they are able to digest more diverse foods. It is also processed into dairy products such as cream, butter, yoghurt, ice-cream, gelato, cheese, casein, lactose, dried milk, and many other food-additive and industrial products.

It can also be used to mean

- the white juice and the processed meat of the coconut in, more or less, liquid form, used especially in Thai, Indian (Keralan), and Polynesian cuisine.
- a non-animal substitute such as soya milk, rice milk, and almond milk.

Human milk is often fed to infants through breastfeeding, either directly or by the female expressing her milk to be saved and fed later. As colostrum, it carries the mother's antibodies and intestinal bacteria to the baby.

Composition and nutrition

The composition of milk varies greatly among different mammals.

- Human breast milk is thin and high in lactose, its primary sugar.
- Cow's milk, in contrast, is lower in sugar and higher in protein, and is composed of about 3.5% to 6.5% milkfat, 4% to 8.5% milk solids and about 88% water. Its main protein (80%) is casein.

Lactose in milk is digested with the help of the enzyme lactase produced by the bodies of infants. In humans, production of lactase falls off towards adulthood (depending on the person's ethnic origin), in many cases to the point where lactose becomes indigestible, leading to lactose intolerance a gastrointestinal condition that afflicts many.

There is some controversy over whether consumption of cow's milk is good for adult humans. While milk is often touted as healthy for its significant amount of calcium, required for healthy bone growth and nerve function, there is some disputed research to suggest that proteins in milk interfere with the use of its calcium to form bones by increasing the acidity level of the blood and triggering a response which balances that acidity level by leeching calcium that is presently in bones. However breeds of cattle produce milk that is significantly different from that of others as do different mammals' from others. Such factors as the lactose content, the proportion of and size of the butterfat globule and the strength of the curd, formed by the human enzymes digesting the milk, can differ from breed to breed and mammal to mammal.

Milk has also been linked in a small number of studies to osteoporosis, cancer, heart disease, obesity and high blood pressure yet in countries where dairy products are plentiful and cheap, New Zealand and Australia, have no particular indications of those diseases.

Cow's milk

Cow's milk is produced on an industrial scale for human consumption.

Varieties and brands

Cow's milk is generally available in several varieties. In some countries these are:

- full cream (or "whole" in North America)
- semi-skimmed ("reduced fat" or "low fat", about 1.5-1.8% fat)
- skimmed (about 0.1% fat)

Milk in the world is sold as

- "whole" varieties
- "2 percent" (reduced fat)

- "1 percent" (low fat)
- "1/2 percent" (low fat)
- "skim" (very low fat)

Full cream, or whole milk, has the full milk fat content (about 3-4% if Friesian- or Holstein-breed are the source). For skimmed or semi-skimmed milk, all of the fat content is removed and then some (in the case of semi-skimmed milk) is returned.

The best-selling variety of milk is semi-skimmed; in some countries full-cream (whole) milk is generally seen as less healthy and skimmed milk is often thought to lack taste.

Whole milk is recommended to provide sufficient fat for developing toddlers who have graduated from breast milk or infant formula.

There are many brands of milk, including:

- Alpenrose
- Anchor (a brand from Fonterra)
- Dairy Farmers
- H.P. Hood
- Leche Caparra
- Leche Suiza
- Lucerne
- Parmalat
- Pauls (a subsidiary of Parmalat in Australia)
- Pura
- Shamrock Milks
- Tenuvah

Milk is the state drink of Minnesota and Pennsylvania.

Common milk animals

In addition to cows, the following animals provide milk for dairy products:

- Sheep
- Goats

- Horses
- Asses (donkeys)
- Camels (including the South American camelids)
- Yaks
- Water buffalo
- Reindeer

Curdling

When raw milk is left standing for a while, it turns sour. This is the result of fermentation: lactic acid bacteria turning the milk sugar into lactic acid. This fermentation process is exploited in the production of various dairy products such as cheese and yogurt.

Pasteurized cow's milk, on the other hand, spoils in a way that makes it unsuitable for consumption, causing it to assume a disgusting odor, which alone may induce vomiting in sensitive persons, and pose a high danger of food poisoning if ingested. The naturally-occurring lactic acid bacteria in raw milk, under suitable conditions, quickly produce large amounts of lactic acid. The ensuing acidity in turn prevents other germs from growing, or slows their growth significantly. Through pasteurization, however, these lactic acid bacteria are mostly destroyed, which means that other germs can grow unfettered and thus cause decomposition.

In order to prevent spoilage, milk can be kept refrigerated and stored between 1 and 4 Celsius. The spoilage of milk can be forestalled by using ultra-high temperature (UHT) treatment; milk so treated can be stored unrefrigerated for several months until opened. Sterilized milk, which is heated for a much longer period of time, will last even longer, but also lose more nutrients and assume a still different taste. The most durable form of milk is milk powder which is produced from milk by removing almost all water.

Distribution

Glass milk bottles used for home delivery service. Prior to the widespread use of plastics, milk was usually commercially distributed to consumers in glass bottles. In the UK, milk can be delivered daily by a milk man who travels round his local milk round on an electric milk float, although this is becoming less popular as a result of supermarkets selling milk at cheaper prices. In New Zealand in some urban areas milk is still delivered to customers' homes.

Glass containers are rare these days and most people purchase milk in plastic jugs or bags or in waxed-paper cartons. Ultraviolet light from fluorescent lighting can destroy some of the proteins in milk, so many companies that once distributed milk in transparent or highly translucent vessels are starting to use thicker materials that block the harmful rays. Many people feel that such "UV protected" milk tastes better. But few people have ever tasted fresh, unprocessed, milk straight from the cow.

In 1856 Gail Borden was granted a patent for his method of condensing, or removing the bulk of the water from, milk. Prior to that development, milk could only be kept fresh for a few days and so was only available in the immediate vicinety of a cow. While returning from a trip to England in 1851, Borden was devastated by the death of several children, apparently due to poor milk from shipboard cows. Without benefit of more than a year of school, following a wake of failures both of his own and others, Borden was inspired by the vacuum pan he had seen used by Sharkers to condense fruit juice and was at last able to reduce milk without scorching or curdling it. Even then, his first two factorys failed and only the third, in Wassaic, New York, produced a usable milk derivative; long lasting without refigeration.

Probably of equal importance for the future of milk, was Borden's requirements for farmers who wanted to sell him raw milk: They were required to wash udders before milking, keep barns swept clean, and scald and dry their strainers morning and night. By 1858 Bordens milk had gained a reputation for purity, durability and economy. The federal government ordered condensed milk as a field ration during the civil war and soldiers returning home spread the word. By the late 1860s milk was a major industry.

Skim milk

The product left after the cream is removed is called skim, or skimmed milk. Reacting skim milk with rennet or with an acid makes casein curds from the milk solids in skim milk, with whey as a residual. In some countries a portion of cream is returned to the skim milk to make low fat milk for human consumption. By varying the amount of cream returned producers can make a variety of low-fat milks to suit their local market. Other products, such as calcium and flavouring, are also added to appeal to consumers.

Obtaining of Milk

People milked cows by hand, in some countries small numbers of cows are still milked by hand. Hand-milking is accomplished by grasping the teats (tits) in the hand and expressing milk by either squeezing the fingers, progressively, from the udder end to the tip or by squeezing the teat between thumb and index finger then moving the hand downward from udder towards the end of the teat. And repeat using both hands for speed. Both methods result in the milk that was trapped in the milk duct being squirted out the end into a bucket that is supported between the knees (or rests on the ground) of the milker who usually sits on a low stool to accomplish the milking task.

In early times the cow, or cows, would stand in the field or paddock while being milked. Young stock, heifers, would have to be trained to remain still to be milked. In many countries the cows were tethered to a post and milked. The problem with this method is that it still relies on quiet animals because the milking end of the cow is not restrained. In northern countries where cows are kept in barns in winter, and much of the rest of the year, they are still tethered only by the neck or head, particularly where they are kept in small numbers.

Casein

Casein is the predominant phosphoprotein found in fresh milk. It has a very wide wide range of uses from being a filler for human foods, such as in ice cream, to the manufacture of products such as fabric, glues and plastics.

Cheese

Cheese is another product made from milk. Whole milk is reacted to form curds that can be compressed, processed and stored to form cheese. In countries where milk is allowed to be processed without pasteurisation a wide range of cheeses can be made using the bacteria naturally in the milk. In most other countries the range of cheeses is smaller and the use of artificial cheese curing is greater. Whey is also the byproduct of this process.

Cheese Humor

Cheese is also a slang which refers to body odor (e.g. toe cheese, dick cheese, head cheese, ass cheese).

Curd is a dairy product obtained by curdling (coagulating) milk with rennet or an edible acidic substance such as lemon juice or vinegar and then draining off the liquid portion (called whey).

Curd products vary by region and include cottage cheese, quark and paneer (the latter by definition being curdled with lemon juice, thus qualifying by some definitions as a vegetarian food).

Cheddar cheese curds are popular in Quebec, Canada and in the Midwest of the United States. They are freshly made morsels of cheddar cheese before being pressed and aged. In Quebec, they are popularly served with french fries and gravy as poutine. In the U.S., they are breaded and fried or are eaten straight. There are also many varieties besides cheddar that are popular, such as white cheeses and flavored cheeses (pepper, garlic, butter, lemon, etc). The cheeses themselves are not flavored but rather lightly coated with a powdered flavor, natural or not, similar to potato chips.

Whey

In earlier times whey was considered to be a waste product and it was, mostly, fed to pigs as a convenient means of disposal. Beginning about 1950, and mostly since about 1980, lactose and many other products, mainly food additives, are made from both casein and cheese whey.

Whey or milk plasma is the liquid remaining after milk has been curdled and strained; it is a byproduct of cheese or casein making with several commercial uses. Whey is used to produce ricotta and gjetost cheeses and is used to make many other products for human consumption and as an animal feed.

The whey protein separated from this mixture is often sold as a nutritional supplement. In addition, liquid whey contains lactose, vitamins, and minerals along with traces of fat.

As the most commonly used curdling agent is rennet, neither whey nor curds nor cheeses made there from automatically qualify as vegetarian foods. Vegetarians generally use vegetable-source rennet or lemon juice (or pure citric acid or sulphuric acid) to separate milk into curds and whey.

Cottage cheese is a cheese curd product with a mild flavor. It is drained, but not pressed so some whey remains. The curd is usually washed to remove acidity giving sweet curd cheese. It is not aged or colored. Different styles of cottage cheese are made from milks with different fat levels and in small curd or large curd preparations. Cottage cheese which is pressed becomes hoop cheese, farmer's cheese, pot cheese or queso blanco.

Cottage cheese is eaten straight where it is like the curds of the nursery rhyme food "curds and whey". It is also eaten in salads, with fruit or as an ingredient in several items of American cuisine like jello salad, lasagna and various desserts. It is popular among dieters and some health food devotees.

Cream cheese is a soft, rich, mild-tasting white cheese usually sold in brick form. Cream cheese differs from other cheese in that it is not allowed time to mature and is meant to be consumed fresh. It is a primary ingredient in the dessert cheesecake, and is often spread on bagels and eaten with lox.

According to the food manufacturer Kraft, "Cream cheese originated in the United States in 1872 when a dairyman in Chester, NY, developed a "richer cheese than ever before," made from cream as well as whole milk. Then in 1880, a New York cheese distributor,

A. L. Reynolds, first began distributing cream cheese wrapped in tin-foil wrappers, calling it Philadelphia Brand." The cheese was inspired by the French cheese Neufchatel.

Fromage frais (also known as fromage blanc) is a dairy product, originating from France. The name literally means 'fresh cheese' (with fromage blanc meaning 'white cheese').

It is made in a similar fashion to cheese, with rennet and a starter culture being added to milk. However, unlike cheese, the curds are not allowed to solidify, but are stirred, giving fromage frais a texture similar to that of yoghurt.

Pure fromage frais is virtually fat free, but cream is frequently added to improve the flavor, which also increases the fat content, frequently up to as high as 8%.

Fromage frais can be served either as a dessert similar to yoghurt, frequently with added fruit, or used in savory dishes.

Casein is the predominant phosphoprotein found in fresh milk. When coagulated with rennet, casein is sometimes called paracasein. British terminology, on the other hand, uses the term caseinogen for the uncoagulated protein and casein for the coagulated protein. As it exists in milk, it is a salt of calcium.

Casein is not coagulated by heat. It is precipitated by acids and by rennet, a proteolytic enzyme obtained from the stomachs of calves. The enzyme trypsin can hydrolyze off a phosphate-containing peptone.

Casein consists of a fairly high number of proline peptides, which do not interact. There are also no disulphide bridges. As a result, it has relatively little secondary structure or tertiary structure. Because of this, it does not denature easily. Another effect is that hydrophobic groups end up on the outside of the protein, making it insoluble in water. It is found in milk as a suspension of particles called micellae, which are held together by calcium ions.

In addition to being consumed in milk casein is used in the manufacture of adhesives, binders, protective coatings, plastics (such as for knife handles and knitting needles), fabrics, food additives and many other products.

The isoelectric point of casein is 4.6. The purified protein is water insoluble. While it is also insoluble in neutral salt solutions, it is readily dispersable in dilute alkalis and in salt solutions such as sodium oxalate and sodium acetate.

Some people with autism and Asperger's syndrome are sensitive to casein and gluten. See more at gluten-free, casein-free diet.

Yoghurt

Yoghurt making is a process similar to cheese making, only the process is arrested before the curd becomes very hard.

Yoghurt (Turkish: yogurt), or yogurt, less commonly yoghourt, or yogourt, is a dairy product produced by bacterial fermentation of milk. Any sort of milk may be used to make yoghurt, but modern production is dominated by cow's milk. It is the fermentation of milk sugar (lactose) into lactic acid that gives yoghurt its gel-like texture and characteristic tang.

Origins

The word derives from the Turkish "yogurt," deriving from the verb yogurtmak, which means "to blend," a reference to how yoghurt is made. In Turkish, the word's g, indicates its pronunciation [yaw-ghurt], where the gh is similar to the ch used in loch but voiced.

Yoghurt making involves the introduction of specific "friendly" bacteria into pasteurised milk under very carefully controlled temperature and environmental conditions. The bacteria ingest the natural milk sugars and release lactic acid as a waste product; the increased acidity, in turn, causes the milk proteins to tangle into a solid mass, (curd). Generally a culture includes two or more different bacteria for more complete fermentation; the most commonly used microbes are Streptococcus salivarius and Lactobacillus bulgaricus, although sometimes another member of the Lactobacillus genus is used, such as Lactobacillus acidophilus. If the yoghurt is not heated to kill the bacteria after fermentation it is sold as containing "live active culture" (or just as "live" in some countries), which some believe to be nutritionally superior. In Spain, the yoghurt producers were divided among those who wanted to reserve the name yogur for live yoghurt and those who wanted to include pasteurised yoghurt under that label.

Pasteurised yoghurt has a shelf life of months and does not require refrigeration. Both sides submitted scientific studies claiming differences or their lack between both varieties. Because live yoghurt culture contains enzymes that break down lactose, some individuals who are otherwise lactose intolerant find that they can enjoy yoghurt without ill effects. Nutritionally, yoghurt is rich in protein as well as several B vitamins and essential minerals, and it is as low in fat as the milk it is made from.

Presentation

Yoghurt is often sold sweetened and flavored, or with added fruit on the bottom, to offset its natural sourness. If the fruit is already stirred into the yoghurt it is sometimes referred to as Swiss-style.

Greek yoghurt is made from milk that has been blended with cream to a fat content of exactly ten percent. It is often served with honey as a dessert.

Lassi is a refreshing yoghurt-based beverage, originally from India where two basic varieties are known: salty and sweet. Salty lassi is usually flavored with ground-roasted cumin and chili peppers; the sweet variety with rosewater and/or lemon, mango or other fruit juice. A lassi-like, salty drink called Ayran is also quite popular in Turkey. It is made by mixing yoghurt with water and adding salt.

History

Yoghurt is traditionally believed to be an invention of the Bulgar people of central Asia, although there is evidence of cultured milk products in other cultures as far back as 2000 BCE. The earliest yoghurts were probably spontaneously fermented, perhaps by wild bacteria residing inside goatskin bags used for transportation.

Yoghurt remained primarily a food of central and eastern Europe until the 1900s, when a Russian biologist named Ilya Ilyich Mechnikov theorised that heavy consumption of yoghurt was responsible for the unusually long lifespans of the Bulgar people. Believing lactobacillus to be essential for good health,

Mechnikov worked to popularise yoghurt as a foodstuff throughout Europe. It fell to a Spanish entrepreneur named Isaac Carasso to industrialise the production of yoghurt. In 1919, he started a commercial yoghurt plant in Barcelona, naming the business Danone after his son.

Yoghurt with added fruit marmalade was invented (and patented) in 1933 in dairy Radlicka Mlekarna in Prague. Originally intention was to protect yoghurt better against decay.

Homemade Yoghurt

Home made yoghurt is consumed by many people throughout the world, and is the norm in countries where yoghurt has an important place in traditional cuisine, such as Turkey, Bulgaria and India. Yoghurt can be made at home using a small amount of store-bought plain live active culture yoghurt as the starter culture. One very simple recipe starts with a litre of low-fat milk, but requires some means to incubate the fermenting yoghurt at a constant 109.4 F (43 C) for several hours. Yoghurt-making machines are available for this purpose. As with all fermentation processes, cleanliness is very important.

- Bring the milk to 185 F (85 C) over a stove and keep it there for two minutes, to kill any undesirable microbes.
- Pour the re-pasteurised milk into a tall, sterile container and allow to cool to 43 C (110 F)
- Mix in cup (120mL) of the warmed yoghurt and cover tightly.
- After about six hours of incubation at precisely 110 F (43 C); the entire mixture will have become a very plain but edible yoghurt with a loose consistency.
- If a precise means of temperature control is not available, put the culture in a warm place such as on top of a water heater or in a gas oven with just the pilot flame burning. The further below 110 F (43 C) the temperature, the longer it will take for the yoghurt to solidify; you can tell it is done when it no longer moves if you tilt the jar.

Gelato is a frozen dessert made from water, milk and/or soy milk, combined with flavourings, sweeteners, and a stabilizing agent.

The Gelato ingredients are first pasteurized then super-cooled while stirring to break up ice crystals as they form. Unlike ice cream, Gelato machinery whips almost no air into the gelato, resulting in a dense and extremely flavorful product. This allows even non-dairy gelato to match and sometimes exceed dairy-based gelato or ice cream for taste.

Gelato, also known as "Italian ice cream," is typically made with fresh fruit or other additives such as chocolate (pure chocolate, flakes, chips, candies, truffles, etc.), nuts, small candies, sweets or cookies. Gelato made with water and no dairy is also known as sorbeto.

Gelato typically contains 3-10% fat depending on the ingredients (nuts, milk, or cream would increase the fat content). North American style ice creams contain more fat than gelato, ranging between 16-30% since cream is used. High end ice creams use more cream, whereas high end gelato combines higher quality ingredients with milk, water or soy milk.

Gelato is typically made from a mixture of:

- 1/2 - 1 liter of water
- 200 - 600 grams of sugar
- 1/2 kilogram of fresh fruit or other ingredients
- 0 - 1/2 liter of milk
- 5-25 grams of stabilizer

The exact proportions vary with the goal of producing a product that is soft: neither frozen solid nor remaining a liquid when frozen.

In its simplest form, ice cream (originally iced cream) is a frozen dessert made from dairy products (milk, cream, or custard) combined with flavourings and sweeteners. This mixture is super-cooled by stirring while reducing its temperature to prevent large ice crystals from forming. Traditionally, the temperature has been reduced by placing the ice cream mixture into a container that is immersed in a mixture of crushed ice and salt. The salt causes a change of state from frozen to liquid water, removing a large amount of heat from the ice cream in the process.

Components

Although the term ice cream is sometimes used to mean frozen desserts and snacks in general, it is usually reserved for frozen desserts and snacks made with a high percentage of milk fat.

Typical definitions for frozen desserts and snacks:

- Ice cream Any frozen dessert product with 10% or more milk fat.
- Ice milk Less than 10% milk fat and lower sweetening content.
- Frozen custard More than 10% milkfat and egg yolk. Considered a kind of ice cream because of the high fat content.
- Sherbert 1-2% milk fat and more sweetener than ice cream.
- Sorbet fruit puree and no milk products
- Pop frozen fruit puree, fruit juice, or flavored sugar water on a stick or in a flexible plastic sleeve.

Many countries, including the United States, regulate the use of these terms based on specific percent quantities of ingredients.

Ice creams come in a wide variety of flavours, often with additives such as chocolate flakes or chips, nuts, fruit, and small candies/ sweets. Some of the most popular ice cream flavours in supermarkets are vanilla, chocolate, strawberry, and Neapolitan (a combination of the three).

Production

Before the development of modern refrigeration by German engineer Carl von Linde during the 1870s, ice cream was a luxury item reserved for very special occasions. Today, ice cream is enjoyed around the world on a daily basis thanks to commercial mass-production and the home freezer. Ice cream is often bought in large tubs from supermarkets/grocery stores, in smaller quantities from ice cream shops, convenience stores, and milk bars, and in individual serves from small carts or vans at public events and places. There are even some ice cream manufacturers who sell ice cream products door-to-door from travelling refrigerated vans.

Modern commercial ice cream is made from a mixture of:

- 10-16% milk fat
- 9-12% milk solids-not-fat: this component, also known as the serum solids, contains the proteins (caseins and whey proteins) and carbohydrates (lactose) found in milk
- 12-16% sweeteners: usually a combination of sucrose and/or glucose-based corn syrup sweeteners
- 0.2-0.5% stabilizers and emulsifiers e.g., agar
- 55%-64% water which comes from the milk or other ingredients

These ingredients make up the solid part of the ice cream, but only 50% of the final volume, the remainder being air incorporated during the whipping process. Generally, the cheaper the ice-cream, the cheaper the ingredients, and the more air is incorporated (since ice cream is sold by volume, it's economically advantageous for producers to reduce the density of the product). Artisan-produced ice creams, such as Berthillon's, often contain none to very little air.

There are several popular legends surrounding the discovery of ice cream. Marco Polo supposedly saw ice cream being made on his trip to China, bringing the recipe home to Italy with him on his return. Charles I was supposedly so impressed by the "frozen snow" that he offered his own ice cream maker a lifetime pension in return for keeping the formula secret, so that ice cream could be a royal prerogative. There is, however, no historical evidence to support this legend, which first appeared during the 19th century and was probably created by imaginative ice cream vendors. Ice cream most likely did originate in China, but it is unknown how and when the idea made its way into the Western world.

The making of ice cream was originally an extremely laborious process. Ice was cut commercially from lakes and ponds during the winter and stored in large heaps in holes in the ground, insulated by straw. Ice cream was made by hand in a large bowl surrounded by packed ice. The hand-cranked churn was invented in 1846, making production simpler, and the world's first commercial ice cream factory opened in Baltimore, Maryland in 1851. A big factor in making the production easier, obviating the need for cutting and storing natural ice, was the development of modern refrigeration during the 1870s (see above). The continuous process freezer was perfected in 1926, allowing commercial mass-production of ice cream and the birth of the modern ice cream industry.

The most common method for producing ice-cream at home is to use an ice-cream machine, generally some electrical device that churns the ice cream while refrigerated inside a household freezer.

A less common method is by mixing liquid nitrogen into the preparation, with vigorous stirring. The preparation is spectacular, since it results in a column of white condensed vapor, reminiscent of movie depictions of witches' cauldrons. The result, due to the extreme rapid cooling of the mixture, is a very smooth ice cream containing only small ice crystals. For obvious reasons, such a method is generally only used by physicists or other scientists with easy access to liquid nitrogen, in particular by graduate students. Important warning: As long as the liquid nitrogen has completely vaporized, the remaining nitrogen bubbles are perfectly harmless, since nitrogen is anyway the major component of air; however, the nitrogen used in laboratories may have been contaminated by other chemicals, possibly harmful. Furthermore, care has to be taken not to leave chunks of very cold ice inside the mix.

Soy, Rice and Non-dairy Ice Cream

Soy ice cream and rice ice cream are ice cream made without dairy, using soy milk or rice milk instead. Brand names include Soy Delicious, Tofutti, and Rice Dream. There are a variety of flavors and novelties. A minority of non-dairy ice creams are nut butter based.

Ice Cream Around the World Today

Ice cream today is a traditional dessert in Italy, where it is still mostly hand-made, even if one of the most known ice cream machine makers is the Italian Carpigiani.

In the United States, one of the most familiar ice cream desserts is the ice cream sundae, which came into being in 1881 when Ed Berners of Two Rivers, Wisconsin decided to make a special dish to sell in his store. Berners charged five cents and only served the dessert on Sundays, hence the name. It is also reported that the first ice cream sundae may have originated in Plainfield, Illinois.

Before the cone became popular for serving ice cream, street vendors would serve the ice cream in a small glass dish referred to as a 'penny lick' or wrapped in waxed paper and known as a hokey-pokey. The use of a cone for serving ice cream can be traced back to Mrs Marshall's Cookery Book published in 1888. Agnes Marshall was a celebrated cookery writer of her day and helped to popularise ice cream. She patented and manufactured an ice cream maker and was the first person to suggest using liquid gases to freeze ice cream after seeing a demonstration at the Royal Institution.

The history of ice cream in the twentieth century is one of great change and increase in availability and popularity. Retail storefront outlets developed as chains of ice cream stores, such as Baskin Robbins.

The popularity of selling ice cream in cones increased greatly after Charles E. Menches of St. Louis, Missouri used them at the St. Louis World's fair in 1904. The story behind why ice creams were sold at the World's Fair is that the ice cream seller had ran out of small cups, and without them could not sell anymore ice cream. Next door to the ice cream booth was the waffle booth, the waffle maker offered to make cones out of stiff waffles, and the new product became extremely popular at the fair and was widely copied by other vendors.

Ice cream became extremely popular throughout the world in the second half of the twentieth century after cheap refrigeration became common, and wages became high enough to indulge in such luxury items. Soon there was an explosion of ice cream stores and of flavours and types.

One important development in the twentieth century was the introduction of soft ice cream. A chemical research team in Britain (of which a young Margaret Thatcher was a member) discovered a method of doubling the amount of air in ice cream. This allowed manufacturers to use less of the actual ingredients, saving money. The ice cream was also very popular amongst consumers who preferred the light flavour, and most major ice cream brands now use this manufacturing process.

Interestingly enough the 1990s saw a return of the older, thicker, ice creams being sold as elite varieties.

Recently, globalisation has brought ice cream styles from around the world to various places. For example, Japanese mochi ice cream is now popular in California, even outside of Japanese restaurants and Little Tokyos.

In the United Kingdom, much of the lower-priced ice cream sold, including that from ice cream vans, has no milk or milk solids content at all. Instead, it is made with vegetable oil, usually hydrogenated palm kernel oil. However, ice cream sold as dairy ice cream must contain milk fat, and many companies make sure that dairy is prominently displayed on their packaging or businesses.

Ice milk is a frozen dessert with less than 10% milk fat and the same sweetener content as ice cream. Ice milk is typically priced lower than ice cream and is typically sold as a generic good.

Products containing less milk fat but higher sweetener content are sold as sherbet, and products with no milk fat or dairy analogues are sold as sorbet. Products which use nonfat or lowfat yoghurt or dairy analogues are sold as frozen yoghurt.

Frozen yoghurt (also frozen yogurt or frogurt or frgrt) is a frozen dessert made from or containing yoghurt or dairy analogues. Typically frozen yoghurt will contain low or no-fat yoghurt, sweetener, gelatin, corn syrup, coloring, and flavoring. Frozen yoghurt is typically made in an ice cream machine. Frozen yoghurt both freezes and melts much more slowly than ice cream since yoghurt has a much higher freezing and melting point than milk.

Frozen yoghurt is flavored typically in the same flavors as ice cream, but since it is made with low-fat or fat-free yoghurt instead of cream or milk it has a much lower fat content. Sugar free versions of frozen yoghurt can be easily purchased. Natural "Sugar Free" frozen yoghurt is often flavored with fructose instead of regular sugar.

Although frozen yoghurt has been made for many years, it did not catch on until the 1990s. Frozen yoghurt is served as a low-fat or fat-free alternative to ice cream

Milk Powders

Milk is also processed by various drying processes into powders. Whole milk and skim-milk powders for human and animal consumption and buttermilk (the residue from butter-making) powder is used for animal food. The main difference between production of powders for human or for animal consumption is in the protection of the process and the product from contamination. Many people in the world today drink milk reconstituted from powdered milk because milk is about 88% water and it is much cheaper to transport the dried product.

Transport of Milk

Historically, the milking and the processing took place in the same place: on a dairy farm. Later, cream was separated from the milk by machine, on the farm, and the cream was transported to a factory for butter making. The skim milk was fed to pigs. This allowed for the high cost of transport, primitive trucks and poor quality of roads. Only farms close to factories could afford to take whole milk to them, which was essential for cheese making in industrial quantities. The development of refrigeration and road transport, in the late 1950s, has meant that most farmers milk their cows and only temporarily store the milk in large refrigerated tanks, whence it is later transported by truck to central processing facilities.

Considerations of Size

In countries where small numbers of cows are kept the number of products made from milk are limited-often to as few as two- and disposal of unusable residuals is a problem. But where large herds are common, say more than 50 cows, the economics of making as many products as possible at a central factory is important. Modern milk-processing factories can make as many as 30 different products from milk, leaving no waste and are able to choose what to make depending on the price of any product combination at any time.

Milking Sheds

Milking sheds are the buildings in which milk is exacted from cows and stored until collected for processing. Shed layouts are important to the milking process, to the cow as much as the farmer. For example when steel pipe rails were first introduced as bail rails (replacing less sanitary wooden rails) the farmers noticed a rapid drop in milk production. This was later found to be because of residual electrical currents in the rails caused from leakages from electric motors operating the milking plant. The cows were more sensitive than the farmers.

Milking Machines

Milking machines are used to extract milk from cows for human consumption. Modern milking machines work using a pulsating vacuum to cause a rubber sleeve round each teat to simulate the effect of hand milking or a suckling calf. The same vacuum transports the flowing milk to a local container, usually sized to the output of one cow, or in series with a mechanical pump to a central storage vat, usually refrigerated in most warmer countries. The pulsations of the teat sleeve are controlled by mechanical devices in older machines but modern ones have electronic controls to enhance the milking action.

Milking machines keep the milk enclosed and safe from external contamination. However keeping the milk-transport pipes clean internally is a problem that is more or less solved by adequate washing with chemical solvents and water rinses. Most metalwork in contact with milk should be stainless steel (corrosion-resistant steel) and synthetic rubber is specially designed for milking and milk contact.

Most milking machines are powered by electricity but in many instances there will be an alternative means of motive power, often internal combustion engines, for the air and milk pumps because milking cows cannot tolerate delays in their scheduled milking without suffering milk production reductions.

Milking Shed Layouts

Bail-style sheds- This type of milking facility was the first development, after open-paddock milking, for many farmers. The building was a long, narrow, lean-to shed that was open along one long side. The cows were held in a yard at the open side and when they were about to be milked they were positioned in one of the bails (stalls). Usually the cows were restrained in the bail with a breech chain and a rope to restrain the outer back leg. The cow could not move about excessively and the milker could expect not to be kicked or trampled while sitting on a (three-legged) stool and milking into a bucket. When each cow was finished it backed out into the yard again.

As herd sizes increased a door was set into the front of each bail so that when the milking was done for any cow the milker could open the door and allow it to exit to the pasture, the next cow walked into the bail and was secured. When milking machines were introduced bails were set in pairs so that a cow was being milked in one paired bail while the other could be prepared for milking. When one was finished the machine's cups are swapped to the other cow. This is the same as for Swingover Milking Parlours as described below except that the cups are loaded on the udder from the side. As herd numbers increased it was easier to double-up the cup-sets and milk both cows simultaneously than to increase the number of bails.

Herringbone Milking Parlours

In herringbone milking sheds, or parlours, cows enter, in single file, and line up almost perpendicular to the central aisle of the milking parlour on both sides of a central pit in which the milker works (you can visualise a fishbone with the ribs representing the cows and the spine being the milker's working area; the cows face outward). After washing the udder and teats the cups of the milking machine are applied to the cows, from the rear of their hind legs, on both sides of the working area. Large herringbone sheds can milk up to 600 cows efficiently with two people.

Swingover Milking Parlours

Swing over parlours are the same as herringbone parlours except they have only one set of milking cups to be shared between the two rows of cows, as one side is being milked the cows on the other side are moved out and replaced with unmilked ones. The advantage of this system is that it is less costly to equip, however it operates at slightly better than half-speed and one would not normally try to milk more than about 100 cows with one person.

Rotary Milking Sheds

Rotary milking sheds consist of a turntable with about 12 to 18 individual stalls for cows around the outer edge. The turntable is turned by an electric-motor drive at a rate that one turn is the time for a cow to be milked completely. As an empty stall passes the entrance a cow steps on, facing the centre, and rotates with the turntable. The next cow moves into the next vacant stall and so on. The operator, or milker, cleans the teats, attaches the cups and does any other feeding or whatever husbanding operations that are necessary. Cows are milked as the platform rotates. The milker, or an automatic device, removes the milking machine cups and the cow backs out and leaves at an exit just before the entrance. The rotary system is capable of milking very large herds-up to a thousand cows.

Temporary Milk Storage

Milk coming from the cow is transported to a nearby storage vessel by the airflow leaking around the cups on the cow. From there it is pumped by a mechanical pump and cooled by a. The milk is then stored in a large vat, or tank, which is usuall / refrigerated until collection for processing.

Waste disposal

In countries where cows are grazed outside year-round there is little waste disposal to deal with. The most concentrated waste is at the milking shed where the animal waste is liquefied (during the water-washing process) and allowed to flow by gravity, or pumped, into composting ponds with anaerobic bacteria to consume the solids. The processed water and nutrients are them pumped back onto the pasture as irrigation and fertilizer. Surplus animals are slaughtered for processed meat and other rendered products.

In the associated milk processing factories most of the waste is washing water that is treated, usually by composting, and returned to waterways. This is much different from half a century ago when the main products were butter, cheese and casein, and the rest of the milk had to be disposed of as waste (sometimes as animal feed).

In areas where cows are housed all year round the waste problem is difficult because of the amount of feed that is bought in and the amount of bedding material that also has to be removed and composted. The size of the problem can be understood by standing downwind of the barns where such dairying goes on.

In many cases modern farms have very large quantities of milk to be transported to a factory for processing. If anything goes wrong with the milking, transport or processing facilities it can be a major disaster trying to dispose of enormous quantities of milk. If a road tanker overturns on a road the rescue crew is looking at accommodating the spill of 10 to 20 thousand gallons of milk (45 to 90 thousand litres) without allowing any into the waterways. A derailed rail tanker-train may involve 10 times that amount. Without refrigeration, milk is a fragile commodity and it is very damaging to the environment in its raw state. A widespread electrical power blackout is another disaster for the dairy industry because both milking and processing facilities are affected.

In dairy-intensive areas the simplest way of disposing of large quantities of milk has been to dig a big hole and allow the clay to filter the milk solids as it soaks away. This is not very satisfactory, but neither the farmer nor the processor wants to loose that much income anyway! In most cases it is an original failure of the infrastructure (electrical distribution or transport system) that caused the initial disaster.

Dairy Cattle

Dairy cattle, generally of the species bos taurus, are domesticated animals bred to produce large quantities of milk.

Terminology

A young dairy animal is known as a calf. A female calf which has not given birth to a calf and is less than thirty months old is called a heifer. When more than seven months pregnant with its first calf, a female heifer is known as a springer. After calving, or when more than thirty months old, a female dairy animal is known as a cow.

A male dairy animal is called a bull at any stage of life, unless castrated, in which case he is known as a steer.

A dairy animal's mother is known as its dam. Similarly, a dairy animal's father is known as its sire.

Historical Background

Cattle were first domesticated around 6,500 B.C. Early cattle served a triple-purpose, providing meat, milk and labor.

Modern Times

Dairy cattle are now specialized animals, focused primarily on producing milk. This milk is made into various products, including cheese, yogurt, and ice cream, and is consumed around the world.

Dairy Farms

Dairy cattle may be found in herds on farms where dairy farmers own, manage, care for, and collect milk from them. These herds range in size from small boutiques of fewer than five cows to large conglomerates of 25,000 cows or more. The average dairy farmer in the United States owns about one hundred cows and is about 53 years old.

Life of Dairy Cattle

Dairy cattle are distinguished by gender at birth. Cows are unique in their ability to produce milk, and thus heifers, young cows, are generally considered more valuable than bulls, which are used solely for beef production and breeding purposes.

Most dairy calves are separated from their dams within a few hours of birth. Such separation ensures decreased risk of disease passing from dam to calf and also allows the dam to begin producing milk for human consumption as soon as possible. However, the dam's first milk, called colostrum, is rich with antibodies unfit for human consumption - but required for newborn calves to survive. A calf must drink two quarts of colostrum within twelve hours of birth or its future may be in jeopardy. The dam's milk quickly changes into that most suitable for humans, and within three days after calving, a cow's milk is already on its way to human hands. Most young stock then subsist on milk replacer, a commercial feed additive used to take the place of the cow's natural milk, until old enough to consume more solid foods.

The Bull

In New Zealand and some other countries male calves are slaughtered at two to four days for their abomasum (fourth stomach) for the rennet that is extracted and sold as a curdling agent for milk.

In Europe and North America most newborn dairy bulls will be slaughtered for veal before reaching six weeks of age. Many bulls, however, will be raised as steers and butchered for dairy-beef when about eighteen months old.

A select few high-quality bulls, however, will be raised for breeding purposes. These bulls will generally have excellent conformation, or type (for the breed), outstanding pedigrees and, early in their breeding life, produce progeny that is superior in dairy production.

Herd bulls, or bulls that live with dairy cows and provide direct, natural breeding, will service up to one hundred and fifty cows at any given time. Such a bull will be used in one herd for up to two years before the risk of inbreeding and the bull's increasingly hostile temperament forces a farmer to move the bull to a new herd.

More recently, since the 1950s, artificial insemination has become the way of the dairy cow. Through artificial insemination, fewer than a thousand elite bulls serve as sires for entire generations of calves. Although conception is less likely through artificial insemination than through use of a herd bull, the outstanding quality of artificial insemination bulls has prompted farmers to use artificial insemination nearly exclusively.

The Cow

Dairy heifers are treated most generously by farmers, as the heifers form the farmer's future herd of cows. As a cow cannot produce milk until after calving (giving birth), most farmers will attempt to breed heifers as soon as they are fit, at about fifteen months of age. A cow's gestation period is about nine months (279 days) long, so most heifers give birth and become cows at about two years of age.

A cow will produce large amounts of milk over its lifetime. Certain breeds, of course, produce more milk than others; however, each breed normally used in dairy production ranges from 28,000 to 18,000 pounds (13 to 8 megagrams or metric tons) of milk per annum.

About 70 days after calving, a cow's milk production will peak. The cow is then bred. The cow's production slowly dwindles until, at about 305 days after calving, the cow is 'dried', when the farmer stops milking her. About sixty days later, one year after her previous calf was born, a cow will give birth again.

When kept inside year-round most dairy cows live to be five or six years old before their annual milk production decreases to the point where it is no longer profitable for a farmer to keep them. Grazing cows have a longer lifetime, up to 12 years depending on production that is measured monthly. The cow is then butchered and sold for its hamburger meat.

Recently, certain practices have been enacted to ensure that high quality cows' progeny is more widespread than what is naturally possible. Some cows are 'flushed', where 7-12 embryos are removed from their reproductive systems. These embryos are then transferred into other cows who serve as surrogate mothers. This process is called an 'embryo transfer' and has been used in New Zealand for many years.

Breeds of Dairy Cattle

In the United States, Dairy Cattle are divided into six major breeds. These are the: Holstein-Friesian, Brown Swiss, Guernsey, Ayrshire, Jersey, and Milking Shorthorn.

Dairy farming is a class of agricultural enterprise, raising female cattle for long-term production of milk, which may be either processed on-site or transported to a dairy for processing and eventual retail sale. Most dairy farms sell the male calves borne by their cows, rather than raising non-milk-producing stock. Many dairy farms also grow their own feed, typically including corn, alfalfa, and hay.

Most milk-consuming countries have a local dairy farming industry, and most producing countries maintain significant subsidies and trade barriers to protect domestic producers from foreign competition. In large countries, dairy farming tends to be geographically clustered in regions with abundant natural water supplies (milk is mostly water) and relatively inexpensive land (even under the most generous subsidy regimes, dairy farms have poor return on capital).

In the United States, dairy farming is an important industry in Vermont, Pennsylvania, Wisconsin, and Minnesota, but the largest state in dairy production is California. In Europe, Denmark, northern France (particularly Normandy), and Switzerland are particularly known as centers of dairy production.

Animal husbandry is the agricultural practice of breeding and raising livestock. As such, it is a vital skill for farmers, and in many ways as much art as it is science. The science of animal husbandry, called animal science, is taught in many universities and colleges around the world. Students of animal science may pursue degrees in veterinary medicine following graduation, or go on to pursue master's degrees or doctorates in disciplines such as nutrition, genetics and breeding, or reproductive physiology. Graduates of these programs may be found working in the veterinary and human pharmaceutical industries, the livestock and pet supply and feed industries, or in academia. Historically, certain sub-professions within the field of Animal Husbandry are specifically named according to the animals which are cared for.

Dairy Technology deals with all methods of handling milk from production and consumption and includes processing, packaging, storage, transport and physical distribution. Based on the sciences of biochemistry, bacteriology, and nutrition, Dairy Technology employs the principles of engineering. Its objectives are to prevent spoilage, improve quality, increase shelf-life, and make milk palatable and safe for human consumption.

The foundation of Anand Milk Union Ltd, more well known by its acronym AMUL, in 1946 led to the development of the dairy industry and gave momentum to education in dairying. Before that, there was not even a single college offering exclusive graduate degree programme in dairying. Traditionally it was the part of veterinary and animal husbandry courses. The first dairy science college was established at the National Dairy Research Institute in Karnal (Haryana) which now offers diploma, undergraduate and postgraduate courses in dairy technology.

Educational Opportunities

At present, there are eleven dairy science colleges which offer first degree level courses leading to BTech (Dairy Technology) of BSc (Dairy Technology). Of these, National Dairy Research Institute (Karnal and Bangalore) and the Sheth MC College of Dairy Science (Anand) have been identified as centres of excellence. The Karnal and Anand colleges have established modern commercial dairies with the financial support of National Dairy Development Board (NDDB). An automated dairy plant having a capacity of one lakh litres named Vidya Dairy became operational at the Dairy Science College, Anand in 1994. All operations in this dairy are carried out by students under the supervision of dairy staff and teachers.

The Bachelor's degree course is of four-year duration. The eligibility requirement is a pass in 10+2 with physics, chemistry and mathematics. In most of the States the admission is made on the basis of entrance test common to other agricultural and animal science courses. There are also diploma level courses in the subject. Three well-known diploma courses leading to Indian Dairy Diploma

(IDD), are offered by the Dairy Science Institute (Aaray, Mumbai), Allahabad Agricultural Institute, and the State Institute of Dairying (Haringhata, West Bengal)., NDRI (Bangalore) has a National Dairy Diploma (NDD) course of two-year duration. Many general universities now offer dairy science as vocational subject at the BSc level. Dairying is also available as a vocational subject for the 10+2 level education.

Master's degree courses in dairy science and dairy technology are offered by 17 institutions which include several agricultural colleges, colleges of veterinary science and animal husbandry. The nomenclature of the awards varies viz., MSc (Dairy Science), MVSc (in Animal Husbandry and Dairying). Admission to postgraduate programmes in such disciplines as Dairy Chemistry, Dairy Microbiology. Quality Control is also offered by Dairy Science Colleges at Karnal and Anand which are also open to general science graduates. In the Indian Institute of Technology (Kharagpur), Dairy Engineering is offered as part of BTech (Hons) in Agricultural and Food Engineering and MTech in Dairy and Food Engineering besides PhD in Dairy Engineering and Dairy Technology. Six universities have introduced PhD courses. Annexure 1 gives a comprehensive list of institutions offering courses at different levels.

Career Opportunities

The establishment in 1965 of the National Dairy Development Board (NDDB) and the promotion of the "Operation Flood" scheme by it, gave a great fillip to the dairy industry in India. The spectacular growth of the dairy industry in the last two decades had created various demands for indigenous production of dairy equipment, increased quality standards and production of varieties of milk products. This has resulted in the progressive development of dairy equipment manufacturing industry and technical consultancy organisations and have also given impetus to research and teaching. Such notable expansion of the dairy processing and related industries has opened up vast career opportunities for dairy technologists and engineers.

2

DAIRY CHEMISTRY AND PHYSICS

COMPOSITION AND STRUCTURE

Overview

The role of milk in nature is to nourish and provide immunological protection for the mammalian young. Milk has been a food source for humans since prehistoric times; from human, goat, buffalo, sheep, yak, to the focus of this section - domesticated cow milk (genus *Bos*). Milk and honey are the only articles of diet whose sole function in nature is food. It is not surprising, therefore, that the nutritional value of milk is high. Milk is also a very complex food with over 100,000 different molecular species found. There are many factors that can affect milk composition such as breed variations. With all this in mind, only an approximate composition of milk can be given:

87.3% water (range of 85.5% - 88.7%)

3.9 % milkfat (range of 2.4% - 5.5%)

8.8% solids-not-fat (range of 7.9 - 10.0%):

protein 3.25% (3/4 casein)

lactose 4.6%

minerals 0.65% - Ca, P, citrate, Mg, K, Na, Zn, Cl, Fe, Cu, sulfate, bicarbonate, many others acids 0.18% - citrate, formate, acetate, lactate, oxalate

enzymes - peroxidase, catalase, phosphatase, lipase

gases - oxygen, nitrogen

vitamins - A, C, D, thiamine, riboflavin, others

The following terms are used to describe milk fractions:

Plasma = milk - fat (skim milk)

Serum = plasma - casein micelles (whey)

solids-not-fat (SNF) = proteins, lactose, minerals, acids, enzymes, vitamins

Total Milk Solids = fat + SNF

Milk Structure

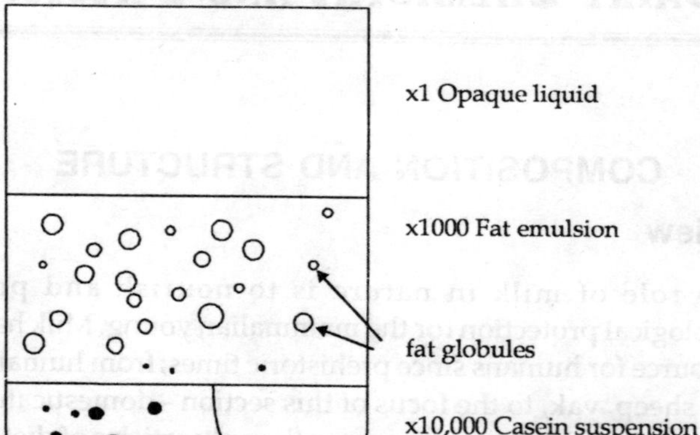

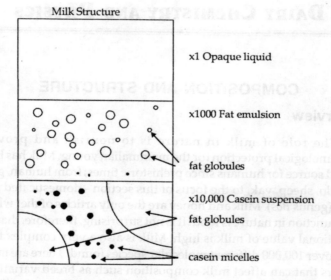

Not only is the composition important in determining the properties of milk, but the physical structure must also be examined. Due to its role in nature, milk is in a liquid form. This may seem curious if one takes into consideration the fact that milk has less water than most fruits and vegetables. Milk can be described as:

- an **oil-in-water emulsion** with the fat globules dispersed in the continuous serum phase
- a **colloid suspension** of casein micelles, globular proteins and lipoprotein partilcles

- a solution of lactose, soluble proteins, minerals, vitamins other components.

Looking at milk under a microscope, at low magnification (5X) a uniform but turbid liquid is observed. At 500X magnification, spherical droplets of fat, known as fat globules, can be seen. At even higher magnification (50,000X), the casein micelles can be observed. The main structural components of milk, fat globules and casein micelles, will be examined in more detail later.

Milk Lipids - Chemical Properties

The fat content of milk is of economic importance because milk is sold on the basis of fat. Milk fatty acids originate either from microbial activity in the rumen, and transported to the secretory cells via the blood and lymph, or from synthesis in the secretory cells. The main milk lipids are a class called **triglycerides** which are comprised of a glycerol backbone binding up to three different fatty acids. The fatty acids are composed of a hydrocarbon chain and a carboxyl group. The major fatty acids found in milk are:

Long Chain

C14 - myristic 11%

C16 - palmitic 26%

C18 - stearic 10%

C18:1 - oleic 20%

Short Chain (11%)

C4 - butyric*

C6 - caproic

C8 - caprylic

C10 - capric

butyric fatty acid is specific for milk fat of ruminant animals and is resposible for the rancid flavour when it is cleaved from glycerol by lipase action.

Saturated fatty acids (no double bonds), such as myristic, palmitic, and stearic make up two thirds of milk fatty acids. Oleic acid is the most abundant **unsaturated fatty acid** in milk with one double bond. While the **cis** form of geometric isomer is the most common found in nature, approximately 5% of all unsaturated bonds are in the **trans** position as a result of rumen hydrogenation.

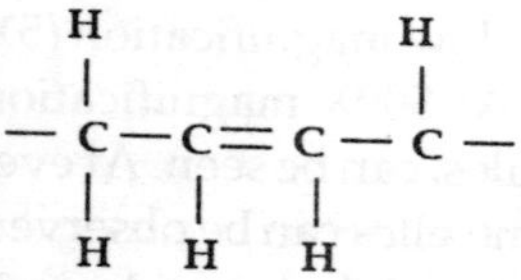

Cis Double Bond

Triglycerides account for 98.3% of milkfat. The distribution of fatty acids on the triglyceride chain, while there are hundreds of different combinations, is not random. The fatty acid pattern is important when determining the physical properties of the lipids. In general, the SN1 position binds mostly longer carbon length fatty acids, and the SN3 position binds mostly shorter carbon length and unsaturated fatty acids. For example:

C4 - 97% in SN3

C6 - 84% in SN3

C18 - 58% in SN1

The small amounts of mono-, diglycerides, and free fatty acids in fresh milk may be a product of early lipolysis or simply incomplete synthesis. Other classes of lipids include **phospholipids** (0.8%) which are mainly associated with the fat globule membrane, and **cholesterol** (0.3%) which is mostly located in the fat globule core.

Milk Lipids - Physical Properties

The physical properties of milkfat can be summerized as follows:

- density at 20° C is 915 kg m(-3)*
- refractive index (589 nm) is 1.462 which decreases with increasing temperature
- solubility of water in fat is 0.14% (w/w) at 20° C and increases with increasing temperature
- thermal conductivity is about 0.17 J m(-1) s(-1) K(-1) at 20° C
- specific heat at 40° C is about 2.1kJ kg(-1) K(-1)
- electrical conductivity is <10(-12) ohm(-1) cm(-1)
- dielectric constant is about 3.1

- the brackets around numbers denote superscript

At room temperature, the lipids are solid, therefore, are correctly referred to as "fat" as opposed to "oil" which is liquid at room temperature. The **melting points** of individual triglycerides ranges from -75° C for tributyric glycerol to 72° C for tristearin. However, the final melting point of milkfat is at 37° C because higher melting triglycerides dissolve in the liquid fat. This temperature is significant because 37° C is the body temperature of the cow and the milk would need to be liquid at this temperature. The melting curves of milkfat are complicated by the diverse lipid composition:

- trans unsaturation increases melting points
- odd-numbered and branched chains decrease melting points

Crystallization of milkfat largely determines the physical stability of the fat globule and the consistency of high-fat dairy products, but crystal behaviour is also complicated by the wide range of different triglycerides. There are four forms that milkfat crystals can occur in; **alpha, ß, ß'1,** and **ß'2,** however, the alpha form is the least stable and is rarely observed in slowly cooled fat.

Milkfat Structure - Fat Globules

More than 95% of the total milk lipid is in the form of a globule ranging in size from 0.1 to 15 um in diameter. These liquid fat droplets are covered by a thin membrane, 8 to 10 nm in thickness, whose properties are completely different from both milkfat and plasma. The **native fat globule membrane** (FGM) is comprised of apical plasma membrane of the secretory cell which continually envelopes the lipid droplets as they pass into the lumen. The major components of the native FGM, therefore, is protein and phospholipids. The phospholipids are involved in the oxidation of milk. There may be some rearrangement of the membrane after release into the lumen as amphiphilic substances from the plasma adsorb onto the fat globule and parts of the membrane dissolve into either the globule core or the serum. The FGM decreases the lipid-serum interface to very low values, 1 to 2.5 mN/m, preventing the globules from immediate flocculation and coalescence, as well as protecting them from enzymatic action.

It is well known that if raw milk or cream is left to stand, it will separate. Stokes Law predicts that fat globules will cream due to the differences in densities between the fat and plasma phases of milk. However, in cold raw milk, creaming takes place faster than is predicted from this fact alone. **IgM**, an immunoglobulin in milk, forms a complex with lipoproteins. This complex, known as **cryoglobulin** precipitates onto the fat globules and causes flocculation. This is known as **cold agglutination**. As fat globules cluster, the speed of rising increases and sweeps up the smaller globules with them. The cream layer forms very rapidly, within 20 to 30 min., in cold milk.

Homogenization of milk prevents this creaming by decreasing the diameter and size distribution of the fat globules, causing the speed of rise to be similar for the majority of globules. As well, homogenization causes the formation of a recombined membrane which is much similar in density to the continuous phase.

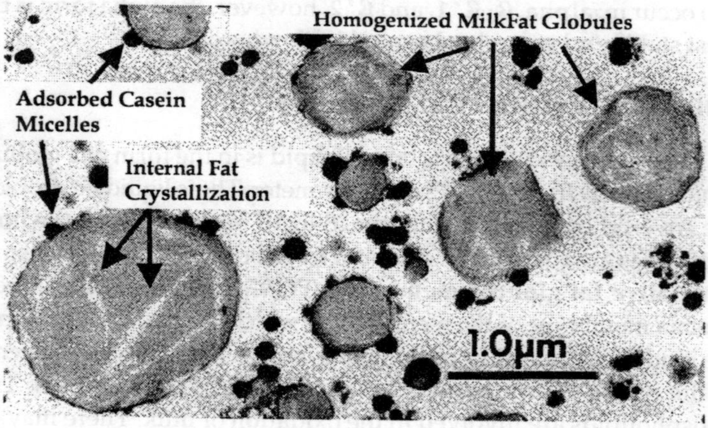

Recombined membranes are very different than native FGM. Processing steps such as homogenization, decreases the average diameter of fat globule and significantly increases the surface area. Some of the native FGM will remain adsorbed but there is no longer enough of it to cover all of the newly created surface area. Immediately after disruption of the fat globule, the surface tension raises to a high level of 15 mN/m and amphiphilic molecules in the plasma quickly adsorb to the lipid droplet to lower this value.

The adsorbed layers consist mainly of serum proteins and casein micelles.

Fat Destabilization

While homogenization is the principal method for acheiving stabilization of the fat emulsion in milk, **fat destabilization** is necessary for structure formation in butter , whipping cream and ice cream. Fat destabilization refers to the process of clustering and clumping (partial coalescence) of the fat globules which leads to the development of a continuous internal fat network or matrix structure in the product. **Fat destabilization (sometimes "fat agglomeration")** is a general term that describes the summation of several different phenomena. These include:

Coalescence: an irreversible increase in the size of fat globules and a loss of identity of the coalescing globules;

Flocculation: a reversible (with minor energy input) agglomeration/clustering of fat globules with no loss of identity of the globules in the floc; the fat globules that flocculate ; they can be easily redispersed if they are held together by weak forces, or they might be harder to redisperse to they share part of their interfacial layers.

Partial Coalescence of Fat Globules

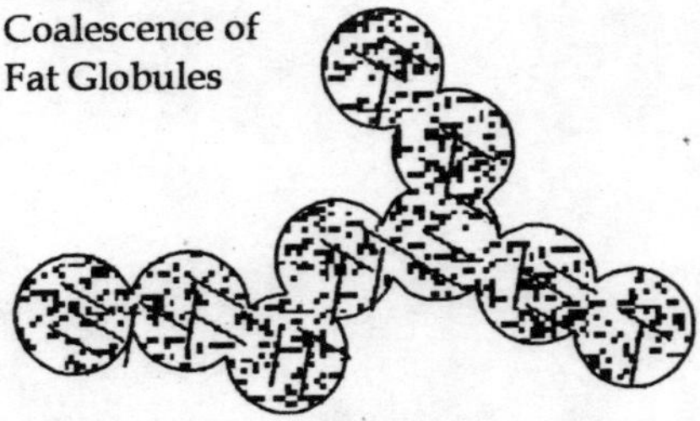

Partial coalescence: an irreversible agglomeration/clustering of fat globules, held together by a combination of fat crystals and liquid fat, and a retention of identity of individual globules as long as the crystal structure is maintained (i.e., temperature dependent, once the crystals melt, the cluster coalesces). They usually come together in a shear field, as in whipping, and it is envisioned that the crystals at the surface of the droplets are responsible for causing colliding globules to stick together, while the liquid fat partially flows between they and acts as the "cement". Partial coalescence dominates structure formation in whipped, aerated dairy emulsions, and it should be emphasized that crystals within the emulsion droplets are responsible for its occurrence.

Milk Lipids - Functional Properties

Like all fats, milkfat provides lubrication. They impart a creamy mouth feel as opposed to a dry texture. Butter flavour is unique and is derived from low levels of short chain fatty acids. If too many short chain fatty acids are hydrolyzed (separated) from the triglycerides, however, the product will taste rancid. Butter fat also acts as a reservoir for other flavours, especially in aged cheese. Fat globules produce a 'shortening' effect in cheese by keeping the protein matrix extended to give a soft texture. Fat substitutes are designed to mimic the globular property of milk fat. The spreadable range of butter fat is 16-24° C. Unfortunately butter is not spreadable at refrigeration temperatures. Milk fat provides energy (1g = 9 cal.), and nutrients (essential fatty acids, fat soluble vitamins).

3

Dairy Microbiology

Basic Microbiology

Microorganisms: Microorganisms are living organisms that are individually too small to see with the naked eye. The unit of measurement used for microorganisms is the micrometer (μ m); 1 μ m = 0.001 millimeter; 1 nanometer (nm) = 0.001 μ m. Microorganisms are found everywhere (ubiquitous) and are essential to many of our planets life processes. With regards to the food industry, they can cause spoilage, prevent spoilage through fermentation, or can be the cause of human illness.

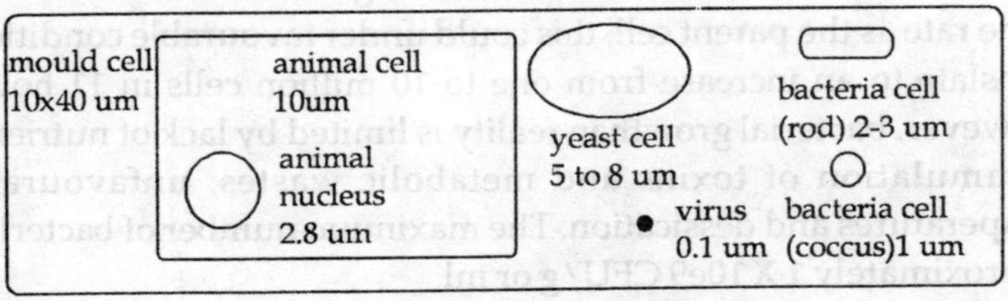

There are several classes of microorganisms, of which bacteria and fungi (yeasts and moulds) will be discussed in some detail. Another type of microorganism, the bacterial viruses or bacteriophage, will be examined in a later section.

Bacteria

Bacteria are relatively simple single-celled organisms. One method of classification is by shape or morphology:

Cocci:

- spherical shape
- 0.4 - 1.5 μ m

Examples: staphylococci - form grape-like clusters; **streptococci** - form bead-like chains

Rods:

- - 0.25 - 1.0 μ m width by 0.5 - 6.0 μ m long

Examples: bacilli - straight rod; **spirilla** - spiral rod

There exists a bacterial system of taxonomy, or classification system, that is internationally recognized with family, genera and species divisions based on genetics.

Some bacteria have the ability to form resting cells known as **endospores**. The spore forms in times of environmental stress, such as lack of nutrients and moisture needed for growth, and thus is a survival strategy. Spores have no metabolism and can withstand adverse conditions such as heat, disinfectants, and ultraviolet light. When the environment becomes favourable, the spore germinates and giving rise to a single vegetative bacterial cell. Some examples of spore-formers important to the food industry are members of ***Bacillus*** and ***Clostridium*** generas.

Bacteria reproduce asexually by **fission** or simple division of the cell and its contents. The doubling time, or **generation time**, can be as short as 20-20 min. Since each cell grows and divides at the same rate as the parent cell, this could under favourable conditions translate to an increase from one to 10 million cells in 11 hours! However, bacterial growth in reality is limited by lack of nutrients, accumulation of toxins and metabolic wastes, unfavourable temperatures and dessication. The maximum number of bacteria is approximately 1 X 10e9 CFU/g or ml.

Note: Bacterial populations are expressed as **colony forming units (CFU)** per gram or millilitre.

Bacterial growth generally proceeds through a series of phases:

- **Lag phase:** time for microorganisms to become accustomed to their new environment. There is little or no growth during this phase.
- **Log phase:** bacteria logarithmic, or exponential, growth begins; the rate of multiplication is the most rapid and constant.
- **Stationary phase:** the rate of multiplication slows down due to lack of nutrients and build-up of toxins. At the same time, bacteria are constantly dying so the numbers actually remain constant.
- **Death phase:** cell numbers decrease as growth stops and existing cells die off.

The shape of the curve varies with temperature, nutrient supply, and other growth factors. This exponential death curve is also used in modeling the heating destruction of microorganism

Yeasts

Yeasts are members of a higher group of microorganisms called fungi. They are single-cell organisms of spherical, elliptical or cylindrical shape. Their size varies greatly but are generally larger than bacterial cells. Yeasts may be divided into two groups according to their method of reproduction:

- **budding:** called Fungi Imperfecti or false yeasts
- **budding and spore formation:** called Ascomycetes or true yeasts

Unlike bacterial spores, yeast form spores as a method of reproduction.

Moulds

Moulds are filamentous, multi-celled fungi with an average size larger than both bacteria and yeasts (10 X 40 μ m). Each filament is referred to as a **hypha**. The mass of hyphae that can quickly spread over a food substrate is called the **mycelium**. Moulds may reproduce either asexually or sexually, sometimes both within the same species.

Asexual Reproduction:

- fragmentation - hyphae separate into individual cells called arthropsores.
- spore production - formed in the tip of a fruiting hyphae, called **conidia**, or in swollen structures called **sporangium.**

Sexual Reproduction: sexual spores are produced by nuclear fission in times of unfavourable conditions to ensure survival.

Microbial Growth

There are a number of factors that affect the survival and growth of microorganisms in food. The parameters that are inherent to the food, or **intrinsic factors**, include the following:

- nutrient content
- moisture content
- pH
- available oxygen
- biological structures
- antimicrobial constituents

Nutrient Requirements: While the nutrient requirements are quite organism specific, the microorganisms of importance in foods require the following:

- water
- energy source
- carbon/nitrogen source
- vitamins
- minerals

Milk and dairy products are generally very rich in nutrients which provides an ideal growth environment for many microorganisms.

Moisture Content: All microorganisms require water but the amount necessary for growth varies between species. The amount of water that is available in food is expressed in terms of water activity (aw), where the aw of pure water is 1.0. Each microorganism has a maximum, optimum, and minimum aw for growth and survival. Generally bacteria dominate in foods with high aw (minimum approximately 0.90 aw) while yeasts and moulds, which require less moisture, dominate in low aw foods (minimum 0.70 aw). The water activity of fluid milk is approximately 0.98 aw.

pH: Most microorganisms have approximately a neutral pH optimum (pH 6-7.5). Yeasts are able to grow in a more acid environment compared to bacteria. Moulds can grow over a wide pH range but prefer only slightly acid conditions. Milk has a pH of 6.6 which is ideal for the growth of many microoorganisms.

Available Oxygen: Microorganisms can be classified according to their oxygen requirements necessary for growth and survival:

- Obligate Aerobes: oxygen required
- Facultative: grow in the presence or absence of oxygen
- Microaerophilic: grow best at very low levels of oxygen
- Aerotolerant Anaerobes: oxygen not required for growth but not harmful if present
- Obligate Anaerobes: grow only in complete absence of oxygen; if present it can be lethal

Biological Structures: Physical barriers such as skin, rinds, feathers, etc. have provided protection to plants and animals against the invasion of microorganisms. Milk, however, is a fluid product with no barriers to the spreading of microorganisms throughout the product.

Antimicrobial Constituents: As part of the natural protection against microorganisms, many foods have antimicrobial factors. Milk has several nonimmunological proteins which inhibit the growth and metabolism of many microorganisms including the following most common:

- lactoperoxidase
- lactoferrin
- lysozyme
- xanthine

More information on these antimicrobials can be found in a chapter on dairy microbiology and safety written by Vasavada and Cousin.

Where the intrinsic factors are related to the food properties, the extrinsic factors are related to the storage environment. These would include temperature, relative humidity, and gases that surround the food.

Temperature: As a group, microorganisms are capable of growth over an extremely wide temperature range. However, in any particular environment, the types and numbers of microorganisms will depend greatly on the temperature. According to temperature, microorganisms can be placed into one of three broad groups:

Psychrotrophs: optimum growth temperatures 20 to 30° capable of growth at temperatures less than 7° C. Psychrotrophic organisms are specifically important in the spoilage of refrigerated dairy products.

Mesophiles: optimum growth temperatures 30 to 40° C; do not grow at refrigeration temperatures

Thermophiles: optimum growth between 55 and 65° C

It is important to note that for each group, the growth rate increases as the temperature increases only up to an optimum, afterwhich it rapidly declines.

Detection and Enumeration of Microorganisms

There are several methods for detection and enumeration of microorganisms in food. The method that is used depends on the purpose of the testing.

Direct Enumeration: Using direct microscopic counts (DMC), Coulter counter etc. allows a rapid estimation of all viable and nonviable cells. Identification through staining and observation of morphology also possible with DMC.

Viable Enumeration: The use of standard plate counts, most probable number (MPN), membrane filtration, plate loop methos, spiral plating etc., allows the estimation of only viable cells. As with direct enumeration, these methods can be used in the food industry to enumerate fermentation, spoilage, pathogenic, and indicator organisms.

Metabolic Activity Measurement: An estimation of metabolic activity of the total cell population is possible using dye reduction tests such as resazurin or methylene blue dye reduction, acid production, electrical impedence etc. The level of bacterial activity can be used to assess the keeping quality and freshness of milk. Toxin levels can also be measured, indicating the presence of toxin producing pathogens.

Cellular Constituents Measurement: Using the luciferase test to measure ATP is one example of the rapid and sensitive tests available that will indicate the presence of even one pathogenic bacterial cell.

Isolation of microorganisms is an important preliminary step in the identification of most food spoilage and pathogenic organisms. This can be done using a simple **streak plate method.**

Microorganisms in Milk

Milk is sterile at secretion in the udder but is contaminated by bacteria even before it leaves the udder. Except in the case of mastisis, the bacteria at this point are harmless and few in number. Further infection of the milk by microorganisms can take place during milking, handling, storage, and other pre-processing activities.

Lactic acid bacteria: this group of bacteria are able to ferment lactose to lactic acid. They are normally present in the milk and are also used as starter cultures in the production of cultured dairy products such as yogurt.

Note: many lactic acid bacteria have recently been reclassified; the older names will appear in brackets as you will still find the older names used for convenience sake in a lot of literature. Some examples in milk are:

- lactococci
- L. delbrueckii subsp. lactis (Streptococcus lactis)
- Lactococcus lactis subsp. cremoris (Streptococcus cremoris)
- lactobacilli
- Lactobacillus casei
- L.delbrueckii subsp. lactis (L. lactis)
- L. delbrueckii subsp. bulgaricus (Lactobacillus bulgaricus)
- Leuconostoc

Coliforms: coliforms are facultative anaerobes with an optimum growth at 37° C. Coliforms are indicator organisms; they are closely associated with the presence of pathogens but not necessarily pathogenic themselves. They also can cause rapid spoilage of milk because they are able to ferment lactose with the production of acid and gas, and are able to degrade milk proteins. They are killed by

HTST treatment, therefore, their presence after treatment is indicative of contamination.*Escherichia coli* is an example belonging to this group.

Significance of microorganisms in milk: Information on the microbial content of milk can be used to judge its sanitary quality and the conditions of production

If permitted to multiply, bacteria in milk can cause spoilage of the product

Milk is potentially susceptible to contamination with pathogenic microorganisms. Precautions must be taken to minimize this possibility and to destroy pathogens that may gain entrance

Certain microorganisms produce chemical changes that are desirable in the production of dairy products such as cheese, yogurt.

Spoilage Microorganisms in Milk

The microbial quality of raw milk is crucial for the production of quality dairy foods. Spoilage is a term used to describe the deterioration of a foods' texture, colour, odour or flavour to the point where it is unappetizing or unsuitable for human consumption. Microbial spoilage of food often involves the degradation of protein, carbohydrates, and fats by the microorganisms or their enzymes.

In milk, the microorganisms that are principally involved in spoilage are psychrotrophic organisms. Most psychrotrophs are destroyed by pasteurization temperatures, however, some like *Pseudomonas fluorescens, Pseudomonas fragi* can produce proteolytic and lipolytic extracellular enzymes which are heat stable and capable of causing spoilage.

Some species and strains of *Bacillus, Clostridium, Cornebacterium, Arthrobacter, Lactobacillus, Microbacterium, Micrococcus* , and *Streptococcus* can survive pasteurization and grow at refrigeration temperatures which can cause spoilage problems.

Pathogenic Microorganisms in Milk

Hygienic milk production practices, proper handling and storage of milk, and mandatory pasteurization has decreased the threat of milkborne diseases such as tuberculosis, brucellosis, and typhoid fever. There have been a number of foodborne illnesses resulting from the ingestion of raw milk, or dairy products made with milk that was not properly pasteurized or was poorly handled causing post-processing contamination. The following bacterial pathogens are still of concern today in raw milk and other dairy products:

- Bacillus cereus
- Listeria monocytogenes
- Yersinia enterocolitica
- Salmonella spp.
- Escherichia coli O157:H7
- Campylobacter jejuni

It should also be noted that moulds, mainly of species of *Aspergillus* , *Fusarium* , and *Penicillium* can grow in milk and dairy products. If the conditions permit, these moulds may produce mycotoxins which can be a health hazard.

HACCP

Raw and end-products may be tested for the presence, level, or absence of microorganisms. Traditionally these practices were used to reduce manufacturing defects in dairy products and ensure compliance with specifications and regulations, however, they have many drawbacks:

- destructive and time consuming
- slow response
- small sample size
- delays in the release of the food

In the 1960's, the Pillsbury Company, the U.S. Army, and NASA introduced a system for assuring pathogen-free foods for the space program. This system, called **Hazard Analysis and Critical Control Points (HACCP)**, is a focus on critical food safety areas as part of total quality programs. It involves a critical examination of the entire food manufacturing process to determine every step where there is a possibility of physical, chemical, or microbiological contamination of the food which would render it unsafe or unacceptable for human consumption. These identified points are the critical control points (CCP). There are seven prinicples to HACCP:

- analyze hazards
- determine CCPs
- establish critical limits
- establish monitoring procedures
- establish deviation procedures
- establish verification procedures
- establish record keeping procedures

Before these principles can be put into place, a prerequisite program and preliminary setup is necessary.

Prerequisite Program:

- premise control
- receiving and storage control
- equipment performance and maintenance control
- personnel training
- sanitation
- recall procedure

Preliminary Setup:

- assemble team
- describe the product
- identify intended use
- construct flow diagram and plant schematic
- verify the diagram on-site

Starter Cultures

Starter cultures are those microorganisms that are used in the production of cultured dairy products such as yogurt and cheese. The natural microflora of the milk is either inefficient, uncontrollable, and unpredictable, or is destroyed altogether by the heat treatments given to the milk. A starter culture can provide particular characteristics in a more controlled and predictable fermentation. The primary function of lactic starters is the production of lactic acid from lactose. Other functions of starter cultures may include the following:

- flavour, aroma, and alcohol production

- proteolytic and lipolytic activities
- inhibition of undesirable organisms

There are two groups of lactic starter cultures:

- simple or defined: single strain, or more than one in which the number is known
- mixed or compound: more than one strain each providing its own specific characteristics
- Starter cultures may be categorized as mesophilic or thermophilic:

Mesophilic

- Lactococcus lactis subsp. cremoris
- L. delbrueckii subsp. lactis
- L. lactis subsp. lactis biovar diacetylactis
- Leuconostoc mesenteroides subsp. cremoris

Thermophilic

- Streptococcus salivarius subsp. thermophilus S.thermophilus)
- Lactobacillus delbrueckii subsp. bulgaricus
- L. delbrueckii subsp. lactis
- L. casei
- L. helveticus
- L. plantarum

Mixtures of mesophilic and thermophilic microorganisms can also be used as in the production of some cheeses.

Bacteriophage

Bacteriophages are viruses that require bacteria host cells for growth and reproduction. Initially, the bacteriophage attaches itself to the bacteria cell wall and injects nuclear substance into the cell. Inside the cell, the nuclear substance produces shells, or phage coats, for the new bacteriophage which are quickly filled with nucleic acid. The bacterial cell ruptures and dies as the new bacteriophage are released.

Bacteriophages are ubiquitous but generally enter the milk processing plant with the farm milk. They can be inactivated heat treatments of 30 min at 63 to 88° C, or by the use of chemical disinfectants.

Bacteriophages are of most concern in cheese making. They attack and destroy most of the lactic acid bacteria which prevents normal ripening known as slow or dead vat.

Starter Culture Preparation

Commercial manufacturers provide starter cultures in lyophilized (freeze-dryed), frozen or spray-dried forms. The dairy product manufacturers need to inoculate the culture into milk or other suitable substrate. There are a number of steps necessary for the propagation of starter culture ready for production:

- Commercial culture
- Mother culture - first inoculation; all cultures will originate from this preparation
- Intermediate culture - in preparation of larger volumes of prepared starter
- Bulk starter culture - this stage is used in dairy product production

4

DAIRY PROCESSING

Clarification and Cream Separation

Centrifugation: Centrifugal separation is a process used quite often in the dairy industry. Some uses include:

- clarification (removal of solid impurities from milk prior to pasteurization)
- skimming (separation of cream from skim milk)
- standardizing
- whey separation (separation of whey cream (fat) from whey)
- bactofuge treatment (separation of bacteria from milk)
- quark separation (separation of quarg curd from whey)
- butter oil purification (separation of serum phase from anhydrous milk fat)

Principles of Centrifugation

Centrifugation is based on Stoke,s Law. The particle sedimentation velocity increases with:

- increasing diameter
- increasing difference in density between the two phases
- decreasing viscosity of the continuous phase

If raw milk were allowed to stand, the fat globules would begin to rise to the surface in a phenomena called **creaming.** Raw milk in a rotating container also has centrifugal forces acting on it. This allows rapid separation of milk fat from the skim milk portion and removal of solid impurities from the milk.

Separation

Centrifuges can be used to separate the cream from the skim milk. The centrifuge consists of up to 120 discs stacked together at a 45 to 60 degree angle and separated by a 0.4 to 2.0 mm gap or separation channel. Milk is introduced at the outer edge of the disc stack. The stack of discs has vertically aligned distribution holes into which the milk is introduced.

Under the influence of centrifugal force the fat globules (cream), which are less dense than the skim milk, move inwards through the separation channels toward the axis of rotation. The skim milk will move outwards and leaves through a separate outlet.

Clarification

Separation and clarification can be done at the same time in one centrifuge. Particles, which are more dense than the continuous milk phase, are thrown back to the perimeter. The solids that collect in the centrifuge consist of dirt, epithelial cells, leucocytes, corpuscles, bacteria sediment and sludge. The amount of solids that collect will vary, however, it must be removed from the centrifuge.

More modern centrifuges are self-cleaning allowing a continuous separation/clarification process. This type of centrifuge consists of a specially constructed bowl with peripheral discharge slots. These slots are kept closed under pressure. With a momentary release of pressure, for about 0.15 s, the contents of sediment space are evacuated. This can mean anywhere from 8 to 25 L are ejected at intervals of 60 min. For one dairy, self-cleaning translated to a loss of 50 L/hr of milk.

The following image is a schematic of both a clarifier and a separator.

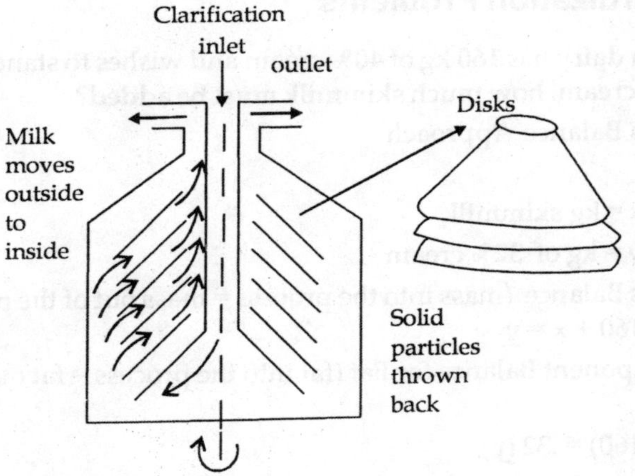

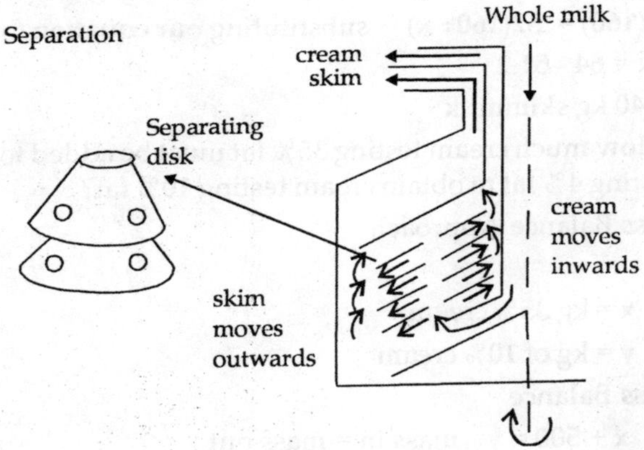

Standardization

The streams of skim and cream after separation must be recombined to a specified fat content. This can be done by adjusting the throttling valve of the cream outlet; if the valve is completely closed, all milk will be discharged through the skim milk outlet. As the valve is progressively opened, larger amounts of cream with diminishing fat contents are discharged from the cream outlet. With direct standardization the cream and skim are automatically remixed at the separator to provide the desired fat content.

Standardization Problems

1. If a dairy has 160 kg of 40% cream and wishes to standardize it to 32% cream, how much skimmilk must be added?

Mass Balance Approach

let

x = kg skimmilk

y = kg of 32% cream

Mass Balance (mass into the process = mass out of the process)

$160 + x = y$

Component Balance for Fat (fat into the process = fat out of the process)

$.40\ (160) = .32\ (y)$

which says 40% of 160 kg comes in and 32% of y goes out

$.40\ (160) = .32(160 + x)$ substituting our equation for y

$.32x = 64 - 51.2$

$x = 40$ kg skimmilk

2. How much cream testing 35% fat must be added to 500 kg of milk testing 4% fat to obtain cream testing 10% fat?

Mass Balance Approach

let

x = kg 35% cream

y = kg of 10% cream

Mass Balance

$x + 500 = y$ mass in = mass out

Component Balance for Fat

$x\ (.35) + 500\ (.04) = y\ (.10)$ again, fat in = fat out

$x\ (.35) + 20 = x(.10) + 50$

$25\ x = 30$

$x = 120$ kg of 35% cream

- Pearson square approach to above problem
- A shortcut for 2-component mass balances
- Place desired percentage in the centre of a rectangle
- Place percentage composition of two available streams in left corners of rectangle

- Cross subtract lower from higher numbers for right corners of triangle (higher number - lower number)
- Use right corners as ratios of two streams

Using the above problem:

Component			Mass
35		6	
	10		
4		25	500
		31	

35% cream $= \dfrac{500 \times 6}{25} = 120$ kg

5

Dairy Products: Overview and Fluid Milk Products

Fluid Milk Processing

Beverage Milks: The production of beverage milks combines the unit operations of clarification, separation (for the production of lower fat milks), pasteurization, and homogenization. The process is simple, as indicated in the flow chart. While the fat content of most raw milk is 4% or higher, the fat content in most beverage milks has been reduced to 3.4%. Lower fat alternatives, such as 2% fat, 1% fat, or skim milk (<0.1% fat) or also available in most markets. These products are either produced by partially skimming the whole milk, or by completely skimming it and then adding an appropriate amount of cream back to achieve the desired final fat content.

Vitamins may be added to both full fat and reduced fat milks. Vitamins A and D (the fat soluble ones) are often supplemented in the form of a water soluble emulsion to offset that quantity lost in the fat separation process.

Creams: During the separation of whole milk, two streams are produced: the fat-depleted stream, which produces the beverage milks as described above or skim milk for evaporation and possibly for subsequent drying, and the fat-rich stream, the cream. This usually comes off the separator with fat contents in the 35-45% range.

Cream is used for further processing in the dairy industry for the production of ice cream or butter, or can be sold to other food processing industries. These industrial products normally have higher fat contents than creams for retail sale, normally in the range of 45-50% fat. A product known as "plastic" cream can be produced from certain types of milk separators. This product has a fat content approaching 80% fat, but it remains as an oil-in-water emulsion (the fat is still in the form of globules and the skim milk is the continuous phase of the emulsion), unlike butter which also has a fat content of 80% but which has been churned so that the fat occupies the continuous phase and the skim milk is dispersed throughout in the form of tiny droplets (a water-in-oil emulsion).

Overview of the Range of Dairy Products from Milk

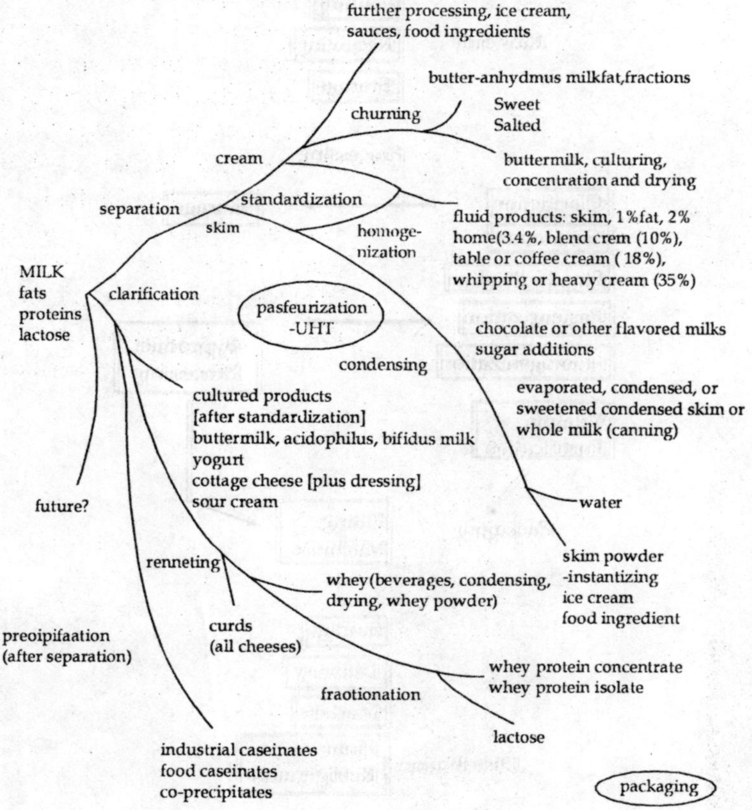

For retail cream products, the fat is normally standardized to 35% (heavy cream for whipping), 18% or 10% (cream for coffee or cereal). Higher fat creams have also been produced for retail sale, a product known as double cream has a fat content of 55% and is quite thick. Creams for packaging and sale in the retail market must be pasteurized to ensure freedom from pathogenic bacteria. Whipping cream is not normally homogenized, as the high fat content will lead to extensive fat globule aggregation and clustering, which leads to excessive viscosity and a loss of whipping ability. This phenomena has been used, however, to produce a spoonable cream product to be used as a dessert topping. Lower fat creams (10% or 18%) can be homogenized, usually at lower pressure than whole milk.

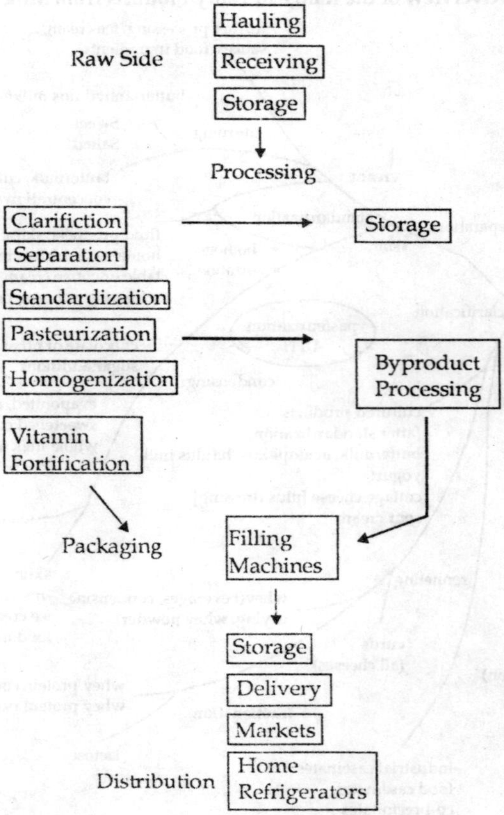

Recombined Milk

Beverage milks can also be prepared by recombining skim milk powder and butter with water. This is often done in countries where there is not enough milk production to meet the demand for beverage milk consumption. The concept is simple. Skim milk powder is dispersed in water and allowed to hydrate. Butter is then emulsified into this mixture by either blending melted butter into the liquid mixture while hot, or by dispersing solid butter into the liquid through a high shear blender device. In some cases, a non-dairy fat source may also be used. The recombined milk product is then pasteurized, homogenized and packaged as in regular milk production. The final composition is similar to that of whole milk, approximately 9% milk solids-not-fat, and either 2% or 3.4% fat. The water source must be of excellent quality. The milk powder used for recombining must be of high quality and good flavour. Care must be taken to ensure adequate blending of the ingredients to prevent aggregation or lumping of the powder. Its dispersal in water is the key to success.

Chocolate Milk

An industry standard for the production of chocolate milk consists of:

93% milk

6.3% sugar

0.65% cocoa powder

0.05% carrageenan

The final product is usually standardized to either 2% fat or 1% fat (meaning, 2.15% or 1.1% fat in the milk before addition of other ingredients). The sugar, cocoa powder and carrageenan are dry blended, and added to cold milk with vigourous agitation, and then pasteurized.

Concentrated and Dried Dairy Products

Fluid milk contains approximately 88% water. Concentrated milk products are obtained through partial water removal. Dried dairy products have even greater amounts of water removed to usually less than 4%. The benefits of both these processes include an increased shelf-life, convenience, product flexibility, decreased transportation costs, and storage.

The following products will be discussed here:

- Concentrated Dairy Products
- Concentrated Dairy Products
- Evaporated Skim or Whole Milk

After the raw milk is clarified and standardized, it is given a pre-heating treatment of 93-100° C for 10 to 25 min or 115-128° C for 1 to 6 min.. There are several benefits to this treatment:

- increases the concentrated milk stability during sterilization; decreases the chance of coagulation taking place during storage
- decreases the initial microbial load
- modifies the viscosity of the final product
- milk enters the evaporator already hot

Milk is then concentrated at low temperatures by **vacuum evaporation**. This process is based on the physical law that the boiling point of a liquid is lowered when the liquid is exposed to a pressure below atmospheric pressure. In this case, the boiling point is lowered to approximately 40-45° C. This results in little to no cooked flavour. The milk is concentrated to 30-40% total solids.

The evaporated milk is then **homogenized** to improve the milkfat emulsion stability. There are other benefits particular to this type of product:

- increased white colour
- increased viscosity
- decreased coagulation ability

A **second standardization** is done at this time to ensure the proper salt balance is present. The ability of milk to withstand intensive heat treatment depends to a great degree on its salt balance.

The product at this point is quite perishable. The fat is easily oxidized and the microbial load, although decreased, is still a threat. The evaporated milk at this stage is often shipped by the tanker for use in other products.

In order to extend the shelf life, evaporated milk can be packaged in cans and then **sterilized** in an autoclave. Continious flow sterilization followed by packaging under aseptic conditions is also done. While the sterilization process produces a light brown colouration, the product can be successfully stored for up to a year.

Sweetened Condensed Milk

Where evaporated milk uses sterilization to extend its shelf-life, sweetened condensed milk has an extended shelf-life due to the addition of sugar. Sucrose, in the form of crystals or solution, increases the osmotic pressure of the liquid. This in turn, prevents the growth of microorganisms.

The only real **heat treatment** (85-90° C for several seconds) this product recieves is after the raw milk has been clarified and standardized. The benefits of this treatment include totally destroying osmophilic and thermophilic microorganisms, inactivating lipases and proteases, decreases fat separation and inhibits oxidative changes. Unfortunately it also affects the final product viscosity and may promote the defect age gelation.

The milk is **evaporated** in a manner similar to the evaporated milk. Although sugar may be added before evaporation, post evaporation addition is recommended to avoid undesirable viscosity changes during storage. Enough sugar is added so that the final concentration of sugar is approximately 45%.

The sweetened evaporated milk is then cooled and **lactose crystallization** is induced. The milk is inoculated, or seeded, with powdered lactose crystals, then rapidly cooled while being agitated. The lactose can crystalize without the seeding but there is the danger of forming crystals that are too large. This would result in a texture defect similar in ice cream called sandiness, which affects the mouthfeel. By seeding, the number of crystals increases and the size of those crystals decreases.

The product is packaged in smaller containers, such as cans, for retail sales and bulk containers for industrial sales.

Condensed Buttermilk

Buttermilk is a by-product of the butter industry. It can be evaporated on its own or it can be blended with skimmilk and dried to produce skimmilk powder. This blended product may oxidise readily due to the higher fat content. Condensed buttermilk is perishable and, therefore, the supply must be fresh and it must be stored cool.

Condensed Whey

In the process of cheesemaking, there is alot of whey that needs to be disposed of. One of the ways of utilizing cheesewhey is to condense it. The whey contains fat, lactose, ß -lactoglobulin, alpha-lactalbumin, and water. The fat is generally removed by centrifugation and churned as whey cream or used in ice cream. Evaporation is the first step in producing whey powder.

Dried Dairy Products

Milk Powder: Milk used in the production of milk powders is first clarified, standardized and then given a heat treatment. This heat treatment is usually more severe than that required for pasteurization. Besides destroying all the pathogenic and most of the spoilage microorganisms, it also inactivates the enzyme lipase which could cause lipolysis during storage.

The milk is then evaporated prior to drying for the following reasons:

- less occluded air and longer shelf life for the powder
- viscosity increase leads to larger powder particles
- less energy required to remove part of water by evaporation; more economical

Homogenization may be applied to decrease the free fat content. Spray drying is the most used method for producing milk powders. After drying, the powder must be packaged in containers able to provide protection from moisture, air, light, etc. Whole milk powder can then be stored for long periods (up to about 6 months) of time at ambient temperatures.

Skim milk powder (SMP) processing is similar to that described above except for the following points:

- contains less milkfat (0.05-0.10%)
- heat treatment prior to evaporation can be more or less severe

- homogenization not required
- maximum shelf life extended to approximately 3 years

Low-heat SMP is given a pasteurization heat treatment and is used in the production of cheese, baby foods etc. **High-heat SMP** requires a more intense heat treatment in addition to pasteurization. This product is used in the bakery industry, chocolate industry, and other foods where a high degree of protein denaturation is required.

Instant milk powder is produced by partially rehydrating the dried milk powder particles causing them to become sticky and agglomerate. The water is then removed by drying resulting in an increased amount of air incorporated between the powder particles.

Whey Powder

Whey is the by-product in the manufacturing of cheese and casein. Disposing of this whey has long been a problem. For environmental reasons it cannot be discharged into lakes and rivers; for economical reasons it is not desirable to simply dump it to waste treatment facilities. Converting whey into powder has led to a number products that it can be incorporated into. It is most desirable, if and where possible, to use it for human food, as it contains a small but valuable protein component. It is also feasible to use it as animal feed. Between the pet food industry and animal feed mixers, hundred's of millions of pounds are sold every year. The feed industry may be the largest consumer of dried whey and whey products.

Whey powder is essentially produced by the same method as other milk powders._Reverse osmosis can be used to partially concentrate the whey prior to vacuum evaporation. Before the whey concentrate is spray dried, lactose crystallization is induced to decrease the hygroscopicity. This is accomplished by quick cooling in flash coolers after evaporation. Crystallization continues in agitated tanks for 4 to 24 h.

A fludized bed may be used to produce large agglomerated particles with free-flowing, non-hygroscopic, no caking characteristics.

Whey Protein Concentrates

Both whey disposal problems and high-quality animal protein shortages have increased world-wide interest in whey protein concentrates. After clarification and pasteurization, the whey is cooled and held to stabilize the calcium phosphate complex, which later decreases membrane fouling. The whey is commonly processed usingultrafiltration, although reverse osmosis, microfiltration, and demineralization methods can be used. During ultrafiltration, the low molecular weight compounds such as lactose, minerals, vitamins and nonprotein nitrogen are removed in the permeate while the proteins become concentrated in the retentate. After ultrafiltration, the retentate is pasteurized, may be evaporated, then dried. Drying, usually spray drying, is done at lower temperatures than for milk in order that large amounts of protein denaturation may be avoided.

6

ENZYMES

Enzymes are a group of proteins that have the ability to catalyze chemical reactions and the speed of such reactions. The action of enzymes is very specific. Milk contains both **indigenous** and **exogenous** enzymes. Exogenous enzymes mainly consist of heat-stable enzymes produced by psychrotrophic bacteria: lipases, and proteinases. There are many indigenous enzymes that have been isolated from milk. The most significant group are the hydrolases:

- lipoprotein lipase
- plasmin
- alkaline phosphatase

Lipoprotein lipase (LPL): A lipase enzyme splits fats into glycerol and free fatty acids. This enzyme is found mainly in the plasma in association with casein micelles. The milkfat is protected from its action by the FGM. If the FGM has been damaged, or if certain cofactors (blood serum lipoproteins) are present, the LPL is able to attack the lipoproteins of the FGM. Lipolysis may be caused in this way.

Plasmin: Plasmin is a proteolytic enzyme; it splits proteins. Plasmin attacks both ß -casein and alpha(s2)-casein. It is very heat stable and responsible for the development of bitterness in pasteurized milk and UHT processed milk. It may also play a role in the ripening and flavour development of certain cheeses, such as Swiss cheese.

Alkaline phosphatase: Phosphatase enzymes are able to split specific phosporic acid esters into phosphoric acid and the related alcohols. Unlike most milk enzymes, it has a pH and temperature optima differing from physiological values; pH of 9.8. The enzyme is destroyed by minimum pasteurization temperatures, therefore, a phosphatase test can be done to ensure proper pasteurization.

Lactose

Lactose is a disaccharide (2 sugars) made up of glucose and galactose (which are both monosaccharides).

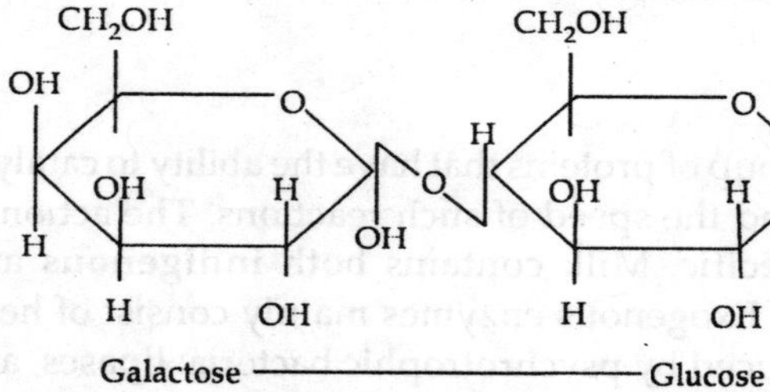

It comprises 4.8 to 5.2% of milk, 52% of milk SNF, and 70% of whey solids. It is not as sweet as sucrose. When lactose is hydrolyzed by **ß -D-galactosidase (lactase)**, an enzyme that splits these monosaccharides, the result is increased sweetness, and depressed freezing point.

One of its most important functions is its utilization as a fermentation substrate. Lactic acid bacteria produce lactic acid from lactose, which is the beginning of many fermented dairy products. Because of their ability to metabolize lactose, they have a competitive advantage over many pathogenic and spoilage organisms.

Some people suffer from **lactose intolerance**; they lack the lactase enzyme, hence they cannot digest lactose, or dairy products containing lactose. Crystallization of lactose occurs in an alpha form which commonly takes a tomahawk shape. This results in the defect called sandiness. Lactose is relatively insoluble which is a problem in many dairy products, ice cream, sweetened condensed milk. In addition to lactose, fresh milk contains other carbohydrates in small amounts, including glucose, galactose, and oligosaccharides.

Vitamins

Vitamins are organic substances essential for many life processes. Milk includes fat soluble vitamins A, D, E, and K. Vitamin A is derived from retinol and ß-carotene. Because milk is an important source of dietary vitamin A, fat reduced products which have lost vitamin A with the fat, are required to supplement the product with vitamin A.

Milk is also an important source of dietary water soluble vitamins:

- B1 - thiamine
- B2 - riboflavin
- B6 - pyridoxine
- B12 - cyanocobalamin
- niacin
- pantothenic acid

There is also a small amount of vitamin C (ascorbic acid) present in raw milk but is very heat-labile and easily destroyed by pasteurization.

The vitamin content of fresh milk is given below:

Vitamin	Contents per litre
A (ug RE)	400
D (IU)	40
E (ug)	1000
K (ug)	50
B1 (ug)	450
B2 (ug)	1750
Niacin (ug)	900
B6 (ug)	500
Pantothenic acid (ug)	3500
Biotin (ug)	35
Folic acid (ug)	55
B12 (ug)	4.5
C (mg)	20

Minerals

All 22 minerals considered to be essential to the human diet are present in milk. These include three families of salts:

- **Sodium (Na), Potassium (K) and Chloride (Cl):** These *free* ions are negatively correlated to lactose to maintain osmotic equilibrium of milk with blood.
- **Calcium (Ca), Magnesium (Mg), Inorganic Phosphorous (P(i)), and Citrate:** This group consists of 2/3 of the Ca, 1/3 of the Mg, 1/2 of the P(i), and less than 1/10 of the citrate in *colloidal* (nondiffusible) form and present in the casein micelle.
- **Diffusible salts of Ca, Mg, citrate, and phosphate:** These salts are very pH dependent and contribute to the overall acid-base equilibrium of milk.

The mineral content of fresh milk is given below:

Mineral	Content per litre
Sodium (mg)	350-900
Potassium (mg)	1100-1700
Chloride (mg)	900-1100
Calcium (mg)	1100-1300
Magnesium (mg)	90-140
Phosphorus (mg)	900-1000
Iron (ug)	300-600
Zinc (ug)	2000-6000
Copper (ug)	100-600
Manganese (ug)	20-50
Iodine (ug)	260
Fluoride (ug)	30-220
Selenium (ug)	5-67
Cobalt (ug)	0.5-1.3
Chromium (ug)	8-13
Molybdenum (u)	18-120
Nickel (ug)	0-50
Silicon (ug)	750-7000
Vanadium (ug)	tr-310
Tin (ug)	40-500
Arsenic (ug)	20-60

1. Physical Properties

Density: The density of milk and milk products is used for the following:

- to convert volume into mass and vice versa
- to estimate the solids content
- to calculate other physical properties (e.g. kinematic viscosity)
- Density, the mass of a certain quantity of material divided by its volume, is dependant on the following:
- temperature at the time of measurement v
- temperature history of the material
- composition of the material (especially the fat content)
- inclusion of air (a complication with more viscous products)

With all of this in mind, the density of milk varies within the range of 1027 to 1033 kg m(-3) at 20° C.

The following table gives the density of various fluid dairy products as a function of fat and solids-not-fat (SNF) composition:

	Product Composition		Density (kg/L) at:			
Product	**Fat (%)**	**SNF (%)**	**4.4°C**	**10°C**	**20°C**	**38.9°C**
Producer milk	4.00	8.95	1.035	1.033	1.030	1.023
Homogenized milk	3.6	8.6	1.033	1.032	1.029	1 . 0 2 2
Skim milk, pkg	0.02	8.9	1.036	1.035	1.033	1.026
Fortified skim	0.02	10.15	1.041	1.040	1.038	1.031
Half and half	12.25	7.75	1.027	1.025	1.020	1,010
Half and half, fort	11.30	8.9	1.031	1.030	1.024	1.014
Light cream	20.00	7.2	1.021	1.018	1.012	1.000
Heavy cream	36.60	5.55	1.008	1.005	0.994	0.978

Viscosity

Viscosity of milk and milk products is important in determining the following:

- the rate of creaming
- rates of mass and heat transfer
- the flow conditions in dairy processes

Milk and skim milk, excepting cooled raw milk, exhibit Newtonian behavior, in which the viscosity is independent of the rate of shear. The viscosity of these products depends on the following:

Temperature: cooler temperatures increase viscosity due to the increased voluminosity of casein micelles temperatures above 65° C increase viscosity due to the denaturation of whey proteins

pH: an increase or decrease in pH of milk also causes an increase in casein micelle voluminosity

Cooled raw milk and cream exhibit **non-Newtonian** behavior in which the viscosity is dependant on the shear rate. Agitation may cause partial coalescence of the fat globules (partial churning) which increases viscocity. Fat globules that have under gone cold agglutination may be dispersed due to agitation, causing a decrease in viscosity.

Freezing Point

Freezing point is a colligative property which is determined by the molarity of solutes rather than by the percentage by weight or volume. In the dairy industry, freezing point is mainly used to determine **added water** but it can also been used to determine lactose content in milk, estimate whey powder contents in skim milk powder, and to determine water activity of cheese. The freezing point of milk is usually in the range of -0.512 to -0.550° C with an average of about **-0.522° C**.

Correct interpretation of freezing point data with respect to added water depends on a good understanding of the factors affecting freezing point depression. With respect to interpretation of freezing points for added water determination, the most significant variables are the nutritional status of the herd and the access to water. Under feeding causes increased freezing points. Large temporary increases in freezing point occur after consumption of large amounts of water because milk is iso-osmotic with blood. The primary sources of non-intentional added water in milk are residual rinse water and condensation in the milking system.

Acid-Base Equilibria

Both titrable acidity and pH are used to measure milk acidity. The pH of milk at 25° C normally varies within a relatively narrow range of **6.5** to **6.7**. The normal range for titratable acidity of herd milks is **13 to 20 mmol/L**. Because of the large inherent variation, the measure of titratable acidity has little practical value except to measure changes in acidity (eg., during lactic fermentation) and even for this purpose, pH is a better measurement. There are many components in milk which provide a buffering action. The major buffering groups of milk are caseins and phosphate.

Optical Properties

Optical properties provide the basis for many rapid, indirect methods of analysis such as proximate analysis by infrared absorbency or light scattering. Optical properties also determine the appearance of milk and milk products. Light scattering by fat globules and casein micelles causes milk to appear turbid and opaque. Light scattering occurs when the wave length of light is near the same magnitude as the particle. Thus, smaller particles scatter light of shorter wavelengths. Skim milk appears slightly blue because casein micelles scatter the shorter wavelengths of visible light (blue) more than the red. The carotenoid precursor of vitamin A, ß -carotene, contained in milk fat, is responsible for the 'creamy' colour of milk. Riboflavin imparts a greenish colour to whey.

Refractive index (RI) is normally determined at 20° C with the D line of the sodium spectrum. The refractive index of milk is 1.3440 to 1.3485 and can be used to estimate total solids.

7

Pasteurization

Introduction

The process of pasteurization was named after **Louis Pasteur** who discovered that spoilage organisms could be inactivated in wine by applying heat at temperatures below its boiling point. The process was later applied to milk and remains the most important operation in the processing of milk.

Definition: The heating of every particle of milk or milk product to a specific temperature for a specified period of time without allowing recontamination of that milk or milk product during the heat treatment process.

Purpose: There are two distinct purposes for the process of milk pasteurization:

Public Health Aspect: to make milk and milk products safe for human consumption by destroying all bacteria that may be harmful to health (pathogens)

Keeping Quality Aspect: to improve the keeping quality of milk and milk products. Pasteurization can destroy some undesirable enzymes and many spoilage bacteria. Shelf life can be 7, 10, 14 or up to 16 days.

The extent of microorganism inactivation depends on the combination of temperature and holding time. Minimum temperature and time requirements for milk pasteurization are based on thermal death time studies for the most heat resistant pathogen found in milk, *Coxelliae burnettii*. Thermal lethality determinations require the applications of microbiology to appropriate processing determinations.

To ensure destruction of all pathogenic microorganisms, time and temperature combinations of the pasteurization process are highly regulated:

Pasteurization Regulations

Milk:

63° C for not less than 30 min.,

72° C for not less than 16 sec.,

or equivalent destruction of pathogens and the enzyme phosphatase as permitted by Ontario Provincial Government authorities. Milk is deemed pasteurized if it tests negative for alkaline phosphatase.

Frozen dairy dessert mix (ice cream or ice milk, egg nog):

at least 69° C for not less than 30 min;

at least 80° C for not less than 25 sec;

other time temperature combinations must be approved (e.g. 83° C/16 sec).

Milk based products- with 10% mf or higher, or added sugar (cream, chocolate milk, etc)

66° C/30 min, 75° C/16 sec

There has also been some progress with low temperature pasteurization methods using membrane processing technology.

Methods of Pasteurization

There are two basic methods, batch or continuous.

Batch method: The batch method uses a vat pasteurizer which consists of a jacketed vat surrounded by either circulating water, steam or heating coils of water or steam.

In the vat the milk is heated and held throughout the holding period while being agitated. The milk may be cooled in the vat or removed hot after the holding time is completed for every particle.

As a modification, the milk may be partially heated in tubular or plate heater before entering the vat. This method has very little use for milk but some use for milk by-products (e.g. creams, chocolate) and special batches. The vat is used extensivly in the ice cream industry for mix quality reasons other than microbial reasons.

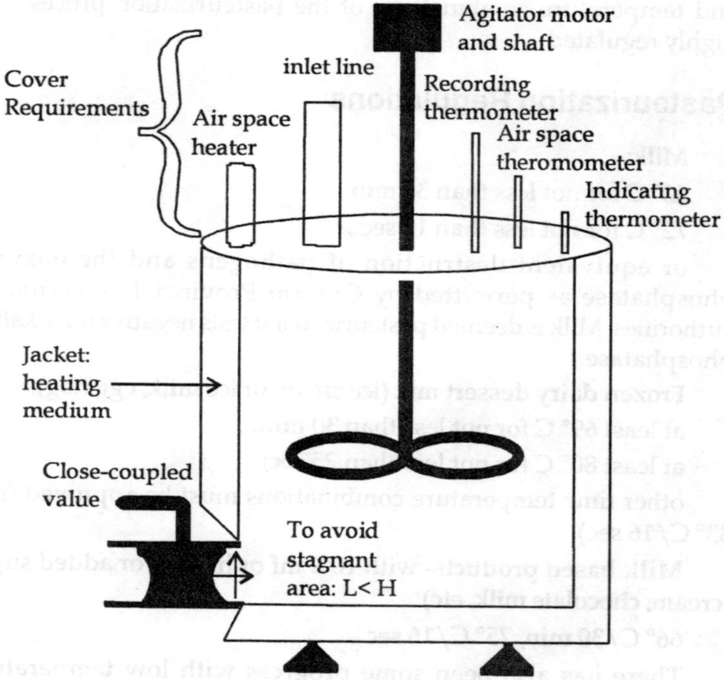

Continuous Method

Continuous process method has several advantages over the vat method, the most important being time and energy saving. For most continuous processing, a high temperature short time (HTST) pasteurizer is used. The heat treatment is accomplished using a **plate heat exchanger**. This piece of equipment consists of a stack of corrugated stainless steel plates clamped together in a frame. There are several flow patterns that can be used. Gaskets are used to define the boundaries of the channels and to prevent leakage. The heating medium can be vacuum steam or hot water.

HTST Milk Flow Overview

This overview is meant as an introduction and a summary. Each piece of HTST equipment will be discussed in further detail later.

Cold raw milk at 4° C in a constant level tank is drawn into the **regenerator** section of pasteurizer. Here it is warmed to approximately 57° C - 68° C by heat given up by hot pasteurized milk flowing in a counter current direction on the opposite side of thin, stainless steel plates. The raw milk, still under suction, passes through a positive displacement **timing pump** which delivers it under positive pressure through the rest of the HTST system.

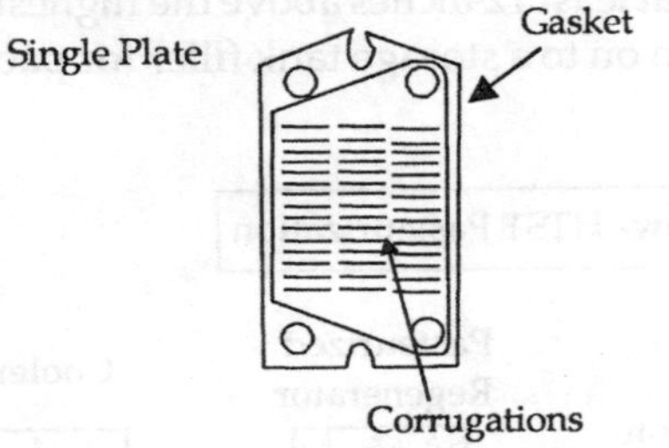

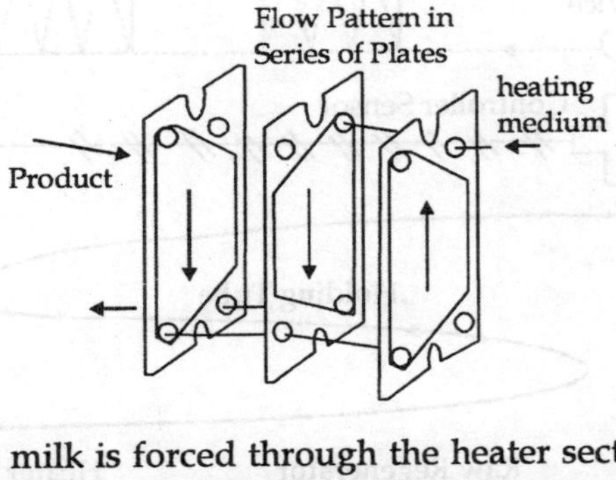

The raw milk is forced through the heater section where hot water on opposite sides of the plates heat milk to a temperature of at least 72° C. The milk, at pasteurization temperature and under pressure, flows through the **holding tube** where it is held for at least 16 sec. The maximum velocity is governed by the speed of the timing pump, diameter and length of the holding tube, and surface friction. After passing temperature sensors of an **indicating thermometer** and a **recorder-controller** at the end of the holding tube, milk passes into the **flow diversion device (FDD)**. The FDD assumes a forward-flow position if the milk passes the recorder-controller at the preset cut-in temperature (>72° C). The FDD remains in normal position which is in diverted-flow if milk has not achieved preset cut-in temperature. The improperly heated milk flows through the diverted flow line of the FDD back to the raw milk **constant level tank.** Properly heated milk flows through the forward flow part of the FDD to the pasteurized milk regenerator section where it gives up heat to the raw product and in turn is cooled to approximately 32° C - 9° C.

The warm milk passes through the cooling section where it is cooled to 4° C or below by coolant on the opposite sides of the thin, stainless steel plates. The cold, pasteurized milk passes through a **vacuum breaker** at least 12 inches above the highest raw milk in the HTST system then on to a storage tank filler for packaging.

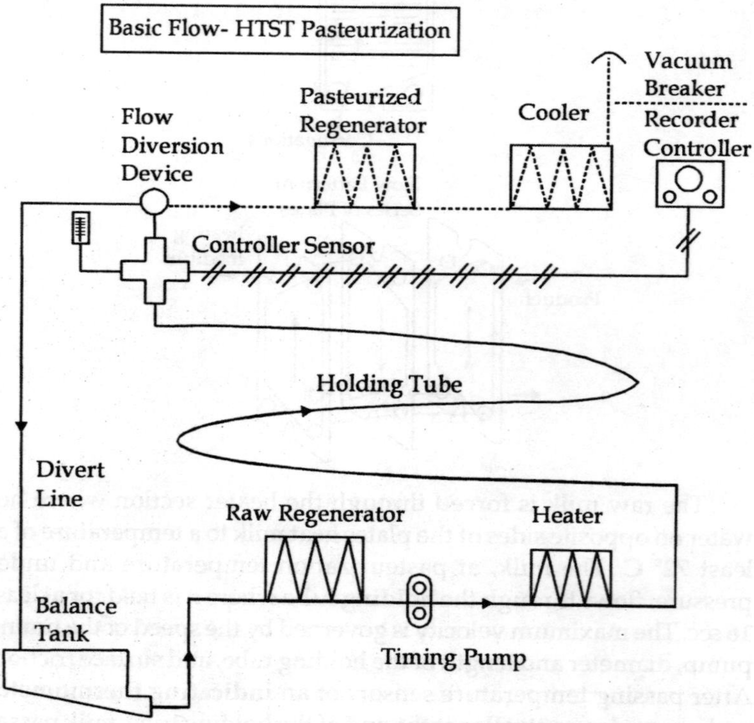

HTST Continuous Plate Pasteurizer

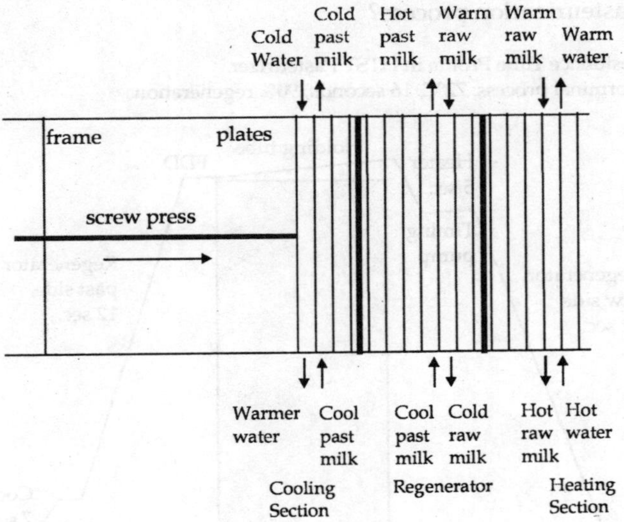

Holding Time

When fluids move through a pipe, either of two distinct types of flow can be observed. The first is known as **turbulent flow** which occurs at high velocity and in which eddies are present moving in all directions and at all angles to the normal line of flow. The second type is streamline, or **laminar flow** which occurs at low velocities and shows no eddy currents. The Reynolds number is used to predict whether laminar or turbulent flow will exist in a pipe:

Re < 2100 laminar

Re > 4000 fully developed turbulent flow

There is an impact of these flow patterns on holding time calculations and the assessment of proper holding tube lengths.

The holding time is determined by timing the interval for an added trace substance (salt) to pass through the holder. The time interval of the fastest particle of milk is desired. Thus the results found with water are converted to the milk flow time by formulation since a pump may not deliver the same amount of milk as it does water.

Note: the formulation assumes flow patterns are the same for milk and water. If they are not, how would this affect the efficiency of the pasteurization process?

Residence Time Profile in HTST Pasteurizer
Norminal process: 72°C, 16 seconds, 90% regeneration

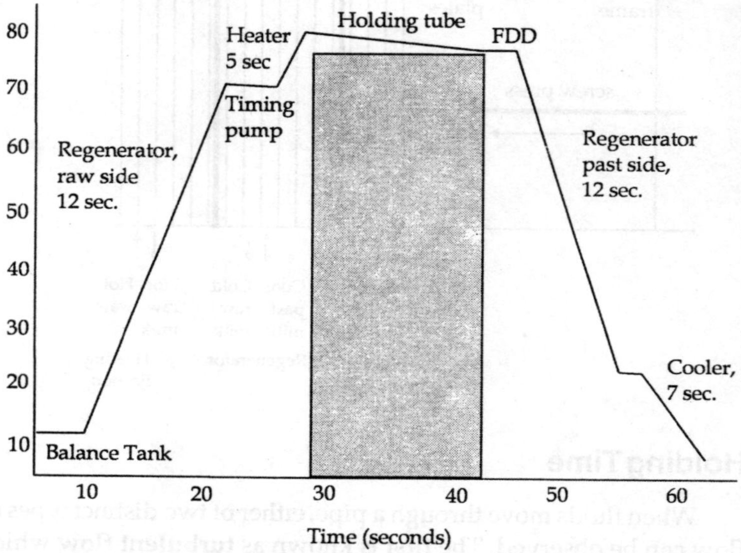

Pressure Differential

For contiunuous pasteurizing, it is important to maintain a higher pressure on the pasteurized side of the heat exchanger. By keeping the pasteurized milk at least 1 psi higher than raw milk in regenerator, it prevents contamination of pasteurized milk with raw milk in event that a pin-hole leak develops in thin stainless steel plates. This **pressure differential** is maintained using a timing pump in simple systems, and differential pressure controllers and back pressure flow regulators at the chilled pasteurization outlet in more complex systems. The position of the timing pump is crucial so that there is suction on the raw regenerator side and pushes milk under pressure through pasteurized regenerator. There are several other factors involved in maintaining the pressure differential:

- The balance tank overflow level must be less than the level of lowest milk passage in the regenerator
- Properly installed booster pump is all that is permitted between balance tank and raw regenerator
- No pump after pasteurized milk outlet to vacuum breaker
- There must be greater than a 12 inch vertical rise to the vacuum breaker
- The raw regenerator drains freely to balance tank at shut-down
- Basic Component Equipment of HTST Pasteurizer

Balance Tank

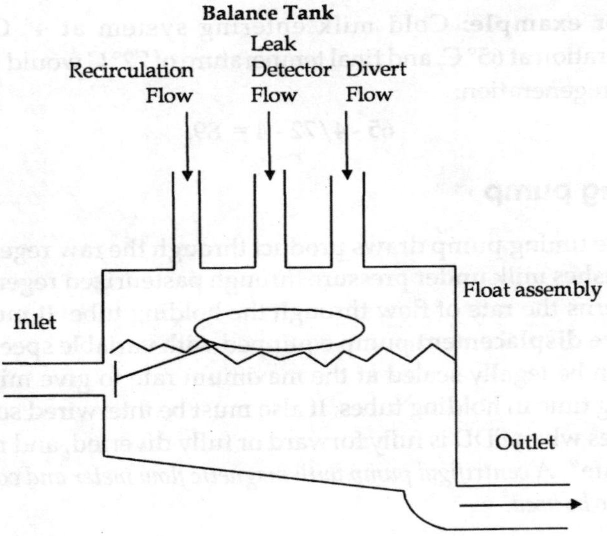

The balance, or constant level tank provides a constant supply of milk. It is equipped with a **float valve assembly** which controls the liquid level nearly constant ensuring uniform head pressure on the product leaving the tank. The overflow level must always be below the level of lowest milk passage in regenerator. It, therefore, helps to maintain a higher pressure on the pasteurized side of the heat exchanger. The balance tank also prevents air from entering the pasteurizer by placing the top of the outlet pipe lower than the lowest point in the tank and creating downward slopes of at least 2%. The balance tank provides a means for recirculation of diverted or pasteurized milk.

Regenerator

Heating and cooling energy can be saved by using a regenerator which utilizes the heat content of the pasteurized milk to warm the incoming cold milk. Its efficiency may be calculated as follows:

% regeneration = temp. increase due to regenerator/total temp. increase

For example: Cold milk entering system at 4° C, after regeneration at 65° C, and final temperature of 72° C would have an 89.7% regeneration:

65 - 4/72 - 4 = 89.

Timing pump

The timing pump draws product through the raw regenerator and pushes milk under pressure through pasteurized regenerator. It governs the rate of flow through the holding tube. It must be a **positive displacement** pump equipped with variable speed drive that can be legally sealed at the maximum rate to give minimum holding time in holding tubes. It also must be interwired so it only operates when FDD is fully forward or fully diverted, and must be "fail-safe". *A centrifigal pump with magnetic flow meter and controller may also be used.*

Holding tube

Must slope upwards 1/4"/ft. in direction of flow to eliminate air entrapment so nothing flows faster at air pocket restrictions.

Indicating Thermometer

The indicating thermometer is considered the most accurate temperature measurement. It is the official temperature to which the

safety thermal limit recorder (STLR) is adjusted. The probe should sit as close as possible to STLR probe and be located not greater than 18 inches upstream of the flow diversion device.

Recorder-controller (STLR)

The STLR records the temperature of the milk and the time of day. It monitors, controls and records the position of the flow diversion device (FDD) and supplies power to the FDD during forward flow. There are both **pneumatic** and **electronic** types of controllers. The operator is responsible for recording the date, shift, equipment, ID, product and amount, indicating thermometer temperature, cleansing cycles, cut in and cut out temperatures, any connects for unusual circumstances, and his/her signature.

Flow Diversion Device (FDD)

Also called the flow diversion valve (FDV), it is located at the downstream end of the upward sloping holding tube. It is essentially a 3-way valve, which, at temperatures greater than 72° C,opens to **forward flow**. This step requires power. At temperatures less than 72° C, the valve recloses to the normal position and diverts the milk back to the balance tank. It is important to note that the FDD operates on the measured temperature, not time, at the end of the holding period. There are two types of FDD:

- **single stem** - an older valve system that has the disadvantage that it can't be cleaned in place.
- **dual stem** - consists of 2 valves in series for additional fail safe systems. This FDD can be cleaned in place and is more suited for automation.

Vacuum Breaker

At the pasteurized product discharge is a vacuum breaker which breaks to atmospheric pressure. It must be located greater than 12 inches above the highest point of raw product in system. It ensures that nothing downstream is creating suction on the pasteurized side.

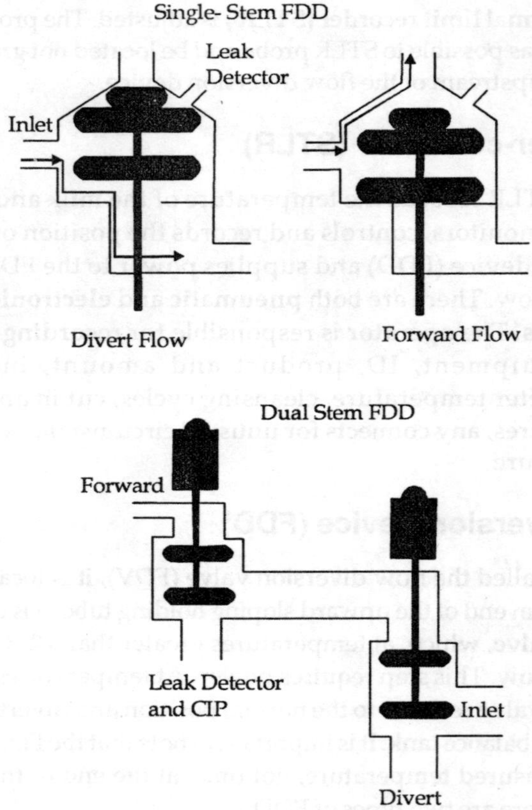

Auxiliary Equipment

Booster Pump: It is centrifugal "stuffing" pump which supplies raw milk to the raw regenerator for the balance tank. It must be used in conjunction with pressure differential controlling device and shall operate only when timing pump is operating, proper pressures are achieved in regenerator, and system is in forward flow.

Homogenizer: The homogenizer may be used as timing pump. It is a positive pressure pump; if not, then it cannot supplement flow. Free circulation from outlet to inlet is required and the speed of the homogenizer must be greater than the rate of flow of the timing pump.

Magnetic flow meter and centrifugal pump arrangements: Magnetic flow meters can be used to measure the flow rate. It is essentially a short piece of tubing (approximately 25 cm long) surrounded by a housing, inside of which are located coils that generate a magnetic field. When milk passes through the magnetic field, it causes a voltage to be induced, and the generated signal is directly proportional to velcoity. Application of the magnetic flow meter in the dairy industry has centered around its replacing the positive displacement timing pump as the metering device in HTST pasteurizing systems, where with certain products the timing pump rotors reportedly wear out in a relatvely short period of time. In operation, the electrical signal is sent by the magnetic flow meter to the flow controller, which determines what the actual flow is compared to the flow rate set by the operator. Since the magnetic flow meter continuously senses flow rate, it will signal the electronic controller if the actual flow exceeds the set flow rate for any reason. If the flow rate is exceeded for any reason, the flow diversion device is put into diverted flow. A significant difference from the normal HTST system (with timing pump) comes into focus at this point. This system can be operated at a flow rate greater than (residence time less than) the legal limit. However, it will be in diverted flow and never in forward flow.

Another magnetic flow meter based system with an AC variable frequency motor control drive on a centrifugal pump is also possible in lieu of a positive displacement metering pump on a HTST pasteurizer.This system does not use a control valve but rather the signal from the magnetic flow meter is transmitted to the AC variable frequency control to vary the speed of the centrifugal pump. The pump, then controls the flow rate of product through the system and its holding time in the holding tube.

Automated Public Health Controllers: These systems are used for time and temperature control of HTST systems. There are concerns that with sequential control, the critical control points are not monitored all the time; if during the sequence it got held up, the CCP's would not be monitored. With operator control, changes can be made to the program which might affect CCP's; the system is not easily sealed. No computer program can be written completely error free in large systems; as complexity increases, so too do errors.

This gives rise to a need for specific regulations or computer controlled CCP's of public health significance:

- dedicated computer - no other assignments, monitor all CCP's at least once/sec
- not under control of any other computer system or override system, i.e., network separate computer on each pasteurizer I/O bus for outputs only, to other computers no inputs from other computers on loss of power - public health computers should revert to fail safe position (e.g. divert) last state switches during power up must be fail safe position
- programs in ROM - tapes/disks not acceptable inputs must be sealed, modem must be sealed, program sealed no operator override switches
- proper calibration procedure during that printing - Public health computer must not leave public health control for > 1 sec and upon return must complete 1 full cycle before returning to printing

FDV position must be monitored and temperature in holding tube recorded during change in FDV position integrated with CIP computer which can be programmed e.g., FDV, booster pump controllable by CIP computer when in CIP made only

Thermal Destruction of Microorganisms

Heat is lethal to microorganisms, but each species has its own particular heat tolerance. During a thermal destruction process, such as pasteurization, the rate of destruction is logarithmic, as is their rate of growth. Thus bacteria subjected to heat are killed at a rate that is porportional to the number of organisms present. The process is dependent both on the temperature of exposure and the time required at this temperature to accomplish to desired rate of destruction. Thermal calculations thus involve the need for knowledge of the concentration of microorganisms to be destroyed, the acceptable concentration of microorganisms that can remain behind (spoilage organisms, for example, but not pathogens), the thermal resistance of the target microorganisms (the most heat tolerant ones), and the temperature time relationship required for destruction of the target organisms.

The extent of the pasteurization treatment required is determined by the heat resistance of the most heat-resistant enzyme or microorganism in the food. For example, milk pasteurization historically was based on *Mycobacterium tuberculosis* and *Coxiella burnetti*, but with the recognition of each new pathogen, the required time temperature relationships are continuously being examined.

A thermal death curve for this process is shown below. It is a logarithmic process, meaning that in a given time interval and at a given temperature, the same percentage of the bacterial population will be destroyed regardless of the population present. For example, if the time required to destroy one log cycle or 90% is known, and the desired thermal reduction has been decided (for example, 12 log cycles), then the time required can be calculated. If the number of microorganisms in the food increases, the heating time required to process the product will also be increased to bring the population down to an acceptable level. The heat process for pasteurization is usually based on a 12 D concept, or a 12 log cycle reduction in the numbers of this organism.

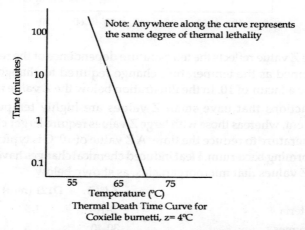

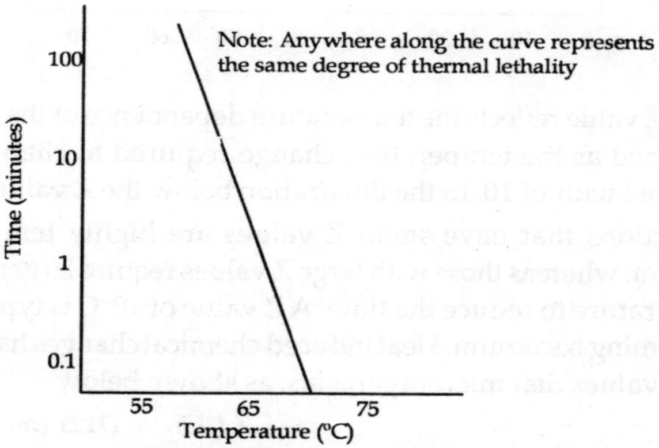

Thermal Death Time Curve for
Coxielle burnetti, z= 4°C

Several parameters help us to do thermal calculations and define the rate of thermal lethality. The D value is a measure of the heat resistance of a microorganism. It is the time in minutes at a given temperature required to destroy 1 log cycle (90%) of the target microorganism. (Of course, in an actual process, all others that are less heat tolerant are destroyed to a greater extent). For example, a D value at 72°C of 1 minute means that for each minute of processing at 72°C the bacteria population of the target microorganism will be reduced by 90%. In the illustration below, the D value is 14 minutes (40-26) and would be representative of a process at 72°C.

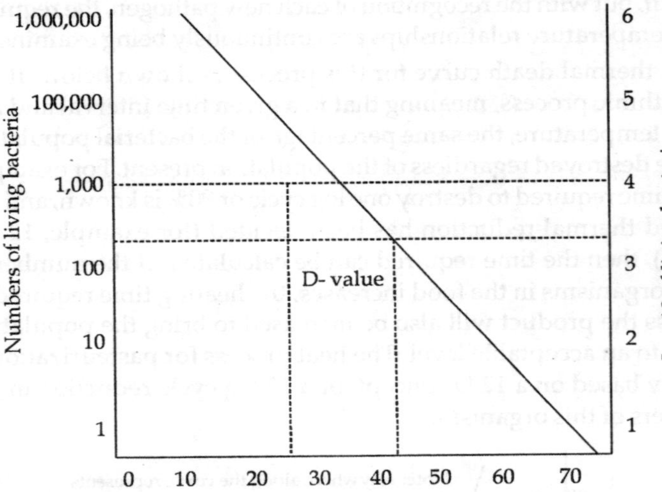

The Z value reflects the temperature dependence of the reaction. It is defined as the temperature change required to change the D value by a factor of 10. In the illustration below the Z value is 10°C.

Reactions that have small Z values are highly temperature dependent, whereas those with large Z values require larger changes in temperature to reduce the time. A Z value of 10°C is typical for a spore forming bacterium. Heat induced chemical changes have much larger Z values that microorganisms, as shown below.

	Z (°C)	D121 (min)
bacteria	5-10	1-5
enzymes	30-40	1-5
vitamins	20-25	150-200
pigments	40-70	15-50

The figure below illustrates the relative changes in time temperature profiles for the destruction of microorganisms. Above and to the right of each line the microorganisms or quality factors would be destroyed, whereas below and to the left of each line, the microorganisms or quality factors would not be destroyed. Due to the differences in Z values, it is apparent that at higher temperatures for shorter times, a region exists (shaded area) where pathogens can be destroyed while vitamins can be maintained. The same holds true for other quality factors such as colour and flavour components. Thus in milk processing the higher temperature, shorter time (HTST) process (72°C/16 sec) is favored compared to a lower temperature longer time (batch or vat) process since it results in a slightly lower loss of vitamins and better sensory quality.

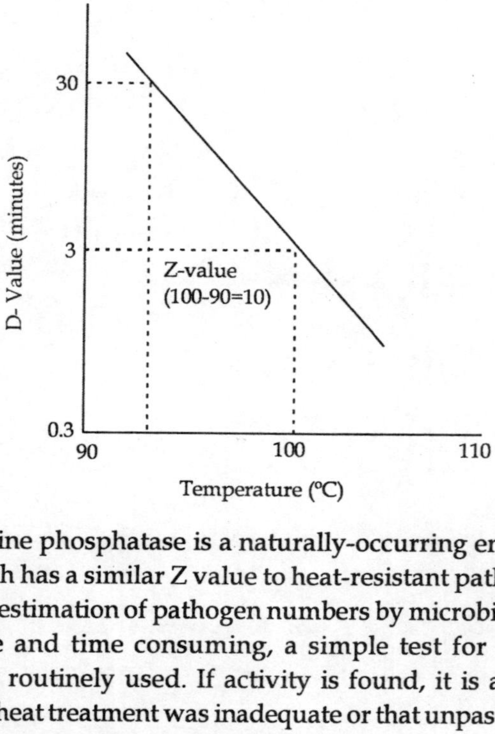

Alkaline phosphatase is a naturally-occurring enzyme in raw milk which has a similar Z value to heat-resistant pathogens. Since the direct estimation of pathogen numbers by microbial methods is expensive and time consuming, a simple test for phosphatase activity is routinely used. If activity is found, it is assumed that either the heat treatment was inadequate or that unpasteurized milk has contaminated the pasteurized product.

A working example of how to use D and Z values in pasteurization calculations: Pooled raw milk at the processing plant has bacterial population of 4x10exp5/mL. It is to be processed at 79°C for 21 seconds. The average D value at 65°C for the mixed population is 7 min. The Z value is 7°C. How many organisms will be left after pasteurization? What time would be required at 65°C to accomplish the same degree of lethality?

Answer: At 79°C, the D value has been reduced by two log cycles from that at 65°C since the Z value is 7°C. Hence it is now 0.07 min. The milk is processed for 21/60=0.35 min, so that would accomplish 5 log cycle reductions to 4 organisms/mL. At 65°C, you would need 35 minutes to accomplish a 5D reduction.

8

ECONOMIC EVALUATION OF DAIRY FEEDS

The FEEDVAL spreadsheet performs the following functions:

- Calculates cost per nutrient for any feed the user enters.
- Estimates a current market value per ton for a feed.

Data requirements:

- Nutrient content of the feed, including crude protein, net energy for lactation, total digestible nutrients (optional), dry matter, and rumen undegradable protein (optional).
- Current market costs of soybean meal and shelled corn.

Terms used in FEEDVAL:

- DM = dry matter
- CP = crude protein
- TDN = total digestible nutrients
- NEL = net energy for lactation
- RUP = rumen undegradable protein

The purpose of the FEEDVAL spreadsheet is to provide a tool to economically evaluate feeds purchased off the farm. It compliments NMSU Extension Guide D-206, Economic Evaluation of Dairy Feeds, which provides further discussion of economic evaluation of dairy feeds. By using this spreadsheet, a dairy producer can determine the value of by-products, concentrates, and forages based on competitive prices of corn and soybean meal. The spreadsheet operates on Microsoft Excel (.xls) or Lotus (.wk3 or .wk4).

When you make entries in the spreadsheet, be sure that numbers are entered as numbers, not text. If a number is entered as text, the spreadsheet assumes the value is 0. Numbers entered as text appear left justified in the cell. Therefore, be sure that all entered numbers appear right justified in the cell. The following example illustrates this point:

Incorrect	Correct
21.0	21.0

The value of the correctly entered cell is 21, the value of the incorrectly entered cell is 0. Also, be sure the percentages are entered as percentages. For instance, 30 percent dry matter must be entered as 30, not 0.30.

Objectives

FEEDVAL will determine:

1. Cost/nutrient.
   a. cost/lb of crude protein
   b. cost/Mcal of net energy
   c. cost/lb of TDN
   d. cost/lb of RUP
1. The value of any feed or forage based on the price of soybean meal and shelled corn.
2. The value of a selected commodity and by- product feeds based on the price of soybean meal and shelled corn.

Running the Program

1. Load the Lotus (FEEDVAL.WK3 or FEEDVAL.WK4) or Excel (FEEDVAL.XLS) version of the spreadsheet from your floppy disk or hard drive.
2. FEEDVAL consists of three sheets (see figs. 1-3). Excel numbers sheets numerically, and Lotus numbers sheets alphabetically. To move between sheets, click the sheet tabs at the bottom

(Excel) or top (Lotus) of the screen. Sheet 1 contains directions for using FEEDVAL. Sheet 2 is where the feed values are entered.

3. At the top of Sheet 2, enter the current market prices for shelled corn and 44% soybean meal.
4. Enter values for feeds in question, as in the corn silage example in the spreadsheet . All feed values must be entered, with the exception of TDN and NEL (one or both of these may be entered). Enter data only in shaded areas.
5. Results are given next to the entered feed values. The last column, value in price per ton, provides a value of a feed using soybean meal and shelled corn as a base of comparison. Calculation of this value requires NEL energy value; TDN will not work.
6. Sheet 3 provides values for specific feeds based on the soybean meal/shelled corn prices.

FEEDVAL can help a producer make feed purchasing decisions, but should not be the sole criteria. The following discussion identifies strong and weak points of each method of economic evaluation.

Cost/Nutrient Method

The cost/nutrient method is useful, but can be misleading. It is important to evaluate feeds based on their most valuable nutrient(s). For example, protein supplements such as soybean meal and cottonseed meal should be evaluated primarily on the basis of their crude protein content, because that is the most valuable nutrient in the feed (that is, the reason the feed is purchased). This does not mean the energy in protein supplements has no value and should be ignored. It simply shouldn't be emphasized as much as protein in that situation. Likewise, energy sources such as shelled corn and fat should be evaluated primarily on energy content. A feed like alfalfa haylage that can supply significant quantities of protein and energy to the total ration should be evaluated on protein and energy cost.

FEEDVAL does not consider palatability, digestibility, and quality of the feed source. A couple of extreme examples illustrate this point. First, consider dairy manure and soybean meal. Dairy manure is certainly a better buy in terms of cost per unit of protein or energy. However, palatability and digestibility are certainly different. Second, consider that on the basis of cost per pound of crude protein, soybean meal is usually a better buy than fish meal. However, fish meal has a high rumen undegradable protein (bypass protein) value, which adds value to the feed.

Cost/nutrient is most useful when comparing feeds of similar use and function.

Value/Ton

FEEDVAL provides a value per ton for a feed, given the prices of shelled corn and soybean meal. Shelled corn and soybean meal are readily available, widely used concentrate feeds in dairy rations throughout the United States. Shelled corn is a high energy concentrate, while soybean meal is a high protein concentrate. Specific equations determine value per ton for selected commodities, while simultaneous equations determine value per ton for any feed. The commodity equations are on Sheet 3 of FEEDVAL. Simultaneous equation results are given in the ivalue/toni column adjacent to cost/nutrient results on Sheet 2.

The value/ton calculation represents the maximum worth of a feed, assuming it to be of equal palatability and digestibility as corn and soybean meal. If a feed is not a good buy, then you would be better off buying soybean meal and corn to supply your energy and protein needs. In the case of wet forages, these values are very liberal price estimates because it assumes the energy and protein of the forage in question to be worth the same as that in corn and soybean meal. This is rarely the case, as wet forages are generally not as marketable as concentrated feeds.

> FEEDVAL will provide economic analysis of feeds. FEEDVAL consists of three sheets. To move between sheets, click the sheet tabs at the bottom of the screen. Sheet one is the current sheet, containing directions for using FEEDVAL. Sheet 2 is where the feed values are entered. At the top, shelled corn and 44% soybean meal prices are entered. Values for the feeds in question must be entered as in the corn silage example. For example, 9% crude protein must be entered as 9, NOT .09. All feed values must be entered, with the exception of TDN and NEL (one or both of these may be entered). Enter only in shaded areas. Results are given next to the entered feed values. The last column, value in

$/ton, provides a value of the feed in question using soybean meal and shelled corn as a base of comparison. Calculation of this value requires NEL energy value; TON will not work. Sheet 3 provides values for specific feeds based on the soybean meal/ shelled corn prices.

The following is a glossary of terms used in FEEDVAL:

DM = dry matter

CP = crude protein

TDN = total digestible nutrients

NEL = net energy lactation RUP = rumen undegradable protein

Fig. 8.1. Approximation of sheet 1 of FEEDVAL spreadsheet (.xls version).

Feedval.xls

44% Soybean Meal Cost = $200.00 /Ton

Shelled Corn Cost = $95.00 /Ton Soybean Meal And Shelled Corn Prices From Screen 2

Feed	Dm %	Cp %	Nel Mcal/ Lb	Value $/Cwt	Value $/Ton
Almond Hulls	90	4.4	0.58	2.75	54.95
Barley	89	13.9	0.87	5.10	101.95
Beet Pulp	91	8.0	0.8	4.17	83.40
Brewers Dried Grains	92	26.0	0.68	6.33	126.51
Brewers Wet Grains	21	26.0	0.69	1.45	29.03
Citrus Pulp	91	6.9	0.80	3.96	79.17
Corn Gluten Feed	90	25.0	0.86	6.70	133.98
Corn Gluten Meal	91	65.9	0.88	12.73	254.51
Cottonseed Hulls	91	4.3	0.37	1.98	39.68
Cottonseed Meal	91	44.8	0.78	9.33	186.51
Cottonseeds	92	24.9	1.04	7.50	150.08
Distillers Grains	92	29.5	0.86	7.68	153.52
Ear Corn	87	9.3	0.84	4.24	84.86
Fish Meal	92	66.6	0.77	12.55	250.90
Hominy	90	11.8	0.97	5.23	104.56
Linseed Meal	90	38.6	0.79	8.40	167.94
Molasses, Beet	77	8.7	0.78	3.4	68.12

(Contd.)

Feed	Dm %	Cp %	Nel Mcal/ Lb	Value $/Cwt	Value $/Ton
Molasses, Sugarcane	75	4.3	0.75	2.79	55.71
Meat & Bone Meal	94	53.8	0.75	10.84	216.73
Oats	89	13.6	0.79	4.78	95.52
Rapeseed Meal	91	43.6	0.71	8.90	178.01
Rice Hulls	92	3.1	0.07	0.71	14.15
Rye	88	13.8	0.84	4.94	98.71
Soybean Hulls	90	12.0	0.81	4.69	93.83
Soybeans	89	41.7	0.99	9.45	188.95
Sunflower Meal	93	50.3	0.87	15.55	311.10
Wheat Bran	90	18.0	0.7	5.03	100.52
Wheat Middlings	90	18.7	0.84	5.91	118.11
Wheat, Soft Winter	89	11.5	0.92	4.96	99.21
Whey	7	14.0	0.8	0.39	7.89

Fig. 8.2. Approximation of Sheet 2 of FEEDVAL spreadsheet (.xls version).

9

FEEDING WASTE MILK TO DAIRY CALVES

Dairy producers feed a variety of liquid feeds to young calves after the initial colostrum. These feeds include whole milk, surplus colostrum, transition milk, waste or discard milk, and milk replacer. Waste or discard milk cannot be sold for human consumption, because it comes from cows treated with antibiotics for mastitis or other illnesses.

Discard milk losses range from 48 to 136 pounds of milk per cow per year. To reduce some of the economic loss, 38 percent of dairy producers feed waste milk to calves.

However, many dairy producers avoid feeding waste milk to calves for fear of increasing calf morbidity or the incidence of heifers calving with mastitis or blind quarters. In early studies, calves generally were housed in pens that enabled them to suckle the rudimentary teats of other calves. This led to an increase in the incidence of mastitis in developing heifers.

Research shows that calves fed waste milk have growth rates and incidences of scouring that are similar to milk-fed controls.

Precautions for Feeding Waste Milk

Waste milk can be a safe liquid feed for calves provided certain precautions are followed .

- Do not feed waste milk to newborn calves on the first day of life. The intestinal wall is permeable to bacteria that could cause illness.
- House calves fed waste milk individually to prevent them from suckling one another. This should reduce the transmission of infectious microorganisms that cause mastitis.
- Use caution when feeding waste milk from antibiotic-treated cows to calves intended for meat production. Antibiotic residues from the milk could be deposited in the calves' tissues.

Waste Milk Storage

When handling large quantities of waste milk, dairy operators need to have the proper equipment. Obtain a small, used bulk tank to store the waste milk produced daily. This allows pooling of all waste milk sources (mastitis and/or transition milk, etc.) and reduces the chances of feeding excessive amounts of antibiotic milk in one feeding. Clean the tank at least every other day.

Pasteurization of Waste Milk Fed to Calves

Young calves are susceptible to diseases. That's why it is important to know the complete health status of introduced cows when expanding herds or buying replacements. Feeding milk from cows of unknown health status could be detrimental to the calves' health.

Pasteurization safely decreases pathogens in all types of milk fed to young calves. Recently, University of California at Davis researchers reported that calves fed pasteurized milk had fewer days with diarrhea and pneumonia than calves fed non-pasteurized milk. Also, calves fed pasteurized milk had greater average weight gain than calves fed non-pasteurized milk. Calves fed pasteurized milk grossed an extra $8.13 per head, attributed to reduced health complications and treatment costs, when compared with calves fed non-pasteurized milk. The researchers calculated that 315 calves (from a dairy of approximately 1,260 cows) need to be fed daily to make pasteurization economically feasible.

Waste milk is an econmomical and nutritious source of liquid feed for young dairy calves if handled properly.

Research from the National Animal Disease Center showed that pasteurization of milk at 162° F (72°C) for 15 seconds killed all Mycobacterium paratuberculosis, the bacteria responsible for Johne's disease. To effectively destroy M. paratuberculosis in milk, a continuous-flow (turbulent) pasteurizer is necessary. A continuous-flow pasteurizer quickly heats and holds milk at temperatures that kill bacteria. The milk is then quickly cooled, maintaining the nutritional components and flavor. Bacterial organisms in milk may clump together and not be pasteurized with a batch-type (static) pasteurization system.

While it is recommended that waste milk be pasteurized, pasteurizing colostrum is discouraged. The elevated temperatures associated with pasteurization can destroy immunoglobulins that are important for passive immunity transfer to young calves. Also, colostrum is more dense than milk, which makes it more difficult to raise pasteurization temperatures high enough to kill bacterial organisms, such as M. paratuberculosis.

Several bacterial organisms, including E. coli, bovine viral diarrhea (BVD), salmonella, Streptococcus species and Staphylococcus species, have been identified in waste milk. Pasteurizing waste milk reduces microbial loads before use as calf feeds. Pasteurization destroys mycoplasma mastitis species, eliminating mycoplasma transmission to calves. Similarly, pasteurization destroys bovine leukosis virus (BLV), so pasteurized milk from BLV-positive cows can be fed to calves when BLV-free milk is not available. Although pasteurization reduces the microbial load of waste milk, pasteurization is not sterilization. A heavy bacterial load in waste milk will not be eliminated completely by pasteurization. Also, pasteurization does not remove potential contamination from antibiotics in waste milk.

House heifer calves separately when feeding waste milk.

Usage Guidelines

Milk from transition and sick cows cannot be sold and must be discarded. Waste milk can be fed to calves, but a few precautions must be followed.

- Before using as a calf feed, pasteurize waste milk to reduce microbial load.
- Do not feed waste milk to newborn calves.
- Use caution when feeding waste milk to calves that are destined for beef production.
- House heifer calves individually (for example, hutches) when feeding waste milk.
- Know the health status of the cows from which waste milk is obtained. Unless milk is pasteurized, do not feed milk from

cows shedding BVD or Johne's or from cows infected with E. coli, Pasteurella or BLV.

- Don't allow waste milk to sit for an extended time without refrigeration.
- Discard waste milk that is excessively bloody, watery or unusual in appearance.

Calves fed pasteurized waste milk have fewer illnesses than those fed unpasteurized waste milk. If handled properly, waste milk is an economical and nutritious source of liquid feed for young dairy calves.

10

Reproductive Status of Your Dairy Herd

The reproductive status of a dairy herd has a dramatic effect on a dairy's profitability and production. Reproductive problems can result in long lactations, long dry periods, or possibly both, thus minimizing profits for the dairy producer. However, the reason these profits were lost may not be easily detected without proper evaluation.

The two most important management factors relating to reproductive performance are heat detection and conception rates. Table 1 illustrates the maximum average number of days between calving and first breeding for a cow herd to maintain a 12.5-month calving interval under varying levels of heat detection accuracy and conception rates.

Table 10.1 Days from calving to first insemination to maintain 12.5-month calving interval as affected by heat detection accuracy (HDA) and conception rate.

% HDA		40	50	60	70	80
Conception	40	-36	16	31	41	48
rate	50	29	36	47	54	61
	60	37	51	58	64	69
	70	52	62	68	73	76

% Conception rate

Evaluation of complete and accurate breeding and heat detection records can assist the dairy producer in achieving maximum reproductive efficiency in the herd. The following eight factors should be considered by the producer to effectively evaluate the reproductive performance of the herd.

Dry Period Length

Exceptionally long or short dry periods will adversely affect the profitability of individual cows. A short dry period will not provide adequate rest and time for mammary regeneration, while long dry periods will result in higher feed costs with no income from milk production. Long dry periods can also result in fat cows that are more prone to problems with health and reproductive performance. Each day dry over 60 days costs $3. However, each day dry under 40 costs $2. Tables 2 and 3 show days dry in relation to milk production.

Table 10.1. Days dry related to milk production in the next lactation (123,181 cows in 808 herds).

Dry Range	Milk per cow
days	lb
<39	17,632
40-49	18,334
50-59	18,463
60-69	17,871
70-79	17,310
80-89	16,474
>90	15,867

Days Open

The number of days a cow is open (DO) may be the best indicator of current reproductive efficiency. A producer's goal is around 100 to 110 DO. Excessive DO costs range from $2 to $5/cow/day for each day beyond 90 days open. For example, if a cow was open 120 days, she would be open 30 excess days, a loss of $90/cow/year at $3/cow/day. Days open can be influenced by factors such as length of voluntary waiting period, heat detection accuracy, semen quality and breeding technique, nutrition, cow fertility, disease, or weather.

Table 10.2. Days dry related to the difference in milk from herdmates' production in the next lactation (expressed as the difference in lactation milk production from herdmates; 281,816 cows).

Days dry	Difference from herdmates
	lb
40	+14
50	+253
60	+315
70	+247
80	+118

Services Per Conception

The number of services per conception (SC) is directly related to the conception rate in a herd. Conception rate influences days open because if a cow does not conceive, she will be open an additional estrous cycle (21 days). Each .1 over 1.5 SC costs approximately $1.50. Cows with an additional .5 SC cost $7.50 more per cow. This may not be a large amount per animal, but in a herd of 1000 cows the total could come to $7500 per year. If problem breeders are not culled, SC will continue to rise. Conception rate problems may be caused by heat detection accuracy, length of voluntary waiting period, semen handling, semen quality, time of insemination, insemination techniques, reproductive tract infection, nutritional status, fertility, or weather. Table 10.3 shows the relationship between conception rates and services per conception.

Days in Milk at First Breeding

Most cows normally show their first estrus by 30-50 days after calving. Recording these early heats will assist in identifying problem breeders. Dairy producers whose herds have good conception rates should set 65-70 days in milk at first breeding as their average goal.

Table 10.3. The relationship between conception rate and services per conception.

Conception rate	Services per conception
95Ð100	1.0
87Ð94	1.1
80Ð86	1.2
75Ð79	1.3
69Ð74	1.4
64Ð68	1.5
61Ð63	1.6

Heats Detected

Heat detection is a constant concern in dairy herds, as poor heat detection is one of the largest contributors to a high days open value. If excessive days open cost $2 to $5 dollars per day, a single missed heat could cost $42 to $105 per cow.

Breeding Interval

Breeding interval is a good indicator of how well heats are being detected after the first service. Dairy producers should strive to maintain an average breeding interval of 25-30 days. Maintaining a breeding interval in this range will reduce costs associated with excessive days open. Use the following formula to calculate the average days between breeding after the first service:

$$\text{Breeding interval} = \frac{\text{days open - DIM at first breeding}}{\text{services per cow - 1}}$$

Calculated breeding intervals are accurate only if all breeding information is reported. Table 10.4 demonstrates how increasing percentages of missed heats affect average breeding interval.

Calving Interval

Calving interval (CI) is the period between two consecutive calving. It is affected by days open and gestation length. Average CI is a good indicator of past reproductive performance because historical data is used to calculate the CI. However, calving interval may not be a good indicator of the present reproductive status of the herd. CI cannot be calculated for cows removed from the herd because there is no later calving date to use as an end point for calculations; therefore, cows removed from the herd for reasons such as failure to conceive do not contribute to the herd's average CI value. Average CI should be kept between 12 and 13 months. Table 10.5 shows the losses associated with CIs over 12.6 months. Table 10.6 shows the relationship between CI and average lactation milk yield.

Table 10.4 The relationship between heat detection rate and average breeding interval (ABI).

ABI	Heats detected	Heats missed
days	%	%
23	90	10
26	80	20
30	70	30
35	60	40
41	50	50
50	40	60
60	30	70

Table 10.5. Loss of returns to management associated with CIs over 12.6 months.

CI months	Loss per cow dollars
12.6	0.00
13.0	0.36
13.3	14.62
13.6	32.96
14.0	57.54
14.3	88.92

Table 10.6. Average lactation milk yield as related to last calving interval (795 herds, 121,773 cows).

Herd average CI range	Rolling herd milk average
month	lb
11.5Ð11.9	15,062
12.0Ð12.4	17,426
12.5Ð12.9	18,330
13.0Ð13.4	18,498
13.5Ð13.9	17,864
14.0Ð14.4	17,733
14.5Ð14.9	17,440
15.0Ð15.4	15,991
15.5Ð15.9	15,814
16.0Ð16.4	14,884

Average Days in Milk

Days in milk (DIM) is related closely to dry period length and is a good indicator of reproductive efficiency and herd management. The 12-month average for DIM should be 160Ð170 days. An average DIM greater than 200 indicates a reproductive problem as a large DIM value results in a lower lifetime milk production per cow due to long lactations and milking of late lactation cows. A short lactation reduces the life-time milk production because of long dry periods.

Summary

These variables will only be useful if accurate records are kept to determine whether a reproductive problem exists in the herd. They can also be used to pinpoint the cause of poor performance. Using records effectively will allow a dairy producer to set achievable goals for a herd.

Lack of accurate reproductive records may result in hidden costs such as fewer calves, lower conception rates, longer lactations and dry periods, poor identification of problem cows, and lost milk production.

11

Dairy Waste Handling

Introduction

The rapid growth in the size of dairy operations has resulted in new laws and regulations governing the handling and disposal of manure (Mitchell and Beddoes 2000). Requirements for nutrient management plans, manure solids disposal, and odor control (HouseBill 2001) make it necessary that new manure management approaches be considered. One of the more promising methods is anaerobic digestion.

Anaerobic digestion is a natural process that converts biomass to energy. Biomass is any organic material that comes from plants, animals or their wastes. Anaerobic digestion has been used for over 100 years to stabilize municipal sewage and a wide variety of industrial wastes. Most municipal wastewater treatment plants use anaerobic digestion to convert waste solids to gas. The anaerobic process removes a vast majority of the odorous compounds (Lusk 1995),(Wilkie 2000),(Wilkie 2000). It also significantly reduces the pathogens present in the slurry (Lusk 1995). Over the past 25 years, anaerobic digestion processes have been developed and applied to a wide array of industrial and agricultural wastes (Speece 1996), (Ghosh 1997). It is the preferred waste treatment process since it produces, rather than consumes, energy and can be carried out in relatively small, enclosed tanks.

The products of anaerobic digestion have value and can be sold to offset treatment costs (Roos 1991).

Anaerobic digestion provides a variety of benefits. The environmental benefits include: ??Odors are significantly reduced or eliminated.

- Flies are substantially reduced.
- A relatively clean liquid for flushing and irrigation can be produced.
- Pathogens are substantially reduced in the liquid and solid products.
- Greenhouse gas emissions are reduced.
- And finally, nonpoint source pollution is substantially reduced.

On the economic side, additional benefits are provided.

- The time devoted to moving, handling, and processing manure is minimized.
- Biogas is produced for heat or electrical power.
- Waste heat can be used to meet the heating and cooling requirements of the dairy.
- Concentrating nutrients to a relatively small volume for export from the site can reduce the land required for liquid waste application.
- The rich fertilizer can be produced for sale to the public, nurseries, or other crop producers.
- Income can be obtained from the processing of imported wastes (tipping fees), the sale of organic nutrients, greenhouse gas credits, and the sale of power.
- Power tax credits may be available for each kWh of power produced.
- Greenhouse tax credits may become available for each ton of carbon recycled.
- Finally the power generated is "distributed power" which minimizes the need to modify the power grid. The impact of new power on the power grid is minimized.

In order to achieve the benefits of anaerobic digestion, the treatment facility must be integrated into the dairy operation. Unfortunately, no single dairy can serve as a model for a manure treatment facility. The operation of the dairy will establish the digester loading and the energy generated from the system. The anaerobic facility must be designed to meet the individual characteristics of each dairy.

This manual provides an introduction to the anaerobic digestion of dairy manure. It is divided into three parts. The first describes the operation and waste management practices of Idaho dairies. The second introduces anaerobic digestion and the anaerobic digestion processes suitable for dairy waste. The third presents typical design applications for different types of dairies and establishes the cost and benefits of the facilities.

Dairy Operations

Dairy operations significantly affect the quantity and quality of manure that may be delivered to the anaerobic digestion system. In addition to the number of milk and dry cows, the housing, transport, manure separation, and bedding systems used by the dairy establishes the amount of material that must be handled and the amount of energy produced.

Housing System

Confined dairy animals may be housed in a variety of systems. Commonly used housing systems include free stalls, corrals with paved feed lanes, and open lot systems. Milk cows, dry cows and heifers may be housed in free stalls, corrals, and open-lots on the same dairy. The type of housing used determines the quantity of manure that can be economically collected.

Free Stall Barns

Free stalls are currently the most popular method for housing large dairy herds. Free stall housing provides a means for collecting essentially all of the manure.

Corrals

Corral systems with paved feed lanes are also commonly used. The manure deposited in the feed lanes can be scraped or flushed daily. From 40 to 55- percent of the excreted manure may be deposited and collected from the corral feed lane. The balance of the manure may be deposited in the milk barn (10 to 15 percent) or the open lot (30 to 50%). Typically the manure deposited in the open lot is removed two to three times a year. It may have little net energy value after being stored in the open lot over prolonged periods of time. For corral systems one must make a reasonable determination of the recoverable manure deposited in the feed lane, corral, and milk barn.

Corral systems also use a considerable amount of bedding material during the winter months. The straw bedding is generally removed in the spring and placed on the fields prior to spring planting.

Milk Barn

Dairy cows are milked two to three times a day. The cows are moved from their stalls to the milk parlor holding area. The milk parlor and holding area are normally flushed with fresh water. From 10 to 15 percent of the manure is deposited in the milk parlor. In addition to the manure that is flushed, the cows may be washed with a sprinkler system. Warm water that is produced by the refrigeration compressors, vacuum pumps, and milk cooling system may be used for drinking water, manure flushing or washing the cows.

It has been estimated that 5 to 150 gallons of fresh water per milk cow is used in the milking center. More common values are 10 to 30 gallons of fresh water per milk cow. The quantity and quality of water discharge from the milk parlor must be accurately measured. In many cases, the waste deposited in the milk barn is processed in a separate waste management system.

Open Lot

In open lot systems the manure is deposited on the ground and scraped into piles. The manure is removed infrequently (once or twice a year). A significant amount of manure degradation occurs resulting in greenhouse gas emissions. In many cases, the open lot degradation produces manure that has little or no net energy value.

Transport System

The commonly used manure transport systems are flush, scrape, vacuum, and loader systems. In free stall barns the manure can be flushed, scraped, or vacuum collected.

Flush Systems: If a flush system is used the manure is substantially diluted. The quantity of water used in a flush system depends on the width, length, and slope of the flush isle. The feed isles are generally 14 feet wide while the back isles are generally 10 feet wide. The slope varies between one and two percent. A flush system will generally reduce the concentration of manure from 12 1/2 percent solids, "as excreted", to less than one percent solids in the flush water. Flush systems are however more economical and less labor-intensive than scrape or vacuum systems.

Scrape Systems Scrape systems are simply systems that collect the manure by scraping it to a sump. Under normal weather conditions the scraped manure has approximately the same consistency as the "as excreted" manure. During the warm dry summer manure may be dewatered on the slab.

Front End Loader

Front-end loaders are used to stack and remove corral bedding and manure.

Vacuum Systems

Vacuum systems collect "as excreted" manure with a vacuum truck. Generally, the trucks collect approximately 4000 gallons per load. The manure can be hauled to a disposal site rather than to an intermediate sump. Vacuum collection is a slow and tedious process. The advantage is that the collected manure is undiluted and approximately equal to the "as excreted" concentration.

Bedding

The type of bedding used can significantly alter the characteristics of the manure being treated. Typically straw, wood chips, sand, or compost are used as bedding material. In some cases paper mixed with sawdust is used. Compost usually has some sand mixed with the organic constituents. If composting is carried out on dirt lots, a significant amount of sand and silt may be incorporated into the compost. Since anaerobic digestion will not degrade the wood chips, sand, or silt, it is necessary to remove those constituents prior to, or during anaerobic digestion process. The quantity of non-degradable, organic and inorganic material can significantly impact the performance of the anaerobic digester.

The quantity of bedding added to the manure is a function of the design and operation of the dairy. Generally only the "kick-out" from the stalls is added to the manure. The quantity that is "kicked-out" is a function of the design of the dairy housing system as well as the type of bedding used.

Manure Processing

Each dairy has its own manure processing system. Scraped or flushed manure may be processed in a system separate from the milk barn waste, or the collected manure waste may be processed with the milk barn waste. In general, current manure processing consists of macerating the waste with a chopper pump, screening the waste to remove the organic fibers, followed by sedimentation to remove the sand, silt, and organic settable particles. Much of the degradable manure is removed during the separation processes. Up to 80% of the COD and 30% of the total Nitrogen and Phosphorous can be lost in the solids removed by the screen and sedimentation process. Detailed sampling and analysis is required to confirm losses.

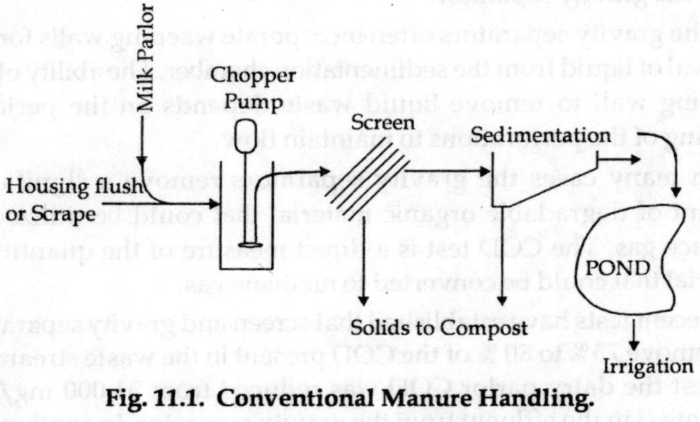

Fig. 11.1. Conventional Manure Handling.

Holding Tanks and Chopper Pumps

A wide variety of holding tanks and chopper pumps are used throughout the dairy industry. Typically, the tanks are relatively small but in some cases they are designed to hold several hours of flush water.

Primary Screens

An equally wide variety of screening systems are used. In many cases the screens are housed in separate enclosures to prevent freezing during the winter months. Outdoor screens are generally problematic during cold weather months. Fan separators (screw press) are also used to provide efficient separation of the fibrous solids. The primary screens will remove a significant amount of degradable organic material that could be converted to gas in an anaerobic digester. The screened materials are generally used to produce bedding after being composted for the required time periods.

Gravity Separators

Gravity separators varying in size from 10 feet wide by 30' long to 24 feet wide by 80 feet long are usually placed after the primary screens. The purpose of the gravity separator is to remove the sands and silt present in the waste stream. If gravity separators are used without screening a thick mat of straw and fibers may develop on top of the gravity separator.

The gravity separators often incorporate weeping walls for the removal of liquid from the sedimentation chamber. The ability of the weeping wall to remove liquid waste depends on the periodic cleaning of the perforations to maintain flow.

In many cases the gravity separators remove a significant amount of degradable organic material that could be utilized to produce gas. The COD test is a direct measure of the quantity of material that could be converted to methane gas.

Recent tests have established that screen and gravity separators can remove 75% to 80 % of the COD present in the waste stream. In one test the dairy parlor COD was reduced from 31,000 mg/l to 8,600 mg/l in the effluent from the gravity separator. In another the flush water influent to a separator system was 10,900 mg/L while the effluent was 1,800 mg/L. While a significant portion of the organic carbon (COD) is retained with the separated solids, an equal percentage of the nitrogen and phosphorus is not. The separation process alters the carbon to nitrogen ratio of both the liquid and solids streams.

The sedimentation process concentrates the organic solids, which are periodically removed. A recent analysis showed the flush water had a COD concentration of 25,500 mg/l while the concentrated solids from the separator had a COD of 115,800 mg/l. (Burke, 2001) Anaerobic decomposition of settled solids can be observed in separators that have a surface covered with methane gas bubbles. It is clear that existing solids handling practices contribute to greenhouse gas emissions and prevent efficient energy recovery from manure waste.

Primary Holding Ponds

Most dairies will discharge the screened and settled waste to a primary holding pond. The primary holding pond is a secondary sedimentation basin where the fine solids are separated from the liquid waste. Eventually the fine solids must be removed from the bottom of the primary holding pond. Odors generally accompany the removal of solids.

Secondary Holding Ponds It is common to have a number of holding ponds that provide the required detention time (180 days) following the primary holding pond. The irrigation and flush pumps are normally installed in one or more of these ponds.

Summary

As indicated above, two separate waste streams, the milk parlor and confinement area wastes, makeup the dairy waste that can be treated through anaerobic digestion. The type of bedding used, as well as the manure transport, and subsequent manure processing will change the characteristics of both waste streams. The dilution of waste will require larger anaerobic digestion facilities.

The removal of organics through screening and sedimentation will reduce the quantity of organic solids that can be converted to gas in the digester. The presence of sand and silts will clog pipes, damage equipment, and fill anaerobic digestion tanks. Sand can only be removed from dilute waste streams. Thick slurries retain sand that precipitate in the digester when the organics are converted to gas and the solids concentration is reduced. If thick slurries are processed in an anaerobic digester, intense mixing is required to maintain the solids in suspension.

Modification of existing dairy management practices may be required to achieve the full benefits of anaerobic digestion. Figure 2 below, shows how a solid waste management facility can be incorporated in an existing dairy waste-processing stream. If low or moderate concentrations of sand are present the entire waste stream may be discharged to an anaerobic digester, bypassing the existing screen and gravity separators. If high concentrations of sand are present, the existing gravity separators may remain in place. Under such conditions, a reduced quantity of organics will be converted to gas.

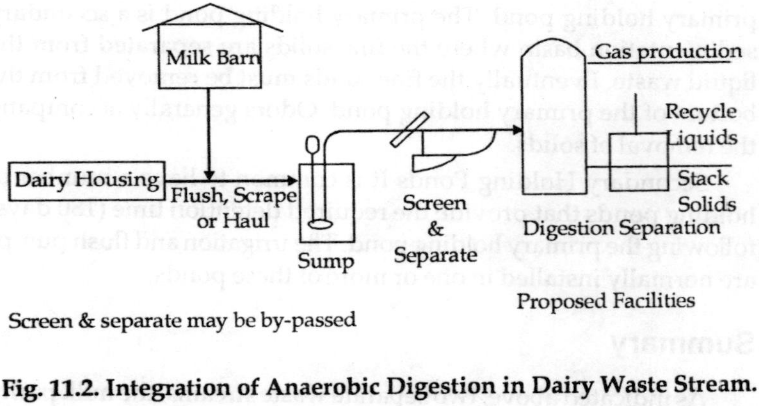

Fig. 11.2. Integration of Anaerobic Digestion in Dairy Waste Stream.

Anaerobic Digestion

Anaerobic digestion is the breakdown of organic material by a microbial population that lives in an oxygen free environment. Anaerobic means literally "without air". When organic matter is decomposed in an anaerobic environment the bacteria produce a mixture of methane and carbon dioxide gas. Anaerobic digestion treats waste by converting putrid organic materials to carbon dioxide and methane gas. This gas is referred to as biogas. The biogas can be used to produce both electrical power and heat. The conversion of solids to biogas results in a much smaller quantity of solids that must be disposed. During the anaerobic treatment process, organic nitrogen compounds are converted to ammonia, sulfur compounds are converted to hydrogen sulfide, phosphorus to orthophosphates, and calcium, magnesium, and sodium are converted to a variety of salts. Through proper operation, the inorganic constituents can be converted to a variety of beneficial products. The end products of anaerobic digestion are natural gas (methane) for energy production, heat produced from energy production, a nutrient rich organic slurry, and other marketable inorganic products.

The effluent containing particulate and soluble organic and inorganic materials can be separated into its particulate and soluble constituents. The particulate solids can be sold or exported from the dairy while the nutrient rich liquids are applied to the land.

Bacterial Consortia

Anaerobic digestion is carried out by a group, or consortia of bacteria, working together to convert organic matter to gas and inorganic constituents. The first step of anaerobic digestion is the breakdown of particulate matter to soluble organic constituents that can be processed through the bacterial cell wall.

Hydrolysis, or the liquification of insoluble materials is the rate-limiting step in anaerobic digestion of waste slurries. This step is carried out by a variety of bacteria through the release of extra-cellular enzymes that reside in close proximity to the bacteria. The soluble organic materials that are produced through hydrolysis consist of sugars, fatty acids, and amino acids. Those soluble constituents are converted to carbon dioxide and a variety of short chain organic acids by acid forming bacteria. Other groups of bacteria reduce the hydrogen toxicity by scavenging hydrogen to produce ammonia, hydrogen sulfide, and methane. A group of methanogens converts acetic acid to methane gas. A wide variety of physical, chemical, and biological reactions take place. The bacterial consortia catalyze these reactions.

Consequently, the most important factor in converting waste to gas is the bacterial consortia. The bacterial consortia are essentially the "bio-enzymes" that accomplish the desired treatment. A poorly developed or stressed bacterial consortium will not provide the desired conversion of waste to gas and other beneficial products.

Factors Controlling the Conversion of Waste to Gas

The rate and efficiency of the anaerobic digestion process is controlled by:

- The type of waste being digested,
- Its concentration,
- Its temperature,
- The presence of toxic materials,
- The pH and alkalinity,
- The hydraulic retention time,
- The solids retention time,
- The ratio of food to microorganisms,
- The rate of digester loading,
- And the rate at which toxic end products of digestion are removed.

Each of these factors is discussed below.

Waste Characteristics

All waste constituents are not equally degraded or converted to gas through anaerobic digestion. Anaerobic bacteria do not degrade lignin and some other hydrocarbons. The digestion of waste containing high nitrogen and sulfur concentrations can produce toxic concentrations of ammonia and hydrogen sulfide. Wastes that are not particularly water-soluble will breakdown slowly.

Dairy wastes have been reported to degrade slower than swine or poultry manure. The manure production from a typical 1,400-pound milk cow is presented in the table below.

Table 11.1. Dairy Manure Production.

Manure Produced by a 1,400 pound Cow	
Manure (pounds)	112
Manure (gallons)	13.5
Total Solids (dry pounds)	14
Volatile Solids (dry pounds)	11.9
COD (pounds)	12.5
TKN (pounds)	0.63
Total Phosphorus (pounds)	0.098
Total Potassium (pounds)	0.36

The composition of the manure solids is presented in Table 2.

Table 11.2. Dairy Manure Composition (Stafford, Hawkes et al. 1980).

Component	% Dry of Matter
Volatile solids	83.0
Ether Extract	2.6
Cellulose	31.0
Hemicellulose	12.0
Lignin	12.2
Starch	12.5
Crude Protein	12.5
Ammonia	0.5
Acids	0.1

As can be observed from Table 11.2, the majority of the volatile solids are composed of cellulose and hemicelluloses. Both are readily converted to methane gas by anaerobic bacteria. As pointed out earlier, lignin will not degrade during anaerobic digestion. Since a substantial portion of the volatile solids in dairy waste is lignin, the percentage of cow manure volatile solids that can be converted to gas is lower when compared to other manure and wastes.

The manure characteristics also establish the percentage of carbon dioxide and methane in the biogas produced. Dairy waste biogas will typically be composed of 55 to 65% methane and 35 to 45% carbon dioxide. Trace quantities of hydrogen sulfide and nitrogen will also be present.

Dilution of Waste

The waste characteristics can be altered by simple dilution. Water will reduce the concentration of certain constituents such as nitrogen and sulfur that produce products (ammonia and hydrogen sulfide) that are inhibitory to the anaerobic digestion process. High solids digestion creates high concentrations of end products that inhibit anaerobic decomposition. Therefore, some dilution can have positive effects.

The literature indicates that greater reduction efficiencies occur at concentrations of approximately 6 to 7 percent total solids. Dairy waste "as excreted" is approximately 12 percent total solids and 10.5 percent volatile solids. Most treatment systems operate at a lower solids concentration than the "as excreted" values.

Dilution also causes stratification within the digester. Undigested straw forms a thick mat on top of the digester while sand accumulates at the bottom. The optimum waste concentration is based on temperature and the quantity of straw and other constituents that are likely to separate within the anaerobic digester. It is desirable to keep the separation or stratification in the digester to a minimum.

Intense mixing involving the consumption of power may reduce the stratification of dilute waste. The use of flush systems to remove the manure from the dairy barns has major economic advantages to the dairy. Flush systems normally use 100 to 200 gallons per cow, per day of dilution water. The flush volumes required are based on the lane or gutter length, width and slope (Fulhage and Martin 1994). The flush water usually contains very low concentrations of total and volatile solids.

At 100 gallons per cow of flush water, the waste has only 12.5 percent of the "as excreted" concentration. At 200 gallons per cow per day of flush water the waste contains only 6.25 percent of the "as excreted" concentration. Table 3 below presents the waste characteristics using various flush volumes.

Table 11.3. Manure Waste Concentration with Various Flush Volumes

	"As Excreted (AE) Manure"	Manure with 100 gal per Cow Flush Water	Manure with 200 gal per Cow Flush Water
Gallons for 1000 milk cows	14,267	114,000	214,000
Total Solids Concentration (mg/l)	120,000	15,000	8,000
Volatile solids Concentration (mg/l)	102,000	12,750	6,800
COD Concentration (mg//)	129,400	16,176	8,627
TKN Concentration (mg/l)	5,294	662	353
Total P Concentration (mg/l)	824	103	55

The milk parlor also produces a substantial amount of dilute waste. Approximately 15% of the animal manure is deposited in the milk parlor. The resulting milk parlor waste has a composition similar to the flush waste presented in Table 11.3.

Foreign Materials

Addition of foreign materials such as animal bedding, sand and silt can have a significant impact on the anaerobic digestion process. For example, the poor performance of the Monroe, WA dairy digester was attributed to the use of cedar wood chip bedding (Ecotope 1979). The quantity and quality of the bedding material added to the manure will have a significant impact on the anaerobic digestion of dairy waste. Sand and silt must be removed before anaerobic digestion. If it is not removed before digestion it must be suspended during the digestion process.

Toxic Materials

Toxic materials such as fungicides and antibacterial agents can have an adverse effect on anaerobic digestion. The anaerobic process can handle small quantities of toxic materials without difficulty. Storage containers for fungicides and antibacterial agents should be placed at locations that will not discharge to the anaerobic digester.

Nutrients

Bacteria require a sufficient concentration of nutrients to achieve optimum growth. The carbon to nitrogen ratio in the waste should be less than 43. The carbon to phosphorus ratio should be less than 187. Hills and Roberts showed that a non-lignin C/N ratio of 20 to 25 is optimum for digester performance. Typically, "as excreted manure has a C/N ratio of 10.

Temperature

The anaerobic bacterial consortia function under three temperature ranges. Psychrophilic temperatures of less than 68 degrees Fahrenheit produce the least amount of bacterial action. Mesophilic digestion occurs between 68 degrees and 105 degrees Fahrenheit. Thermophilic digestion occurs between 110 degrees Fahrenheit and 160 degrees Fahrenheit. The optimum mesophilic temperature is between 95 and 98 degrees Fahrenheit. The optimum thermophilic temperature is between 140 and 145 degrees Fahrenheit. The rate of bacterial growth and waste degradation is faster under thermophilic conditions. On the other hand, thermophilic digestion produces an odorous effluent when compared to mesophilic digestion. Thermophilic digestion substantially increases the heat energy required for the process. In most cases, sufficient heat is not available to operate in the thermophilic range. This is especially true if flush systems are used or the milk parlor waste is mixed with the scraped manure. Large quantities of dilution flush water must be heated to the digester's operating temperature.

During cold weather, control of the flush volume is critical in maintaining adequate digester temperatures.

Seasonal and diurnal temperature fluctuations significantly affect anaerobic digestion and the quantities of gas produced. Bacterial storage and operational controls must be incorporated in the process design to maintain process stability under a variety of temperature conditions.

Temperature is a universal process variable. It influences the rate of bacterial action as well as the quantity of moisture in the biogas. The biogas moisture content increases exponentially with temperature. Temperature also influences the quantity of gas and volatile organic substances dissolved in solution as well as the concentration of ammonia and hydrogen sulfide gas.

pH

Methane producing bacteria require a neutral to slightly alkaline environment (pH 6.8 to 8.5) in order to produce methane. Acid forming bacteria grow much faster than methane forming bacteria. If acid-producing bacteria grow too fast, they may produce more acid than the methane forming bacteria can consume. Excess acid builds up in the system. The pH drops, and the system may become unbalanced, inhibiting the activity of methane forming bacteria. Methane production may stop entirely. Maintenance of a large active quantity of methane producing bacteria prevents pH instability. Retained biomass systems are inherently more stable than bacterial growth based systems such as completely mixed and plug flow digesters.

Hydraulic Retention Time (HRT)

Most anaerobic systems are designed to retain the waste for a fixed number of days. The number of days the materials stays in the tank is called the Hydraulic Retention Time or HRT. The Hydraulic Retention Time equals the volume of the tank divided by the daily flow (HRT=V/Q). The hydraulic retention time is important since it establishes the quantity of time available for bacterial growth and subsequent conversion of the organic material to gas. A direct relationship exists between the hydraulic retention time and the volatile solids converted to gas. Such a relationship for dairy waste is shown in Figure 11.3.

Solids Retention Time (SRT)

The Solids Retention Time (SRT) is the most important factor controlling the conversion of solids to gas. It is also the most important factor in maintaining digester stability. Although the calculation of the solids retention time is often improperly stated, it is the quantity of solids maintained in the digester divided by the quantity of solids wasted each day.

$$SRT = \frac{(V)(C_d)}{(Q_w)(C_w)}$$

where V is the digester volume; Cd is the solids concentration in the digester; Qw is the volume wasted each day and Cw is the solids concentration of the waste.

In a conventional completely mixed, or plug flow digester, the HRT equals the SRT. However, in a variety of retained biomass reactors the SRT exceeds the HRT. As a result, the retained biomass digesters can be much smaller while achieving the same solids conversion to gas.

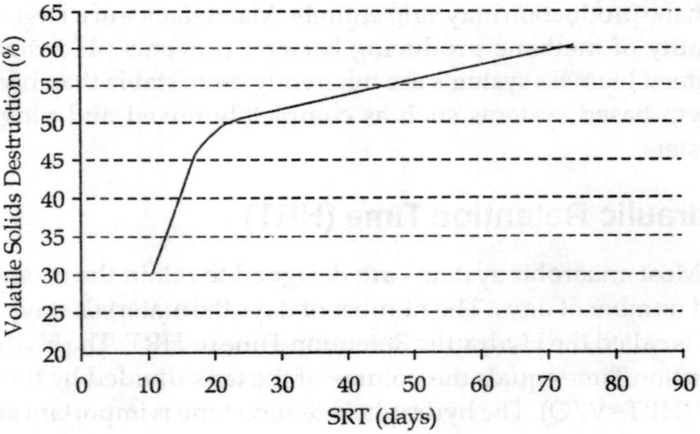

Fig. 11.3. Dairy Waste Volatile Solids Destruction.

The volatile solids conversion to gas is a function of SRT (Solids Retention Time) rather than HRT. At a low SRT sufficient time is not available for the bacteria to grow and replace the bacteria lost in the effluent. If the rate of bacterial loss exceeds the rate of bacteria growth, "wash-out" occurs. The SRT at which "wash-out" begins to occur is the "critical SRT".

Jewel established that a maximum of 65 percent of dairy manure's volatile solids could be converted to gas with long solids retention times. Burke established that 65 to 67 percent of dairy manure COD could be converted to gas. Long retention times are required for the conversion of cellulose to gas.

The goal of process engineers over the past twenty years has been to develop anaerobic processes that retain biomass in a variety of forms such that the SRT can be increased while the HRT is decreased. The goal has been to retain, rather than waste the biocatalyst (bacterial consortia) responsible for the anaerobic process. As a result of this effort, gas yields have increased and digester volumes decreased. A measure of the success of biomass retention is the SRT/HRT ratio. In conventional digesters, the ratio is 1.0. Effective retention systems will have SRT/HRT ratios exceeding 3.0. At an SRT/HRT ratio of 3.0 the digester will be 1/3rd the size of a conventional digester.

Digester Loading (kg / m3 / d)

Neither the hydraulic retention time (HRT), nor the solids retention time (SRT) tells the full story of the impact that the influent waste concentration has on the anaerobic digester. One waste may be dilute and the other concentrated. The concentrated waste will produce more gas per gallon and affect the digester to a much greater extent than the diluted waste. A more appropriate measure of the waste on the digester's size and performance is the loading. The loading can be reported in pounds of waste (influent concentration x influent flow) per cubic foot of digester volume. The more common units are kilograms of influent waste per cubic meter of digester volume per day (kg / m3 / d). One (kg / m3 / d) is equal to 0.0624 (lb / ft3 / d).

The digester loading can be calculated if the HRT and influent waste concentration are known. The loading in (kg / m3 / d) is simply:

$$L = \left(\frac{1}{HRT}\right)(C_1)$$

where CI is the influent waste concentration in grams. Increasing the loading will reduce the digester size but will also reduce the percentage of volatile solids converted to gas.

Food to Microorganism Ratio

The food to microorganism ratio is the key factor controlling anaerobic digestion. At a given temperature, the bacterial consortia can only consume a limited amount of food each day. In order to consume the required number of pounds of waste one must supply the proper number of pounds of bacteria. The ratio of the pounds of waste supplied to the pounds of bacteria available to consume the waste is the food to microorganism ratio (F/M). This ratio is the controlling factor in all biological treatment processes. A lower the F/M ratio will result in a greater percentage of the waste being converted to gas.

Unfortunately, the bacterial mass is difficult to measure since it is difficult to differentiate the bacterial mass from the influent waste. The task would be easier if all of the influent waste were converted to biomass or gas. In that case, the F/M ratio would simply be the digester loading divided by the concentration of volatile solids (biomass) in the digester (L / Cd). For any given loading, the efficiency can be improved by lowering the F/M ratio by increasing the concentration of biomass in the digester. Also for any given biomass concentration within the digester, the efficiency can be improved by decreasing the loading. Unfortunately, a portion of the influent waste is not processed or converted to biomass or gas by the bacteria. In that case the F/M ratio is equal to the VS loading divided by the digester VS measured (VSD) minus the unprocessed Volatile Solids (VSUP). The unprocessed volatile solids may include refractory or non-degradable biological products produced by the bacteria.

$$\frac{F}{M} = \frac{L_{VS}}{VS_D - VS_{UP}}$$

End Product Removal

The end products of anaerobic digestion can adversely affect the digestion process. Such products of anaerobic digestion include organic acids, ammonia nitrogen, and hydrogen sulfide. For any given volatile solids conversion to gas, the higher the influent waste concentration, the greater the end product concentration. End product inhibition can be reduced by lowering the influent waste concentration or by separately removing the soluble end products from the digester through elutriation. Elutriation is the process of washing the solids (bacteria) with clean water to remove the products of digestion. The contact process provides an efficient means of removing the end products of digestion. End product removal can be enhanced by elutriation, which is easily incorporated into the contact process (Burke 1997).

Digester Types

A vast array of anaerobic digesters have been developed and placed in operation over the past fifty years. A variety of schemes could be used to classify the digestion processes. For dairy waste, the most important classification is whether or not it can be used to convert dairy waste solids to gas while meeting the goals of anaerobic digestion. The goals of dairy waste anaerobic digestion are as follows:

1. Reduce the mass of solids
2. Reduce the odors associated with the waste products
3. Produce clean effluent for recycle and irrigation
4. Concentrate the nutrients in a solid product for storage or export
5. Generate energy
6. Reduce pathogens associated with the waste In addition, the digester must be able to handle or process the dairy waste stream.

Dairy waste is a semi-solid slurry. Much of the energy value is in the solids. Consequently, the process must be able to convert solids to gas without clogging the anaerobic reactor. The process must also be able to handle bedding material, sand and other foreign materials associated with typical dairy waste. In addition, if the dairy manure is a dilute waste, the process must be capable of mitigating stratification and solids separation within the reactor.

Processes that are not Appropriate for Digesting Dairy Manure

A variety of high rate anaerobic processes, which retain bacteria have been developed to treat soluble organic industrial wastes. These "high rate" digesters have reduced hydraulic detention times from 20 days to a few hours. They include anaerobic filters, both upflow and downflow, and a variety of biofilm processes such as fixed film packed bed reactors. Bacteria are retained in these reactors as films on carriers such as plastic beads, or sand, or on support media of all configurations. The waste washes past the retained bacteria. The bacteria convert the soluble constituents to gas but have little opportunity to hydrolyze and degrade the particulate solids, unless the solids become attached to the biomass.

These reactors are not suitable for digesting dairy waste since they are not effective in converting particulate solids to gas and tend to clog while digesting dairy manure slurries. These high rate reactors can treat the soluble component of dairy waste. But only a fraction of the available energy will be recovered.

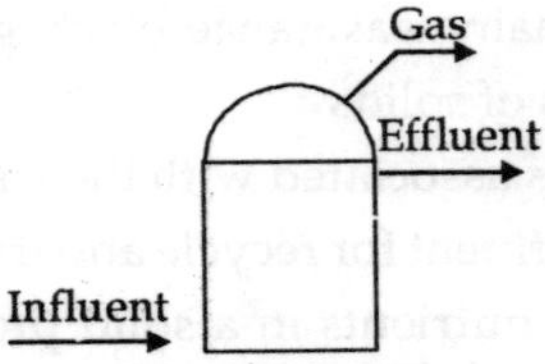

Fig. 11.4. Packed Fixed Film Reactor.

A widely used industrial waste anaerobic digester is the UASB or "Upflow Anaerobic Sludge Blanket", reactor. The process stores the anaerobic consortia as pellets, approximately the size of a pea. The upflow anaerobic sludge blanket reactor (UASB) is widely used in industrial treatment processes throughout the world. It is an extremely effective process for converting soluble organic materials, such as sugar to methane gas. It has not been used for processing dairy waste since it is ineffective in converting solids to gas. It is primarily used to convert non-particulate or soluble waste to gas.

Influent Effluent Gas UASB Reactor The anaerobic baffled reactor is a horizontal version of the upflow anaerobic sludge blanket reactor. Both store large quantities of anaerobic bacteria as pellets approximately the size of a pea. Unfortunately, these very successful anaerobic reactors are not effective in digesting particulate waste.

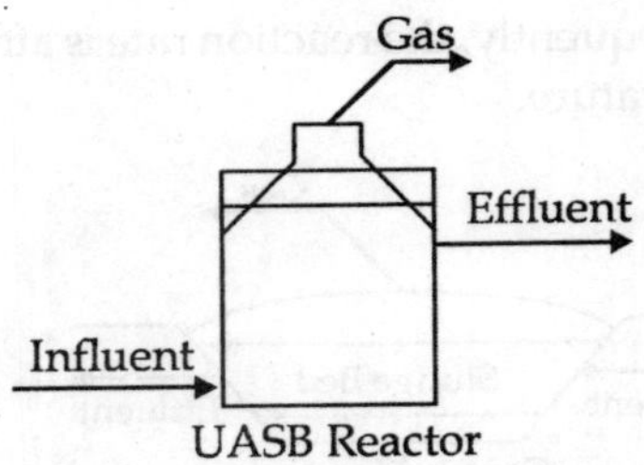

Fig. 11.5. Upflow Anaerobic Sludge Blanket Reactor.

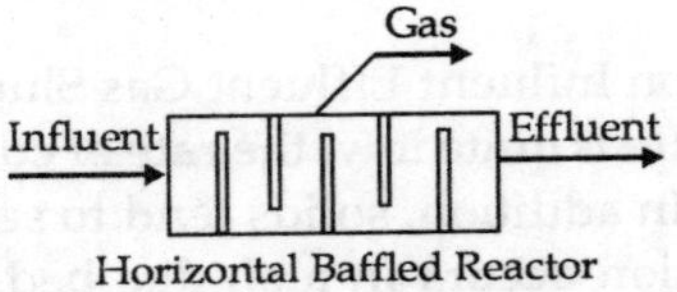

Fig. 11.6. Baffled Reactor.

Particulate solids tend to settle in the horizontal baffled reactor (HBR) while organic fibers will form a mat on the surface. There are no known instances of the HBR being used for the treatment of dairy waste. Unless the dairy waste was thoroughly screened and all particulate matter removed the HBR would tend to become clogged. The removal of solids by screening and gravity sedimentation will eliminate up to 80% of the energy generating potential from dairy waste.

Processes that can be used for Digesting Dairy Manure

The processes that have been used for digesting dairy waste can be subdivided into high rate and low rate processes. Low rate processes consist of covered anaerobic lagoons, plug flow digesters, and mesophilic completely mixed digesters. High rate reactors include the thermophilic completely mixed digesters, anaerobic contact digesters, and hybrid contact/fixed film reactors.

Anaerobic Lagoons (Very Low Rate): Anaerobic lagoons are covered ponds. Manure enters at one end and the effluent is removed at the other. The lagoons operate at psychrophilic, or ground temperatures. Consequently, the reaction rate is affected by seasonal variations in temperature.

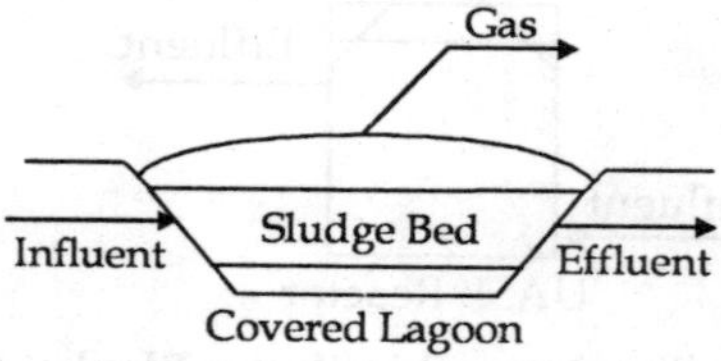

Fig. 11.7. Anaerobic Lagoons.

Covered Lagoon Influent Effluent Gas Sludge Bed Since the reaction temperature is quite low, the rate of conversion of solids to gas is also low. In addition, solids tend to settle to the bottom where decomposition occurs in a sludge bed. Little contact of bacteria with the bulk liquid occurs. The biomass concentration is low, resulting in very low solids conversion to gas (High F/M ratio with poor growth rates at low temperatures). Little or no mixing occurs. Consequently, lagoon utilization is poor. Anaerobic lagoons have been used to treat parlor and free stall flush water. Gas production rates have been low and seasonal. Solids may be screened and removed prior to entering the lagoon. A considerable amount of energy potential is lost with the removal of particulate solids. The advantage of anaerobic lagoons is the lowcost. The low cost is offset by the lower energy production and poor effluent quality. Periodically the covered lagoons must be cleaned at considerable cost. Nuisance odors may be generated while cleaning the lagoons.

Completely Mixed Digesters (Low Rate)

The most common form of an anaerobic digester is the completely mixed reactor. Most sewage treatment plants and many industrial treatment plants use a completely mixed reactor to convert waste to gas. The completely mixed reactor is a tank that is heated and mixed.

Most completely mixed reactors operate in the mesophilic range. All of the initial anaerobic digesters used to treat dairy manure were completely mixed mesophilic digesters. The cost of mixing is high, especially if sand, silt, and floating materials, present in the waste stream, must be suspended throughout the digestion period.

Some completely mixed reactors operate in a thermophilic range where sufficient energy is available to heat to reactor. Highly concentrated readily degradable waste is required in order to generate sufficient heat for the thermophilic range of operation. Completely mixed thermophilic digesters are used in the EEC to treat animal manure(Ahring, Ibrahim et al. 2001). Recently, completely mixed thermophilic digesters were proposed in Oregon to treat dairy manure(Tillamook 1999).

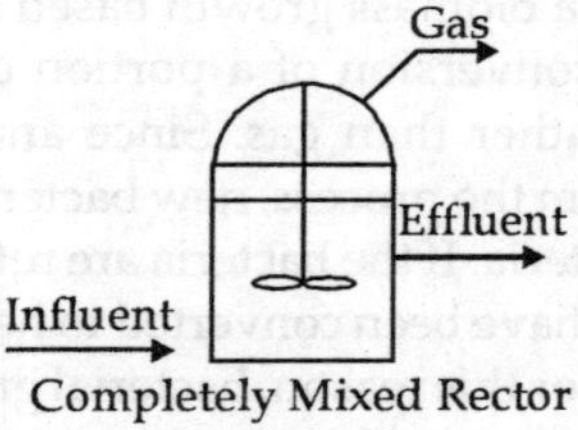

Fig. 11.8. Completely Mixed Reactor.

Most completely mixed reactors are heated with spiral flow heat exchangers. These heat exchangers apply hot water to one side of the spiral and the anaerobic slurry to the other. The spiral heat exchangers have proven to be a successful method of efficiently transferring heat.

Completely mixed reactors can be constructed of a variety of materials. In the U.S. most completely mixed reactors have a low profile with a diameter greater than the height. Some municipal digesters in the U.S., and most in Europe have an egg shape with a height much greater than the diameter. The egg shape enhances mixing while eliminating much of the stratification. Completely mixed reactors can have fixed covers, floating covers, or gas holding covers. Most municipal digesters have floating covers. Floating covers are more expensive than fixed covers.

Mixing can be accomplished with a variety of gas mixers, mechanical mixers, and draft tubes with mechanical mixers or simply recirculation pumps. The most efficient mixing device in terms of power consumed per gallon mixed is the mechanical mixer. Most municipal digesters are intensely mixed to reduce the natural stratification that occurs in a low profile tank. A large amount of evidence has been accumulated over the past 10 years indicating that intense mixing may inhibit the bacterial consortia. But, intense mixing is required to keep sands and silts in suspension.

The advantage of the completely mixed reactor is that it is a proven technology that achieves reasonable conversion of solids to gas. It can be applied to the treatment of slurry waste such as dairy manure (Ecotope 1979). The disadvantage of the completely mixed reactor is the high cost of installation, and the energy cost associated with mixing the digester. The completely mixed conventional anaerobic digester is a biomass growth based system. The process requires a constant conversion of a portion of the feed solids to anaerobic bacteria rather than gas. Since anaerobic bacteria are constantly wasted from the process, new bacteria must be produced to replace the lost bacteria. If the bacteria are retained, the portion of the waste that would have been converted to new bacterial cells will be converted to gas. For this reason, bacterial growth based systems are not as efficient as retained biomass systems.

The advantage of the completely mixed thermophilic reactor is the rapid conversion of solids to gas and biomass (Ratkowsky, Olley et al. 1981). Some claim that the rate of conversion is three times greater with thermophilic reactors.

Consequently, the HRT can be lower and the gas production greater. The disadvantage of the thermophilic reactor is the energy required to heat cold dairy manure to thermophilic temperatures. Additional costs are incurred in tank insulation and heat exchangers. Sufficient heat may not be available from the gas produced unless the solids are highly concentrated. Thermophilic digestion of dairy manure cannot be used with manure diluted with parlor or flush water since sufficient energy will not be available to meet the heat requirements. In addition, the higher temperature thermophilic reactors increase end product inhibition, especially ammonia and organic acids (Ahring, Ibrahim et al. 2001).

Plug Flow Digesters (Low Rate)

The plug flow anaerobic digester is the simplest form of anaerobic digestion(Jewell, Kabrick et al. 1981). Consequently, it is the least expensive (Jewell, Dell-Orto et al. 1981). The plug flow digester can be a horizontal or vertical reactor. The horizontal reactor shown in Figure 9 is the most commonly used configuration. The waste enters on one side of the reactor and exits on the other. Since bacteria are not conserved, a portion of the waste must be converted to new bacteria, which are subsequently wasted with the effluent. Since the plug flow digester is a growth based system, it is less efficient than a retained biomass system. It converts less waste to gas.

Plug flow systems are subject to stratification wherein the sands and silts settle to the bottom and the organic fibers migrate to surface. The stratification can be partially inhibited by maintaining a relatively high solids concentration in the digester. Periodically, solids must be removed from the plug flow reactor. Since there is no easy way of removing the solids, the reactor must be shut down during the cleaning period. The cost of cleaning can be considerable. Since the solids concentration must be maintained at high levels, dilute milk barn waste is normally excluded from the digester. Plug flow reactors are normally heated by a hot water piping system within the reactor. The hot water piping system can complicate the periodic cleaning of the reactor.

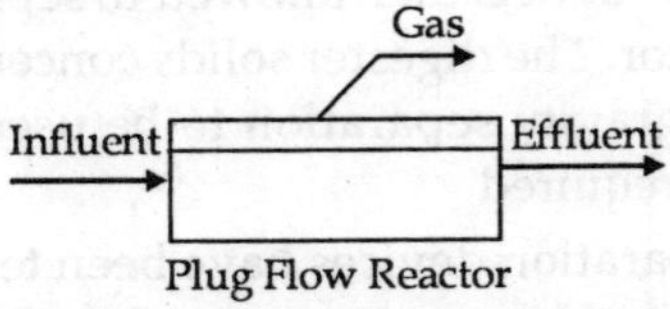

Fig. 11.9. Plug Flow Reactor.

The plug flow reactor is a simple, economical system. Applications are limited to concentrated dairy manure containing a minor amount of sand and silt. If stratification occurs because of a dilute waste or excess sand, significant operating costs will be incurred.

Contact Digesters (High Rate)

The contact reactor is a high rate process that retains bacterial biomass by separating and concentrating the solids in a separate reactor and returning the solids to the influent (Ettinger, Witherow et al. 1957; Eckenfelder 1966; Loehr 1974). More of the degradable waste can be converted to gas since a substantial portion of the bacterial mass is conserved. The contact digester can be either completely mixed or plug flow. It can be operated in the thermophilic or mesophilic range. The contact reactor can treat both dilute and concentrated waste provided the separator can concentrate the digester effluent solids sufficiently to enhance the process.

A wide variety of separators have been tested over the past 30 years. Initially gravity separators (settling tanks), or solids thickeners were used. It was soon discovered that the solids could not be sufficiently concentrated in a gravity separator without degassing to remove the gas bubbles attached to the solids.

Actively fermenting digester effluent containing gas bubbles floated rather than settled in the separator. Lamella or plate separators have also been used to concentrate the biomass after degassing. Both of these gravity-settling techniques are not effective for concentrated digester solids. Gravity separation techniques are effective with dilute waste following a completely mixed reactor.

Separation requires several days of detention(Duke Engineering & Services 2001). The completely mixed digester will prevent stratification. The effluent is then allowed to separate by gravity in the separation reactor. The digester solids concentration should be less than 2.5% for gravity separation to be used. Long separator detention times are required.

Mechanical separation devices have been tested to reduce the detention time required by gravity separation. Centrifuges, gravity belts, membranes, and other mechanical separators have been used with limited success. These disruptive devices have been shown to inhibit the bacterial consortia and thus limit the effectiveness of the contact process.

Burke used gas flotation to separate and concentrate the digester effluent for the efficient and tranquil recovery of the anaerobic consortia. The process has been used for the digestion of dairy manure(Burke 1998), sewage sludge (Burke and Yokers 1999), and potato waste(Burke 1997). It has been shown to be effective for concentrating the biomass from actively fermenting digester liquors without the need for degassing. The process has been referred to as the AGF or "anoxic gas flotation" process. Gas flotation can achieve significantly greater biomass concentrations than gravity separation without the adverse consequences associated with disruptive separation techniques.

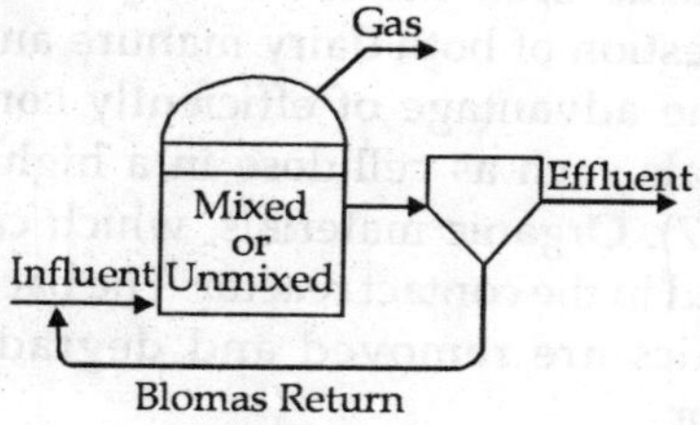

Fig. 11.10. Contact Reactor.

Gas flotation can also remove enzymes(Burke, Butler et al. 1997), organic acids (Burke 1997), and other products of digestion that cannot be removed through settling or other mechanical means. Finally, gas flotation can be performed in a non-mechanical manner, which is simple to operate and maintain.

During the contact process, refractory organic and inorganic solids accumulate within the system. The accumulated sands, silts, and non-degradable organic fibers dictate the rate of solids wasting. Wasting the nonbiodegradable solids causes the loss of bacterial mass and reduced process efficiency. The anaerobic contact process can utilize mechanical separating devices to remove refractory solids from the digestion system (Burke 2000).

Sequencing Batch Reactors (High Rate)

A sequencing batch reactor is a contact digester, which utilizes the same tank for digestion as well as separation. In a sequencing batch reactor the same tank is used to digest the waste and separate the biomass from the effluent liquor (Dugba, Zhang et al. 1997). Generally, two or more tanks are used. The tanks are operated in a fill and draw mode. The separation is accomplished by gravity.

Consequently, a more dilute, screened waste is treated. Laboratory scale sequencing batch reactors have been used to digest dairy manure.

Contact Stabilization Reactors (High Rate)

The anaerobic contact stabilization process is a more efficient contact process. Burke used the anaerobic contact stabilization process for the digestion of both dairy manure and potato waste. The process has the advantage of efficiently converting slowly degradable materials such as cellulose in a highly concentrated reactor (Burke 1997). Organic materials, which can be degraded rapidly, are digested in the contact reactor. The bacteria and slowly degradable organics are removed and degraded in a highly concentrated reactor.

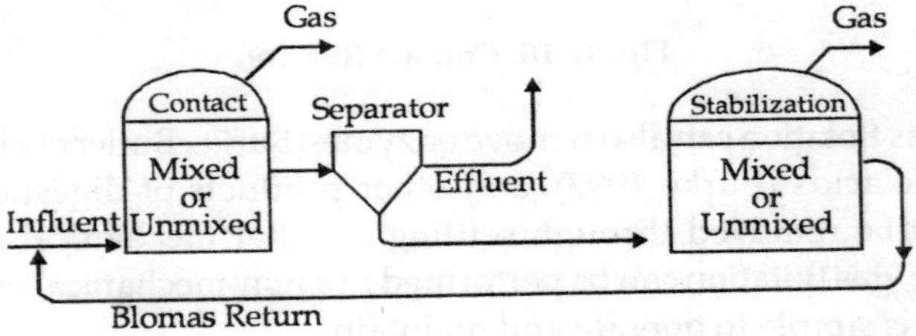

Fig. 11.11. Contact Stabilization Reactor.

Phased Digesters

Both acid phased and temperature phased digestion have been used to convert municipal sludge to gas. Acid phased digestion (Ghosh 1987) takes advantage of the fact that the acid forming bacteria have a much higher growth rate than the methanogens.

Consequently, the initial reactor can be much smaller than the subsequent methane producing digester. Acid phased digestion offers greater efficiency in the size of the anaerobic digesters. Acid phased digestion has not been applied to dairy waste.

Temperature phased digestion has been applied to the digestion of sewage sludge. The initial digester is operated in the thermophilic mode followed by a second digester, which is operated in the mesophilic mode. In the first thermophilic digester, pathogens are destroyed. In the second mesophilic digester, the mesophilic bacteria consume the organic acids created in the thermophilic reactor.

Consequently, the odors associated with a thermophilic effluent are eliminated while achieving the desired pathogen destruction.

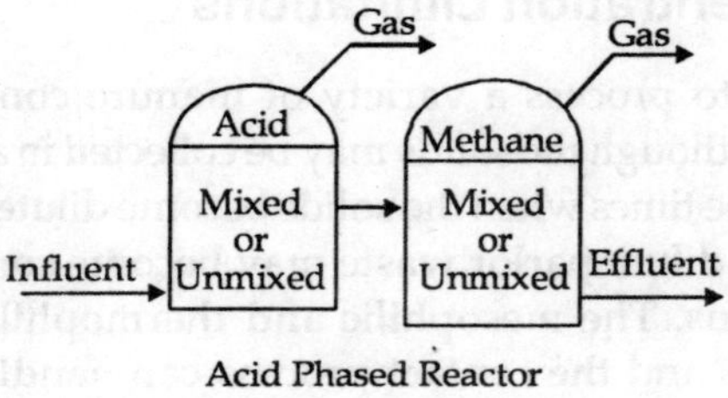

Fig. 11.12. Acid Phased Digester.

Temperature phased digestion has been used to digest dairy manure (Dugba, Zhang et al. 1997). In addition it must be pointed out that completely mixed reactors are not completely effective in removing pathogens.

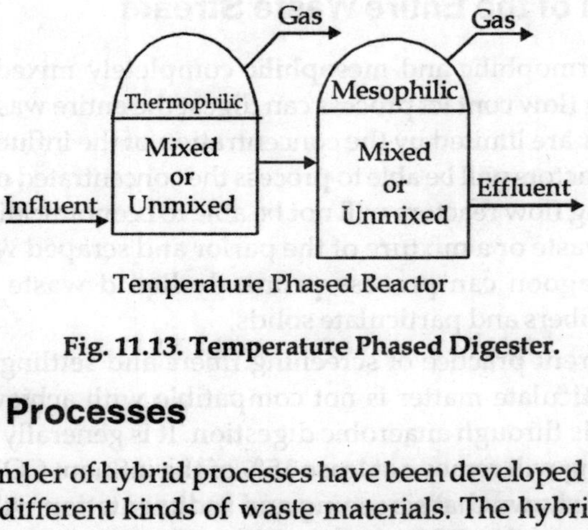

Fig. 11.13. Temperature Phased Digester.

Hybrid Processes

A number of hybrid processes have been developed and applied to many different kinds of waste materials. The hybrid processes incorporate a combination of the previously described configurations.

Qualitative Analysis of Anaerobic Processes

In order to assess the various digester configurations one must define their limitations for dairy waste digestion. The following pages describe the attributes as well as the limitations of each digester configuration.

Solids Concentration Limitations

The ability to process a variety of manure concentrations is important. Even though the solids may be collected in a concentrated form, there will be times when the solids become diluted. The inverse is also true. The dilute parlor waste may become concentrated for variety of reasons. The mesophilic and thermophilic completely mixed processes and the contact process can handle a variety of influent manure concentrations. Their operating performance is not limited by the manure concentration. On the other hand the plug flow digester and the anaerobic lagoon are limited by the influent manure concentration. The plug flow digester will stratify at low feed concentrations. The anaerobic lagoon will accumulate non-degraded solids at high influent solids concentrations.

Digestion of the Entire Waste Stream

The thermophilic and mesophilic completely mixed reactors and the plug flow contact process can digest the entire waste stream since neither are limited by the concentration of the influent waste. Plug flow reactors will be able to process the concentrated or scraped manure. Plug flow reactors will not be able to economically process the parlor waste or a mixture of the parlor and scraped waste. The anaerobic lagoon can process primarily liquid waste after the removal of fibers and particulate solids.

The current practice of screening fibers and settling solids to remove particulate matter is not compatible with achieving high energy yields through anaerobic digestion. It is generally accepted that screening will remove at lease 15% of the influent COD. Recent analysis has shown that screening and sedimentation will remove 60% or more of the COD that could be converted to gas. Solids separation should follow, rather than precede anaerobic digestion.

Foreign Material Processing

High concentrations of sand and silt are not compatible with the plug flow digester or the anaerobic lagoon. Completely mixed reactors can operate with minor concentrations of foreign material by maintaining the material in suspension through intense mixing. The contact process incorporating grit removal as described by Burke (Burke 2000) is not limited by the concentration of foreign material.

Odor Control

Most properly operated anaerobic digesters will eliminate the generation of odors from the site(Wilkie 2000). However, both plug flow anaerobic digesters and the anaerobic lagoon must be periodically cleaned. During the cleaning process odors are generated. The thermophilic completely mixed reactors produce an effluent that is far more odorous than mesophically digested waste. Contact and completely mixed digesters significantly reduce odors and may not require cleaning, especially if refractory inorganic and organic solids removal is practiced (Burke 2000).

Stability, Flexibility, and Reliability

Each type of anaerobic reactor imposes requirements for its proper operation. The inability to meet those requirements, such as operating temperature, may result in process failure. The mesophilic process is more reliable than the thermophilic process because of the greater risk associated with meeting the thermophilic temperature requirements utilizing a cold waste at cold temperatures.

The anaerobic process has been labeled an unreliable process because of frequent toxic upsets. The contact process is a more reliable process in preventing process failure, foaming, and loss of biomass. Retained biomass systems are the least likely to fail because of a large quantity and diversity of the biocatalyst in the digestion system. The addition of elutriation, or the washing of biological solids to remove inhibitory products, adds further stability to the process.

The contact stabilization process is the least likely to be upset by changes in hydraulic flow, or organic loading. Since mixing is essential to any completely mixed process, mixing failures, or inadequacies may result in poor performance. The plug flow contact process also poses little risk of failure due to mixing inadequacies or solids accumulation in the digester.

The complexity of the process will also affect its reliability. The thermophilic digestion of dairy manure must incorporate a complex heating and heat recovery system. Its reliability will be less than a system that does not have such complexity. The contact process and the contact stabilization process are also more complex systems. They have more of an opportunity to fail. Redundant equipment and robust controls are essential to improving the reliability of complex systems.

Nutrient Concentration and Retention

The process of anaerobic digestion will convert nutrients from an organic form to an inorganic form. In plug flow, completely mixed, and thermophilic reactors the quantity of nutrients entering the reactor equals the quantity of nutrients exiting the reactor. However, in retained biomass digesters such as the contact process, sequencing batch reactors, and fixed film reactors, nutrients may be concentrated in a separate waste solids stream. Dugba demonstrated that the effluent from a sequencing batch reactor contained less than 50 percent of the influent phosphorus (Dugba, Zhang et al. 1997). The balance of the phosphorus was concentrated in the biosolids. Burke demonstrated the retention and concentration of 90 percent of the influent phosphorus and 43 percent of the influent total nitrogen in the waste solids that was only 1/5 of the influent volume.

The ability to concentrate nutrients is an important characteristic of the selected anaerobic process since it provides the dairy operator with the control necessary to manage nutrient application to the land.

Additional Substrate Processing

Hobson studied the effect of adding cellulose to dairy manure (Hobson and Taiganides 1983). His research indicated that the volatile solids conversion to gas would be substantially improved through the addition of cellulose. At a 16- day hydraulic retention time the volatile solids conversion to gas increased from 30 percent with no cellulose to 51 percent with a manure containing six percent cellulose. Many commercial digesters supplement the influent with food waste or food processing waste. Collection of tipping fees improves the economic viability of anaerobic facilities. The Tillamook project in Oregon proposed to supplement the influent waste with municipal solid waste to increase revenues. The proposed Myrtle Point project in Oregon (Duke Engineering & Services 2001) may treat milk-processing waste to increase revenues. The ability to treat a wide variety of influent substrates, and thereby enhance the economics, is an important process characteristic. The completely mixed and contact processes can process a variety of added substrates.

Energy Production

The quantity of energy produced from each gallon of waste processed is strictly a function of the percentage conversion of volatile solids to gas. Each pound of volatile solids destroyed will produce 5.62 cubic feet of methane. Each cubic foot of methane will contain 1000 Btu's of energy. Therefore, each pound of volatile solids converted will produce 5620 Btu's of energy. At 35 percent conversion efficiency, each pound of volatile solids destroyed will produce 0.58 kWh of energy. It is therefore important to look at the conversion efficiencies of the various anaerobic processes.

As pointed out earlier, the conversion of volatile solids to gas is a function of the organic loading to the digester. Higher percentage conversions to gas are achieved at lower organic loadings. Low loadings however, translate into larger digestion facilities. However, it is possible to achieve a higher volatile solids conversion to gas by increasing the digester loading while maintaining a higher biomass concentration in the digester. In other words, the food to microorganism (F/M) ratio remains low resulting in a higher rate of conversion. The rate of volatile solids conversion to gas is related to the type of anaerobic digester used.

Conventional completely mixed and plug flow digesters, which do not retain biomass, should have comparable volatile solids destructions. Anaerobic lagoons will have a lower rate of conversion, while high rate retained biomass reactors will have higher rates of solids conversion to gas. Each is discussed separately below.

Conventional Digesters

A review of recent dairy waste anaerobic digestion studies has established that most engineers anticipate a 50 percent conversion of volatile solids to gas. The planned Three-Mile Farm (Oregon) dairy waste thermophilic anaerobic digestion facility is expected to achieve a 50 percent volatile solids conversion to gas. The C. Bar M. (Idaho) plug flow anaerobic digester facility anticipated a 50 percent conversion of dairy waste volatile solids to gas. The recently completed Myrtle Point (Oregon) feasibility study utilizing the gravity separation contact process anticipated a 50 percent conversion of dairy waste volatile solids to gas.

Relatively high loading rates were anticipated in each case. The organic loading rates varied between 5.6 and 6.4 kg per cubic meter per day. The available literature does not support such high volatile solids conversions to gas at high organic loading rates. A summary is as follows: The Monroe Honor Farm (Ecotope 1979) completely mixed anaerobic digester achieved a maximum of 40 percent volatile solids conversion to gas at a loading rate of 6 kg / m3 / d. Jewel operated a plug flow anaerobic digesters at an organic loading rate of 2.37 and achieved a 32.4 percent conversion to volatile solids to gas(Jewell, Dell'Otto et al. 1980), (Jewell, Dell-Orto et al. 1981).

Converse operated both thermophilic and mesophilic completely mixed anaerobic digesters at a loading rate of 4.2 kg / m3 / d (Converse, Zeikus et al. 1975). Both thermophilic and mesophilic digesters achieved a 41 percent conversion of volatile solids to gas. Bryant (1977) on the other hand, operated completely mixed thermophilic digesters at loadings of 6.5 to 10.78 kg / m3 / d and achieved 50 percent volatile solids conversion to gas. Recently, Ahring reported a 28% volatile solids conversion in a thermophilic digester operated at a loading of 3 kg / m3 / d (Ahring, Ibrahim et al. 2001). Ghaly operated a dairy waste completely mixed mesophilic digester at a loading of 3.6 kg / m3 / d (Ghaly and Pyke 1992). He achieved a 46 percent conversion of volatile solids to gas.

Qasim operated a completely mixed mesophilic digester at an organic loading rate of 3.2 kg / m3 / d and achieved a 52.9 percent volatile solids conversion to gas(Quasim, Warren et al. 1984). Echiegu operated a completely mixed dairy waste digester at an organic loading rate of 2 kg / m3 / d but only achieved a 40 percent conversion (Echiegu, Ghaly et al. 1992). Robbins also operated a completely mixed mesophilic digester at an organic loading rate of 2.6 kg per cubic meter per day that achieved a 30 percent conversion of volatile solids to gas (Robbins, Armold et al. 1983). Hills and Kayhanian (1985) operated a completely mixed mesophilic digester at a 1.8 kg / m3 / d loading that achieved a 31 percent volatile solids destruction and a 38 percent conversion at 1.0 kg / m3 / d. On the other hand, Pigg operated a completely mixed mesophilic anaerobic digester at an organic loading rate of 1.0 kg / m3 / d and achieved a peak volatile solids conversion to gas of 64 percent (Pigg 1977).

As can be observed the published literature values are highly variable. The results generally confirm Smith's conclusion that mesophilic digesters can achieve a 40% conversion of volatile solids at a loading of 5.7 kg / m3 / d (Smith, Greiner et al. 1980). Better conversions can be achieved at lower loadings.

Thermophilic reactors appear to achieve greater conversions at high loadings while mesophilic reactors appear to achieve greater conversions at lower loadings.

Lusk (1998) provided information on the performance of full-scale plug flow and completely mixed anaerobic digesters treating dairy manure. The loading and percent volatile solids conversion can be calculated from the information he presented. Figure 14 below presents the results of the analysis of the Lusk data.

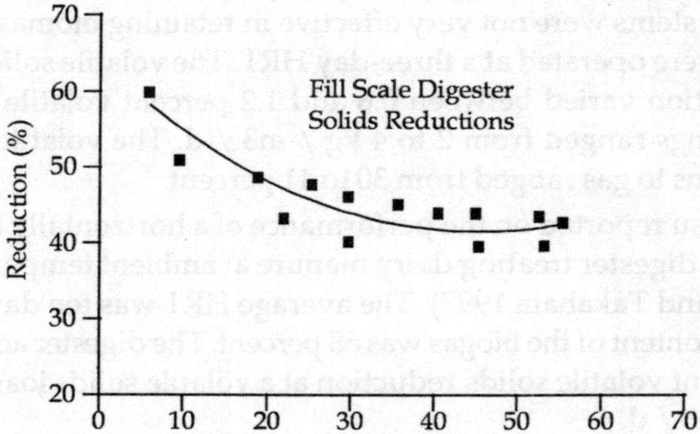

Fig. 11.14. Full Scale Mesophilic Digester VS Reductions.

Lagoons

California Polytechnic State University in San Luis Obispo constructed an anaerobic lagoon to treat flush waste from a 350 animal dairy (equivalent of 250 animals). The screening system removed 15 percent of the manure volatile solids. The lagoon was projected to achieve a 35 percent volatile solids conversion to gas at a loading of 0.04 kg / m3 / d.

High Rate Anaerobic Reactors

Wilkie reported the use of a fixed film reactor treating screened dairy manure having the volatile solids concentration of 3.2 g per liter (Wilkie 2000). The fixed film reactor achieved a 57 % COD conversion to gas. The gas contained 78 % methane. On a COD basis, the loading was approximately 10.7 kg / m3 / d. The hydraulic retention time was three days. Unfortunately, most of the potential gas production was lost in the screened and settled manure that was not processed by the fixed film digester.

Dugba reported on the use of a temperature phased anaerobic sequencing batch reactor system treating dairy manure (Dugba, Zhang et al. 1997). The systems were operated at a three-day hydraulic retention time. The dairy manure was screened utilizing a 2 by 2 mm screen opening. The biogas had a methane concentration of 62 to 66 %. The sequencing batch reactors reportedly had a SRT/HRT ratio of 3 to 4. (Observation of phosphorus retention indicated that the systems were not very effective in retaining biomass.) The systems were operated at a three-day HRT. The volatile solids feed concentration varied between 0.6 and 1.2 percent volatile solids. The loadings ranged from 2 to 4 kg / m3 / d. The volatile solids conversions to gas ranged from 30 to 41 percent.

Umetsu reported on the performance of a horizontally baffled anaerobic digester treating dairy manure at ambient temperatures (Umetsu and Takahata 1997). The average HRT was ten days. The methane content of the biogas was 58 percent. The digester achieved a 25 percent volatile solids reduction at a volatile solids loading of 7.3 kg / m3 / d.

Wuhou reported on the anaerobic digestion of dairy manure from a 2900 cow dairy (Wuhou, Wenying et al. 1997). The digester was a mesophilic up flow mixing reactor operated at a volatile solids loading of 3.7 kg per cubic meter per day. The digester achieved a 78.2 percent volatile solids conversion to gas.

Burke operated a mesophilic AGF contact reactor at an average loading of 2.13 kg per cubic meter per day. The average COD conversion to gas was 66.3 percent. The maximum COD conversion to gas was 69 % at a loading of 2.4 kg per cubic meter per day. The minimum conversion was 59.2 percent during the startup period. The biogas had a methane concentration between 60 and 65 percent. A summary of the expected performance for each type of anaerobic reactor is presented in the table below.

Table 11.4. Expected Percentage VS Conversion to Gas.

Process	Load	Conversion to Gas
Entire Waste Stream		
Completely mixed mesophilic	High	35 to 45 %
Completely mixed thermophilic	High	45 to 55 %
Contact	High	50 to 65 %
Partial Waste Stream		
Plug mesophilic	High	35 to 45 %
Fixed film	High	55 to 65 %
Lagoon	Low	35 to 45 %

Table 11.5 presents a summary of the attributes of the anaerobic processes that can be used to convert all or a fraction of dairy manure to gas.

Table 11.5. Summary of Process Attributes.

Attribute	Comp. mix-meso philic	Comp. mix-meso philic	Cont. Meso-philic	Plug Flow Meso-philic	Lag-oon	Fixed Film
Not Limited by Solids Concentration	X	X	X			
Not Limited by Foreign Material	X	X	X			
Digest Entire Dairy Waste Stream	X	X	X			

(Contd.)

Attribute	Comp. mix-meso philic	Comp. mix-meso philic	Cont. Meso-philic	Plug Flow Meso-philic	Lag-oon	Fixed Film
Sand & Floating Solids Processing	X	X	X			
Best at Odor Control	X		X			
Concentrate Nutrients in Solids			X			X
Treat Additional Substrate	X	X	X			
Stability			X	X	X	X
Simplicity				X	X	
Flexibility			X			
Net Energy Production		X	X			X

Cost of Anaerobic Processes for Dairy Waste

The cost of a dairy waste management system can be subdivided into the following elements:

- Housing - Determines the percentage of manure actually collected
- Collection - A means of collecting the waste by manual, or automatic scraper, vacuum truck, or flush.
- Pre-processing - Screening and or sedimentation prior to digestion
- Anaerobic Digestion - The solids conversion process
- Post-processing - The concentration of solids after digestion
- Energy Production - Engine Generator or Turbine with heat recovery
- Liquid Handling & Irrigation - The storage and disposal of liquid waste
- Solids Disposal

As pointed out earlier, use of any particular system will have an effect on the other. For example, if a flush system is used the anaerobic digester must be larger. If pre screening and sedimentation are used, the amount of energy produced will be lower. Post processing will establish the cost of ultimate solids disposal. In many cases, solids must be exported from the site. The use of an anaerobic digestion system may eliminate the need for pre-processing or screening and sedimentation.

The cost of a complete dairy waste management system may exceed $1,200 per cow. Anaerobic digestion system costs however, are confined to the cost of the anaerobic process, post solids handling, and energy production.

A review of the anaerobic digestion system costs at U.S. dairies compiled by Lusk has established that the typical anaerobic system constructed in the U.S. had an average cost of $470 per cow. The proposed thermophilic digestion project at Three Mile Farm (21,000 cows) in Oregon projected a cost of $710 per cow. The proposed contact process at Myrtle Point (4,500 cows) Oregon has a proposed cost of $678 per cow for digestion, solids handling, and power generation. The recently constructed Cal Polly flush system anaerobic lagoon had a cost of $800 per cow. Anaerobic systems for digestion, solids processing, and generation are expected to cost $500 to $800 per cow.

The per-cow capital cost estimates can be deceptive since some processes treat the entire waste stream while others treat only a portion of the waste stream. For example, the plug flow systems documented by Lusk treat only the concentrated portion of the manure while excluding the milk parlor waste (15% of dairy manure). The table below presents the corrected capital costs for the entire waste stream (100% of cow manure).

Table 11.6. Adjusted Capital Costs.

System	% Treated	Reported Cost $ / Cow	Adjusted Cost $ / Cow
Lusk U.S. Average	85	$470	$552
Three Mile Farm Thermo	80	$710	$887
Myrtle Point Oregon	80	$678	$847
Cal Poly (lagoon)	100	$800	$800

Even the adjusted capital cost per cow does not tell the full economic story. Some systems are far more efficient than others in producing power and sequestering nutrients. The best approach is to report the capital costs in terms of dollars per MBtu generated during the first year of operation or dollars per net kW of power sale capacity. There is little data available in those units for US systems. The costs of a wide variety of European systems have been reported in those units. The capital costs of European systems vary from country to country.

Germany produces anaerobic digesters for the least cost per gallon while the Danish systems produce greater amounts of biogas per pound of solids introduced to the digester. German digester systems are constructed for an average cost of $1.52 per gallon. Danish digesters have a capital cost of $50 per GJ or $5.26 per annual biogas therm (100,000 Btu or 1.06 GJ). Power is produced for a capital cost of $10,000 per kW of export capacity. The table below presents the capital and operating cost of European systems for a large facility and a small on farm system.

Table 11.7. Capital and Operating Costs of European Digestion Systems.

	Large 1 MW 5000 Cow Facility	Small 25 kW 125 Cow Farm
Capital Cost	$9,113,000	$500,000
Annual Operating Cost	$643,000	$8,800
Power Sale Rate $/kW	$0.06	$0.06
Heat Sale $/kW	$0.01	$0.01
Solids Sales	$700,000	$20,000

It must be noted that the capital and operation and maintenance costs are considerably greater in Europe than those reported the US. On the other hand, income derived from the sale of the solids is considerably greater in Europe. The capital cost of dairy waste systems in Idaho are expected to be from $2,700 / kW to $6,000 / kW exclusive of sales tax, power connection to the site and financing costs (27 to 60% of the European cost).

Alternative Waste Management Systems

A Dairyman has many choices in designing and operating in modern dairy. Figure 15 presents the basic options for housing cows, the collection of manure, the pretreatment and treatment of manure, the post treatment and final disposal. Each of the options must be judged by the goals of the Dairymen to maintain animal health, recover nutrients, minimize odors, produce energy, and reduce operation and maintenance costs. The following paragraphs summarize the advantages and disadvantages of each alternative. The better alternatives are shaded in the accompanying figure.

Existing Manure Handling

Existing manure handling consists of screening, and gravity separating the solids for subsequent composting. The existing system is shown in Figure 11.1 and in Figure 11.15 (red boxes). The compost produced by existing systems can either be exported or used for bedding material. Up to 70 percent of the phosphorus nutrients can be diverted from the farm through the use of the existing solids removal processes. However, the conventional solids handling process does not reduce the quantity of material to be handled. It simply separates the material into a solid fraction that can be stacked and hauled and a liquid fraction that can be placed in a holding pond for the required 180-day detention time with a minimum of sedimentation. The system does not control odors since the liquid fraction containing large quantities of organic acids is discharged to an open lagoon for further decomposition. The system does not produce any energy.

Large quantities of energy are consumed in separating the solids and subsequent composting. The operation and maintenance costs are high but the capital costs are low. Overall the commonly used manure handling system does not pay for self nor meet the environmental goals of the Dairymen.

Housing

This type of housing establishes the quantity of manure that can be collected economically. Free stall barns permit the collection of 85 percent of the manure.

The remaining 15 percent is normally deposited in the milk parlor where it is collected through a flush system. In corral systems only 40 to 50 percent of the manure can be collected from the feed lanes, which are either scraped or flushed. Manure deposited in the open lot portion of the corral is normally collected once or twice a year. While in the open lot, the manure is degraded both aerobically and anaerobically depending on the moisture content. The degradation process produces odors and greenhouse gases that are discharged to the atmosphere. There is little net energy available from the manure after it has remained in the open lot for 8 to 12 months.

The free stall system is better for animal health since it provides the greatest separation between manure and cow. Since the free stall system provides an opportunity to collect the maximum amount of manure it also provides the opportunity to recover most of the phosphorus nutrients and generate the most energy.

Free stall barns are more expensive to construct than corral or open lot systems. The operation and maintenance cost of the free stall barn is less than corral or open lot systems. Overall the free stall system provides the best manure processing option.

Collection

Manure can be collected by flush, scrape, or vacuum collection. Scrape and vacuum collection systems have a higher capital and operation and maintenance costs. Flush systems have the lowest capital and operation and maintenance costs. Flush systems also remove substantially all of the manure. The vacuum and scrape systems do not clean the barns as efficiently as a flush system.

Flush systems significantly increase the quantity of waste that must be processed through an energy recovery system. The increased quantity of cold, dilute manure can result in much larger treatment facilities and lower temperatures within the anaerobic digesters. Flush systems have also been associated with severe odor problems. Wet flush aisles promote bacterial activity leading to organic degradation and the generation of odors. The large quantity of untreated wastewater that is discharged to open ponds is an additional source of odorous degradation products. The problems associated with flush systems can be mitigated to a great extent by flushing once a day. By flushing the aisles once a day the volume of flush water will be significantly reduced such that it can be heated and effectively treated with the anaerobic contact process. Flushing once a day will also provide the opportunity for the aisles to dry, eliminating the generation of odors from open-air microbial degradation.

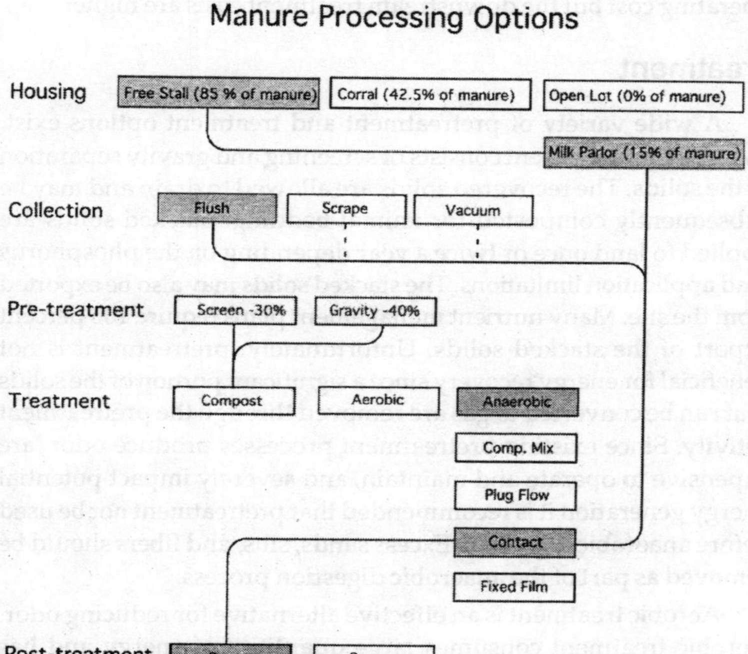

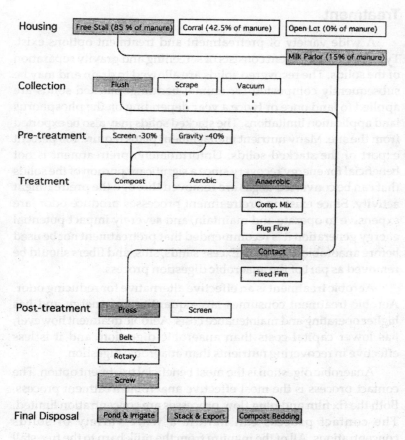

Fig. 11.15. Manure Processing Alternatives.

Scrape and vacuum systems provide a concentrated waste flow, which minimizes the size of down-stream treatment facilities. The choice of which collection system to use will be based on economics since all collection systems, if properly operated, provide an opportunity to recover nutrients, enhance animal health, and minimize odors. Scrape and vacuum systems have a higher capital, and operation and maintenance costs. The downstream treatment costs however are lower. Flush systems have a lower capital and operating cost but the downstream treatment costs are higher.

Treatment

A wide variety of pretreatment and treatment options exist. Typically pretreatment consists of screening and gravity separation of the solids. The recovered solids are allowed to drain and may be subsequently composted for animal bedding. Stacked solids are applied to land once or twice a year depending on the phosphorus land application limitations. The stacked solids may also be exported from the site. Many nutrient management plans require 100 percent export of the stacked solids. Unfortunately, pretreatment is not beneficial for energy recovery since a significant portion of the solids that can be converted to gas are removed through the pretreatment activity. Since existing pretreatment processes produce odor, are expensive to operate and maintain, and severely impact potential energy generation it is recommended that pretreatment not be used before anaerobic digestion. Excess sands, silts, and fibers should be removed as part of the anaerobic digestion process.

Aerobic treatment is an effective alternative for reducing odor. Aerobic treatment consumes large quantities of energy and has higher operating and maintenance costs. Aerobic treatment however, has lower capital costs than anaerobic digestion, and it is less effective in recovering nutrients than anaerobic digestion.

Anaerobic digestion is the most beneficial treatment option. The contact process is the most effective anaerobic treatment process. Both the fix film and plug flow processes are concentration limited. The contact process can handle a wide variety of solids concentrations. All of the manure from the milk barn to the free stall can be processed through the contact process. In addition to processing a larger percentage of manure, a greater percentage of the solids will be converted to energy. It provides greater load flexibility, allowing dairymen to process other waste materials for additional gas production.

The contact process requires little operation and maintenance. It can be an automated process. Both the contact process and completely mixed processes can handle sand and floating fibers. The contact process and completely mixed digester use more energy than the plug flow process. However, a greater percentage of the solids will be converted to energy. The plug flow process is less expensive than either the contact process or the completely mixed reactor.

The contact process however, uses less energy than the completely mixed reactor and has a much lower capital costs. All mesophilic anaerobic treatment processes are effective in reducing or eliminating odors. All anaerobic processes can sequester most of the nutrients. Since the contact process produces a relatively clear effluent, additional nutrients can be removed. All anaerobic processes produce energy. The contact process will provide the greatest solids retention time leading to a higher energy yield.

The plug flow process has the lowest capital costs followed by the contact process. The plug flow reactor also has the lowest operation and maintenance costs. The contact process will have the highest operation and maintenance costs because of the reagents that are used in the biomass separation process. Overall, the contact process offers a greatest benefit.

Post-Treatment

The final product from the treatment process consisting of undigested solids, biomass, and inorganic precipitates must be separated such that the solids containing a majority of the nutrients can be stored, stacked, and exported if required. The post-treatment process fulfills the same need as conventional pretreatment process. However, after passing through an anaerobic digestion process the solids are substantially reduced and the nutrients are concentrated.

A number of options exist for post-treatment. They include screens and a variety of presses. The screw press requires the least amount of operation and maintenance. Consequently, the recommended post-treatment is to pass the digested solids through a screw press, separate the solids from the liquid, and either export the solids or compost them for bedding. The contact process provides more effective liquid solids separation. If the contact process were used, the liquid from the screw press would be recycled to the contact separator.

The clean particle free effluent would be discharged from the contact process separator to the storage pond for irrigation.

Final Disposal

The final products consisting of a liquid stream and a solid stream must be disposed in accordance with the nutrient management plan. The liquid stream will contain inorganic nitrogen as ammonia and a small amount of phosphorus.

The solid stream will contain organic nitrogen and a vast majority of the phosphorus. Both the solid and liquid streams will be fully stabilized and odorless. The solids can be stacked for export or composted for bedding.

Evaluation

Table 11.8 summarizes the attributes of the alternative waste management systems in terms of the dairyman's goals. The most advantageous housing system is the free stall since it is the best system for animal health, nutrient recovery, odor minimization, energy production, and operation and maintenance cost.

The flush system may be the most effective collection system, provided the number of flush cycles can be minimized. The most effective option is to flush once per day. Scrape systems are the most beneficial in terms of net energy production and overall performance. Vacuum systems are also advantageous but consume a considerable amount of energy while collecting the manure.

Treatment can consist of solids composting, aerobic treatment, and anaerobic treatment. Anaerobic treatment is the most effective for nutrient recovery, minimizing odors, and energy production. Aerobic treatment is effective in reducing odors. Composting has the lowest capital cost followed by aerobic treatment. Anaerobic treatment has the lowest operation and maintenance cost.

Table 11.5 presented an evaluation of the various anaerobic processes. The contact process was the most advantageous for a variety of reasons.

As indicated in Table 11.8, screw presses provide the most effective post treatment since they are the least costly while producing a highly concentrated stackable residual.

Table 11.8. Evaluation of Alternative Waste Management Systems.

	Animal Health	Nutrient Recovery	Odor	Energy	Capital Cost	O & M Cost
Housing						
Free Stall	X	X	X	X		X
Corral						
Open Lot					X	
Collection						
Flush	X	X			X	X
Scrape	X	X	X	X		
Vacuum	X	X	X			
Treatment						
Compost	X				X	
Aerobic	X		X			
Anaerobic	X	X	X	X		X
Comp Mix						
Plug flow					X	X
Contact		X	X	X		
Fixed Film						
Lagoon						
Post Treatment						
Screen				X	X	X
Press		X	X			
Screw				X	X	X
Belt						
Rotary						

12

Sanitation

Cheese makers are frequently too relaxed about sanitation because they assume that the active cultures and development of acidity in cheese offer adequate protection against pathogenic organisms. It's true that well made cheese normally offers significant hurdles to most pathogens, however, several pathogens are well known to survive and may grow under the conditions of cheese manufacture and curing. Cheese with minimal acid development such as Latin American White Cheese (Queso Blanco) and cheese which undergo increased pH during curing (Brie, Camembert and, to a lesser extent, Blue) are especially susceptible to growth of pathogens.

1. Culture room separate from plant positive air pressure totally clean at all times restricted access
2. Drains must have traps must be adequate for peak periods to avoid any pooling of whey and/or wash water
3. Surfaces all surfaces clean and sanitizable all food contact surfaces must be stainless exceptions are curing boards and rooms for surface ripened cheese
4. Personnel clean clothes, clean person, especially hands Staphylococcus aureus and fecal coliforms are often from people

5. Plant Environment ideally have positive air pressure separate raw milk operations from rest of the plant no implements or equipment or persons move from raw to pasteurized sections check coliform counts of equipment and employees on regular basis
6. Cleaning Systems Depend on:
   (1) Soil to be removed: fat, protein or milk stone
   (2) Surface to be cleaned note that stainless steel is not a smooth surface to the eye of the microscope nor to a microorganism from the perspective of a coliform organism, a stainless steel surface is world of mountains and valleys stretching out into infinity mechanical abrasion only further roughens the surface and makes cleaning those valleys more difficult must let the chemistry do its work chlorinated alkaline cleaners will remove both fat and protein if applied for sufficient time check vat surfaces with a flourescent light; if the surfaces reflect bluish/purple light you know there is a residual protein film

- **Cleaning Action:**
  (1) Water rinse: removes loose soil collection of first rinse, especially from milk storage tanks, will substantially reduce biological oxygen demand (BOD) loads in the drain
  (2) Chlorinated alkaline detergent with chelator detergent provides wetability chelator softens water and removes milk stone alkali swells and loosens proteins rinsing action is then sufficient to remove soil
  (3) Water rinse
  (4) Acid rinse: nitric, phosphoric complete removal of milk stone and water hardness
  (5) Rinse
  (6) Disinfectant

13

Proper Semen Handling of Dairy Cows

Artificial insemination (AI) has greatly enhanced production potential in the dairy industry since its implementation in the United States in the late 1930s. However, improper semen handling can result in low conception rates, minimizing the advantages of an AI program. Semen is most frequently damaged during handling after thawing and prior to insemination of the cow. The following practices should help minimize semen damage that occurs due to improper handling procedures.

Caring for Insemination Equipment

Several items are necessary to perform successful artificial insemination, including an AI gun, plastic sheaths, shoulder-length gloves, straw cutter, thermometer, thaw box, tweezers, paper towels, and lubricant. Plastic or stainless steel boxes are good containers in which to keep equipment clean and dry. Clean equipment after each use with 70 percent isopropyl alcohol to prevent spread of disease. Disinfectants and soaps are lethal to semen and should not be used as lubricants or to clean equipment.

Removing Semen from the Liquid Nitrogen Tank

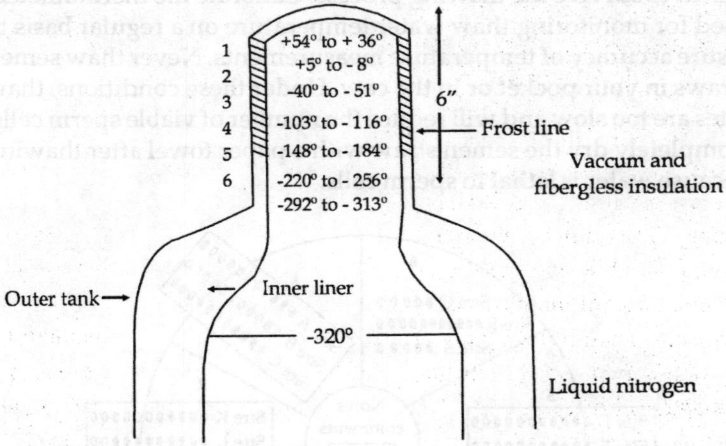

Fig. 13.1. Temperatures found in the neck of a semen tank.

Time spent removing semen from the liquid nitrogen (LN) tank must be kept to a minimum to reduce semen damage. Temperatures can reach +54°F in the neck of the LN tank (1 inch from the top). If the entire canister of semen (10 straws) is withdrawn above the frost line (2 to 3 inches from the top of the tank), all straws of semen can be damaged. When the desired straw of semen cannot be located within 10 seconds of raising the canister, lower the canister back into the LN for 10 to 15 seconds to cool completely. Remove semen from the tank with tweezers, not with the hands. Note the location of the semen in the tank before removing the plug from the tank. This can be accomplished by maintaining a tank inventory with a wall chart or inventory wheel. Quantity of semen remaining in the LN tank also can be accounted for with such a system.

Thawing Semen

Unfortunately, recommended procedures for thawing semen are not the same for all AI companies. Dairy producers usually use semen from several companies but use only one protocol for thawing semen. The National Association of Animal Breeders (NAAB) recommends thawing semen at about 90° to 95°F for at least 40 seconds. Thawing semen between these temperatures allows more semen to survive the thawing process. Calibrate the thermometers used for monitoring thaw water temperature on a regular basis to insure accuracy of temperature measurements. Never thaw semen straws in your pocket or in the cow. Under these conditions, thaw rates are too slow and will reduce the number of viable sperm cells. Completely dry the semen straw with a paper towel after thawing because water is lethal to sperm cells.

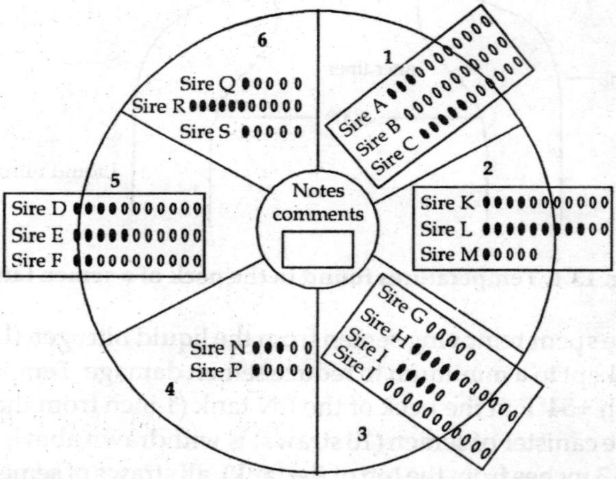

Fig. 13.2. Semen inventory wheel made from Plexiglas or laminated cardboard. Sire number can be written on adhesive labels and attached to the wheel or written directly on the wheel with erasable markers. Circles represent straws of semen and can be darkened after each straw is used.

In large herds, it is not uncommon for several cows to exhibit estrus on the same day, so it is likely that numerous straws of semen will be thawed at one time. Researchers at Washington State University reported that as many as 15 to 20 straws of semen can be thawed simultaneously in a thermos without reducing semen quality. However, the inner semen straws of a group of straws that had frozen together demonstrated reduced motility, suggesting the thaw water should be agitated so that straws do not freeze together during thawing. A larger volume of water (more than 1 quart) is recommended if more than five straws of semen are thawed simultaneously. The number of straws of semen thawed should not exceed the quantity that can be used within 10 to 15 minutes.

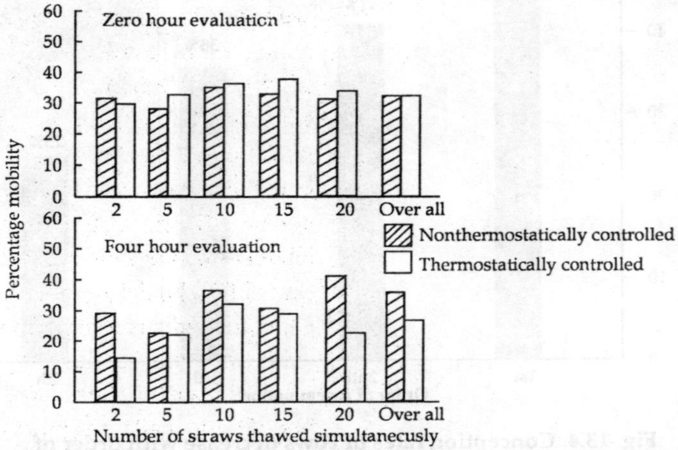

Fig. 13.3. Effect of thawing groups of straws and type of thawing bath on percentage of sperm motility 0 hours and 4 hours after thawing at 97°F. Thawing semen in groups did not significantly damage sperm cells.

Loading the AI Gun

Before loading the semen in the AI gun, warm the gun by rubbing it with a paper towel to avoid cold-shocking the semen. Cut the semen straw at the crimped end, not at the end with the cotton plug. Then place a plastic sheath over the semen and gun. Place the semen gun close to your body under clothing (such as a shirt or jacket) to avoid cold-shocking semen.

A preliminary study from Hawaii indicates loading multiple AI guns may be detrimental to conception rates in hot environments. In this study, four cows were bred in about 6 minutes. Cows bred last (at 6 minutes) had lower conception rates than cows bred first, second, and third. It should be noted that these conception rates were not statistically different. Further research with more cows is needed to confirm effects on conception rates of time from thawing to insemination. It still is recommended that cows be inseminated as soon as possible after thawing semen.

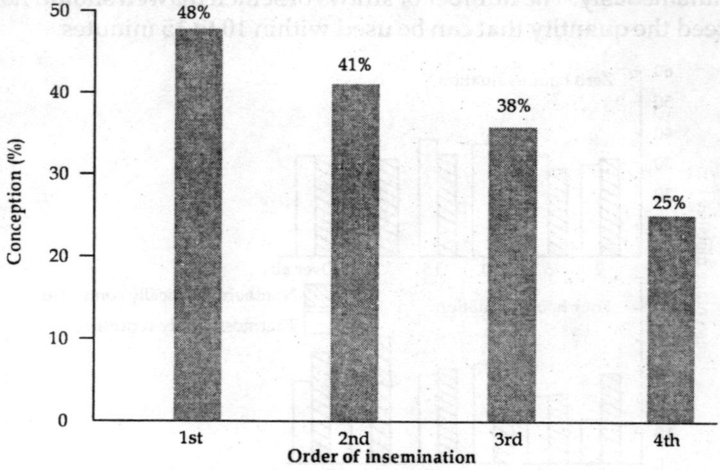

Fig. 13.4. Conception rates of cows decrease with order of insemination.

Proper Semen Handling on Large Dairy Operations

On large operations, dairy personnel not acquainted with AI techniques sometimes are recruited to help inseminate cows. But only people who have been adequately trained in artificial insemination should be allowed to breed cows. Untrained personnel can become fatigued, reducing the accuracy of semen deposition.

General recommendations include thawing semen at 95¡F in a water bath, not in the pocket or cow, for at least 30 seconds but not more than 15 minutes. If several straws of semen are thawed at one time, stir the water bath so that straws do not freeze together. Use the same caution when thawing several straws of semen as you would when thawing a single straw.

Do not load too many AI guns simultaneously. Conception rates could be reduced. Inseminate cows as soon as possible after semen is thawed. Dairies using lock-up stanchions should develop some form of an AI cart or wagon. A golf cart or other small vehicle (such as a mail truck) can be used to transport the AI equipment to the cow. This will allow less time between removing the semen from the thaw bath and inseminating the cow.

Artificial insemination techniques of people responsible for breeding cows should be reevaluated on a regular basis (such as monthly or quarterly). It is important to remember that proper AI

14

Artificial Insemination of Dairy Goats

Introduction

Artificial Insemination (A.I.) involves collection of semen from a buck and transfer of the semen to the reproductive tract of the doe. Does can be inseminated with either fresh semen or with commercially available frozen semen. This publication discusses use of frozen semen to artificially inseminate does.

Reasons the dairy goat producer may consider using A.I. include the following:

1. Eliminate or reduce the cost of maintaining bucks.
2. Increase the rate of genetic improvement.
3. Increase the number of does to which a buck could be bred.
4. Through use of estrous synchronization, A.I. allows several does to be bred the same day.

Whatever the reasons for using A.I., it is important the producer fully understands the reproductive cycle of the doe, and correct semen handling and insemination procedures.

Reproductive Cycle of the DOE

In general, dairy goats are seasonal breeders. The breeding season is initiated by decreasing daylight and runs from late August to January in the United States. Estrous cycles can be initiated out of season by controlling artificial lights to simulate decreasing daylight. The goat's average estrous cycle is 21 days. However, individual does can have either longer and shorter intervals between heat periods. For this reason, it is important to keep individual reproductive records on each doe. The duration of heat or estrus is typically 24 to 36 hours with ovulation occurring near the end of estrus.

Heat Detection

A producer's heat detection program is an important factor in determining whether an artificial insemination program will succeed. Knowing when a doe comes into estrus lets the technician time insemination so it more nearly coincides with ovulation.

Symptoms of does in heat are:

1) does that are unusually aggressive, noisy or active,
2) females that stand to be mounted by herdmates,
3) decreased appetite and milk production, and
4) a clear mucous discharge from the vulva.

It is important establish a heat detection schedule during the breeding season. Does that are to be inseminated should be observed twice daily for 15-20 minutes. Early morning and late afternoon are good times to observe estrus. Observing does for heat detection only during chore time may result in estrus ewes being overlooked because of their change in behavior as they anticipate feeding.

Accurate records should be maintained, including time of heat, length of heat and length of time between heat periods. These records will help a producer accurately anticipate and detect heat in individual does, and time insemination with ovulation.

Time of Insemination

As discussed earlier, a doe is a seasonal breeder that cycles about every 21 days. The average heat or estrus will last from 24 to 36 hours with ovulation occurring near the end of estrus. The standard A.I. recommendation is to breed does two (or three) times at 12-hr intervals. This breeding schedule increases the possibility of a healthy sperm contacting a healthy ovum. It is essential that does be inseminated before ovulation so that sperm cells can undergo a process called capacitation. If records establish the average length of a particular doe's heat period, one can breed the doe once using the schedule shown in table 1 and probably achieve satisfactory fertility:

Table 14.1. Breeding time chart.*

If doe's normal heat period length (hrs.) is:	Breed her at this time after first observed signs of heat:
24	As soon as the doe show estrus
36	Within 12 hr estrus
48	24 hr after estrus
72	48 hr after estrus

*In all cases, if doe is still in heat 24 hrs after first breeding, breed her again.

Equipment Needed to Inseminate Does With Frozen Semen

1. Liquid nitrogen tank
2. Speculum (25 x 175 mm for doelings or 25 x 200 mm for does)
3. A.I. light
4. Straw tweezers
5. Sterile lubricant (non-spermicidal)
6. Insemination gun (for straws)
7. Breeding stand or facilities to restrain the doe
8. Thaw box
9. Paper towels
10. Straw cutter
11. Thermometer

These supplies can be obtained from several livestock supply companies. The liquid nitrogen tank will be the largest single expense, and will cost approximately $500.

Semen Thawing and Insemination Procedures

The first step is to restrain the doe to be inseminated. This can be done with a breeding stand or any other satisfactory facility. After the doe is restrained, the semen is thawed and the insemination gun is prepared. Frozen semen should be thawed according to the processor's recommendations. If these recommendations are not available, remove the frozen straw from the liquid nitrogen tank with a straw tweezers, and place it in a thaw box filled with warm water (95F) for 30 seconds. After thawing, dry the straw thoroughly with a paper towel. Semen must be kept warm and must not be exposed to sunlight or water during the thawing and inseminating process to prevent damaging or killing sperm cells. Pull the plunger back 4 to 6 inches on the insemination gun and place the straw into the gun with the cotton plug toward the plunger. After the straw has been secured in the gun, the sealed end of the straw must be cut off with the straw cutter. The cover sheath should now be placed over the insemination gun and secured with an 0 ring.

The next step is the actual insemination process. It may be necessary to lift the does 's hindquarters if she will not stand. If working alone, hold the insemination gun in your mouth, or have an assistant hand the insemination gun to you at the appropriate time. Turn your headlight on.

Lubricate the speculum with a non-spermicidal lubricant. Clean the doe's vulva with a dry paper towel and insert the lubricated speculum slowly into the vulva. Insert the speculum at an upward angle to prevent vaginal irritation.

Once the speculum has been inserted, visually locate the cervix. The cervix should have a red-purple color and white mucus will be present if the doe is in heat. Center the speculum over the opening of the cervix.

Insert the insemination gun into the speculum and thread it into the opening of the cervix. Use a circular motion and slight pressure to work the insemination gun through the rings of the cervix. Do not penetrate the cervix more than 1.5 inches. It is a good idea to draw a red ring around the cover sheath of the insemination gun 1 1/2 inches from the tip. This mark lets you to know how far you have penetrated the cervix.

Deposit the semen slowly by pushing the plunger forward. Remove the insemination gun slowly and remove the speculum.

15

UHT Processing

Introduction

While pasteurization conditions effectively eliminate potential pathogenic microorganisms, it is not sufficient to inactivate the thermoresistant spores in milk. The term sterilization refers to the complete elimination of all microorganisms. The food industry uses the more realistic term "commercial sterilization"; a product is not necessarily free of all microorganisms, but those that survive the sterilization process are unlikely to grow during storage and cause product spoilage.

In canning we need to ensure the "cold spot" has reached the desired temperature for the desired time. With most canned products, there is a low rate of heat penetration to the thermal centre. This leads to overprocessing of some portions, and damage to nutritional and sensory characteristics, especially near the walls of the container. This implies long processing times at lower temperatures.

Milk can be made commercially sterile by subjecting it to temperatures in excess of 100° C, and packaging it in air-tight containers. The milk may be packaged either before or after sterilization. The basis of UHT, or ultra-high temperature, is the sterilization of food before packaging, then filling into pre-sterilized containers in a sterile atmosphere. Milk that is processed in this way using temperatures exceeding 135° C, permits a decrease in the necessary holding time (to 2-5 s) enabling a continuous flow operation.

Some examples of food products processed with UHT are:

- liquid products - milk, juices, cream, yoghurt, wine, salad dressings
- foods with discrete particles - baby foods; tomato products; fruits and vegetables juices; soups
- larger particles - stews

Advantages of UHT

High quality: The D and Z valves are higher for quality factors than microorganisms. The reduction in process time due to higher temperature (UHTST) and the minimal come-up and cool-down time leads to a higher quality product.

Long shelf life: Greater than 6 months, without refrigeration, can be expected.

Packaging size: Processing conditions are independent of container size, thus allowing for the filling of large containers for food-service or sale to food manufacturers (aseptic fruit purees in stainless steel totes).

Cheaper packaging: Both cost of package and storage and transportation costs; laminated packaging allows for use of extensive graphics

Difficulties with UHT

Sterility: Complexity of equipment and plant are needed to maintain sterile atmosphere between processing and packaging (packaging materials, pipework, tanks, pumps); higher skilled operators; sterility must be maintained through aseptic packaging

Particle Size: With larger particulates there is a danger of overcooking of surfaces and need to transport material - both limits particle size

Equipment: There is a lack of equipment for particulate sterilization, due especially to settling of solids and thus overprocessing

Keeping Quality: Heat stable lipases or proteases can lead to flavour deterioration, age gelation of the milk over time - nothing lasts forever! There is also a more pronounced cooked flavour to UHT milk.

UHT Methods

There are two principal methods of UHT treatment:

- Direct Heating
- Indirect Heating

Direct heating systems: The product is heated by direct contact with steam of potable or culinary quality. The main advantage of direct heating is that the product is held at the elevated temperature for a shorter period of time. For a heat-sensitive product such as milk, this means less damage.

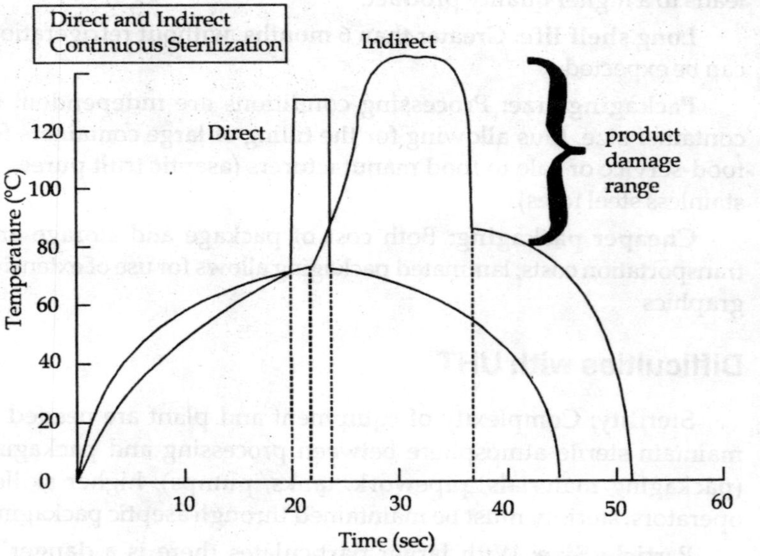

There are two methods of direct heating:

- injection
- infusion

Injection: High pressure steam is injected into pre-heated liquid by a steam injector leading to a rapid rise in temperature. After holding, the product is flash-cooled in a vacuum to remove water equivalent to amount of condensed steam used. This method allows fast heating and cooling, and volatile removal, but is only suitable for some products. It is energy intensive and because the product comes in contact with hot equipment, there is potential for flavour damage.

Infusion: The liquid product stream is pumped through a distributing nozzle into a chamber of high pressure steam. This system is characterized by a large steam volume and a small product volume, distributed in a large surface area of product. Product temperature is accurately controlled via pressure. Additional holding time may be accomplished through the use of plate or tubular heat exchangers, followed by flash cooling in vacuum chamber. This method has several advantages:

- instantaneous heating and rapid cooling
- no localized overheating or burn-on
- suitable for low and higher viscosity products

Indirect heating systems: The heating medium and product are not in direct contact, but separated by equipment contact surfaces. Several types of heat exchangers are applicable:

- plate
- tubular
- scraped surface
- double-cone

Plate Heat Exchangers: Similar to that used in HTST but operating pressures are limited by gaskets. Liquid velocities are low which could lead to uneven heating and burn-on. This method is economical in floor space, easily inspected, and allows for potential regeneration.

Tubular Heat Exchangers: There are several types:

- shell and tube
- shell and coil
- double tube
- triple tube

All of these tubular heat exchangers have fewer seals involved than with plates. This allows for higher pressures, thus higher flow rates and higher temperatures. The heating is more uniform but difficult to inspect.

Scraped Surface Heat Exchangers: The product flows through a jacketed tube, which contains the heating medium, and is scraped from the sides with a rotating knife. This method is suitable for viscous products and particulates (< 1 cm) such as fruit sauces, and can be adjusted for different products by changing configuration of rotor. There is a problem with larger particulates; the long process time for particulates would mean long holding sections which are impractical. This may lead to damaged solids and overprocessing of sauce.

Double-cone Heat Exchangers: Suitable for large particulates because it involves separation of solids/liquids and combines indirect heating in double cone (batch) with direct heating of liquid portion (maybe also scraped surface if too viscous). The solid pieces are fed into a double-cone, rotated slowly on horizontal axis with steam injection and heated surfaces. There is no burn-on because they are the same temperature. The liquid is directly heated with steam separately, then added after pre-cooling. The double cone acts as a blender and coats solids. The product is then discharged to an aseptic filler by overpressure with sterile air. Used for soups, stews, carrots, and vegetables.

Packaging for Aseptic Processing

The most important point to remember is that it must be sterile! All handling of product post-process must be within the sterile environment.

There are 5 basic types of aseptic packaging lines:

- **Fill and seal:** preformed containers made of thermoformed plastic, glass or metal are sterilized, filled in aseptic environment, and sealed
- **Form, fill and seal:** roll of material is sterilized, formed in sterile environment, filled, sealed e.g. tetrapak
- **Erect, fill and seal:** using knocked-down blanks, erected, sterilized, filled, sealed. e.g. gable-top cartons, cambri-bloc
- **Thermoform, fill, sealed** roll stock sterilized, thermoformed, filled, sealed aseptically. e.g. creamers, plastic soup cans

- **Blow mold, fill, seal:**

There are several different package forms that are used in aseptic UHT processing:

- cans
- paperboard/plastic/foil/plastic laminates
- flexible pouches
- thermoformed plastic containers
- flow molded containers
- bag-in-box
- bulk totes

It is also worth mentioning that many products that are UHT heat treated are not aseptically packaged. This gives them the advantage of a longer shelf life at refrigeration temperatures compared to pasteurization, but it does not produce a shelf-stable product at ambient temperatures, due to the possibility of recontamination post-processing.

Homogenization of Milk and Milk Products

Introduction: Milk is an oil-in-water emulsion, with the fat globules dispersed in a continuous skimmilk phase. If raw milk were left to stand, however, the fat would rise and form a cream layer. Homogenization is a mechanical treatment of the fat globules in milk brought about by passing milk under high pressure through a tiny orifice, which results in a decrease in the average diameter and an increase in number and surface area, of the fat globules. The net result, from a practical view, is a much reduced tendency for creaming of fat globules. Three factors contribute to this enhanced stability of homogenized milk: a decrease in the mean diameter of the fat globules (a factor in Stokes Law), a decrease in the size distribution of the fat globules (causing the speed of rise to be similar for the majority of globules such that they don't tend to cluster during creaming), and an increase in density of the globules (bringing them closer to the continuous phase) oweing to the adsorption of a protein membrane. In addition, heat pasteurization breaks down the cryo-globulin complex, which tends to cluster fat globules causing them to rise.

Homogenization Mechanism

Auguste Gaulin's patent in 1899 consisted of a 3 piston pump in which product was forced through one or more hair like tubes under pressure. It was discovered that the size of fat globules produced were 500 to 600 times smaller than tubes. There have been over 100 patents since, all designed to produce smaller average particle size with expenditure of as little energy as possible. The homogenizer consists of a 3 cylinder positive piston pump (operates similar to car engine) and homogenizing valve. The pump is turned by electric motor through connecting rods and crankshaft.

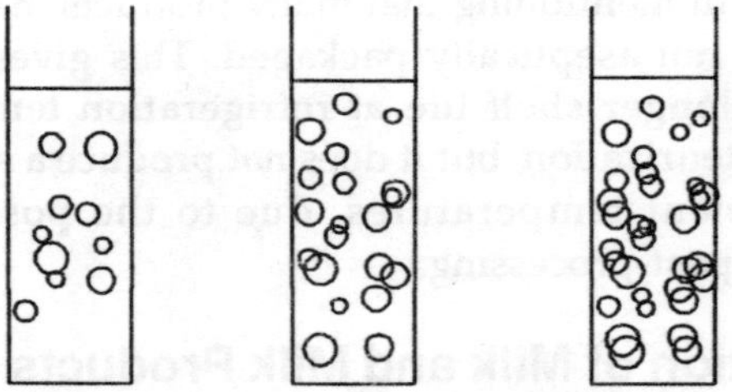

Raw milk | Cold, raw milk after 1 hour | Homogenized milk during storage

To understand the mechanism, consider a conventional homogenizing valve processing an emulsion such as milk at a flow rate of 20,000 l/hr. at 14 MPa (2100 psig). As it first enters the valve, liquid velocity is about 4 to 6 m/s. It then moves into the gap between the valve and the valve seat and its velocity is increased to 120 meter/sec in about 0.2 millisec. The liquid then moves across the face of the valve seat (the land) and exits in about 50 microsec. The homogenization phenomena is completed before the fluid leaves the area between the valve and the seat, and therefore emulsification is initiated and completed in less than 50 microsec. The whole process occurs between 2 pieces of steel in a steel valve assembly. The product may then pass through a second stage valve similar to the first stage. While most of the fat globule reduction takes place in the first stage, there is a tendency for clumping or clustering of the reduced fat globules. The second stage valve permits the separation of those clusters into individual fat globules.

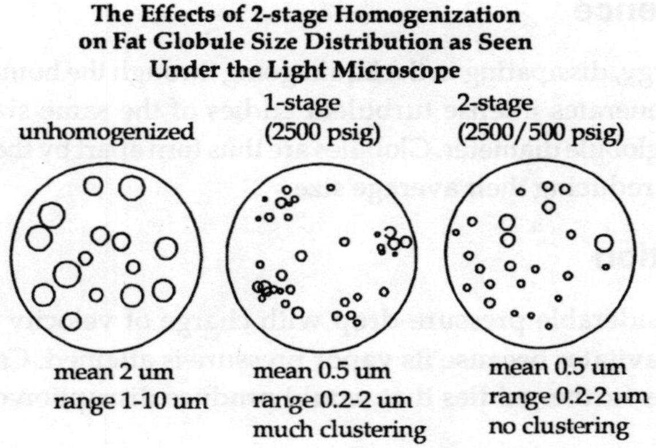

It is most likely that a combination of two theories, turbulence and cavitation, explains the reduction in size of the fat globules during the homogenization process.

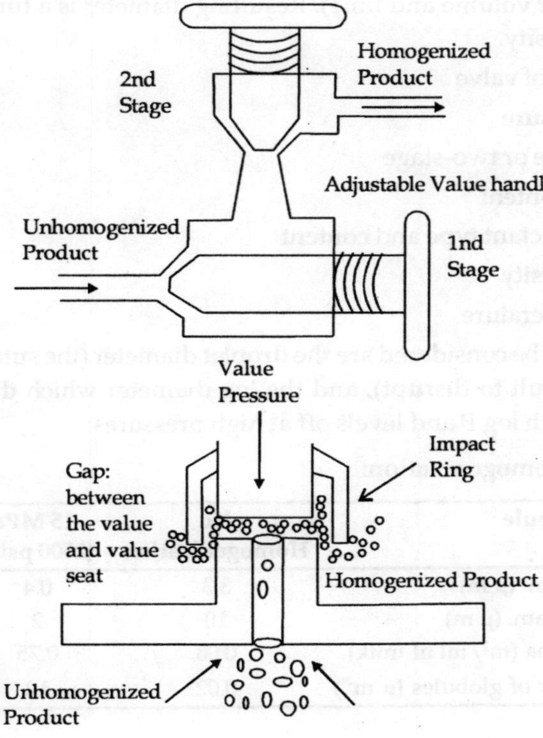

Turbulence

Energy, dissipating in the liquid going through the homogenizer valve, generates intense turbulent eddies of the same size as the average globule diameter. Globules are thus torn apart by these eddie currents reducing their average size.

Cavitation

Considerable pressure drop with charge of velocity of fluid. Liquid cavitates because its vapor pressure is attained. Cavitation generates further eddies that would produce disruption of the fat globules.

The high velocity gives liquid a high kinetic energy which is disrupted in a very short period of time. Increased pressure increases velocity. Dissipation of this energy leads to a high energy density (energy per volume and time). Resulting diameter is a function of energy density.

- type of valve
- pressure
- single or two-stage
- fat content
- surfactant type and content
- viscosity
- temperature

Also to be considered are the droplet diameter (the smaller, the more difficult to disrupt), and the log diameter which decreases linearly with log P and levels off at high pressures.

Effect of Homogenization:

Fat globule	No Homogenization	15 MPa (2500 psig)
Av. diam. (μ m)	3.3	0.4
Max. diam. (μ m)	10	2
Surf. area (m^2/ml of milk)	0.08	0.75
Number of globules (μ m^{-3})	0.02	12

Surface Layer

The milk fat globule has a native membrane, picked up at the time of secretion, made of amphiphilic molecules with both hydrophilic and hydrophobic sections. This membrane lowers the interfacial tension resulting in a more stable emulsion. During homogenization, there is a tremendous increase in surface area and the native milk fat globule membrane (MFGM) is lost. However, there are many amphiphilic molecules present from the milk plasma that readily adsorb: casein micelles (partly spread) and whey proteins. The interfacial tension of raw milk is 1-2 mN/m, immediately after homogenization it is unstable at 15 mN/m, and shortly becomes stable (3-4 mN/m) as a result of the adsorption of protein. The transport of proteins is not by diffusion but mainly by convection. Rapid coverage is achieved in less than 10 sec but is subject to some rearrangement.

Surface excess is a measure of how much protein is adsorbed; for example 10 mg/m^2 translates to a thickness of adsorbed layer of approximately 15 nm.

Membrane Processing

Membrane processing is a technique that permits concentration and separation without the use of heat. Particles are separated on the basis of their molecular size and shape with the use of pressure and specially designed semi-permeable membranes. There are some fairly new developments in terms of commercial reality and is gaining readily in its applications:

- proteins can be separated in whey for the production of whey protein concentrate
- milk can be concentrated prior to cheesemaking at the farm level
- apple juice and wine can be clarified
- waste treatment and product recovery is possible in edible oil, fat, potato, and fish processing
- fermentation broths can be clarified and separated
- whole egg and egg white ultrafiltration as a preconcentration prior to spray drying

The following topics will be covered in this section:

Principle of Operation: When a solution and water are separated by a semi-permeable membrane, the water will move into the solution to equilibrate the system. This is known as osmotic pressure. If a mechanical force is applied to exceed the osmotic pressure (up to 700 psi), the water is forced to move down the concentration gradient i.e. from low to high concentration. **Permeate** designates the liquid passing through the membrane, and **retentate** (concentrate) designates the fraction not passing through the membrane.

Membrane Processing

Reverse Osmosis: Reverse osmosis designates a membrane separation process, driven by a pressure gradient, in which the membrane separates the solvent (generally water) from other components of a solution. The membrane configuration is usually cross-flow. With reverse osmosis, the membrane pore size is very small allowing only small amounts of very low molecular weight solutes to pass through the membranes. It is a **concentration process** using a 100 MW cutoff, 700 psig, temperatures less than 40°C with cellulose acetate membranes and 70-80°C with composite membranes. Please click above link for a schematic diagram of these membrane processes.

Member Processing

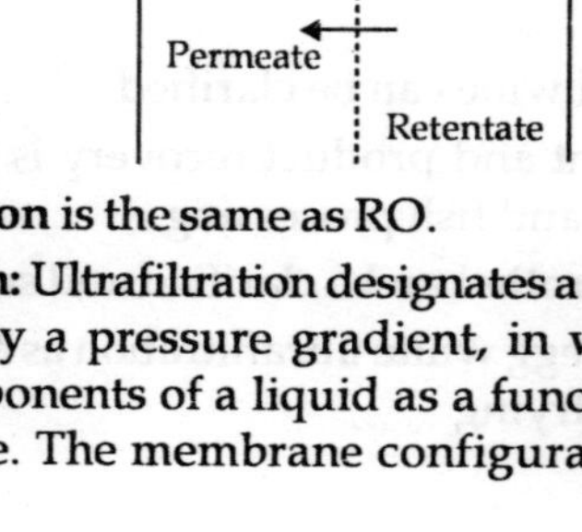

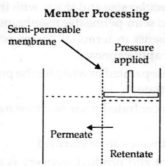

Hyperfiltration is the same as RO.

Ultrafiltration: Ultrafiltration designates a membrane separation process, driven by a pressure gradient, in which the membrane fractionates components of a liquid as a function of their solvated size and structure. The membrane configuration is usually cross-flow. In UF, the membrane pore size is larger allowing some components to pass through the pores with the water. It is a **separation/fractionation process** using a 10,000 MW cutoff, 40 psig, and temperatures of 50-60°C with polysulfone membranes. In UF milk, lactose and minerals pass in a 50% separation ratio; for example, in the retentate would be 100% of fat, 100% of protein, 50% of lactose, and 50% of free minerals.

Diafiltration is a specialized type of ultrafiltration process in which the retentate is diluted with water and re-ultrafiltered, to reduce the concentration of soluble permeate components and increase further the concentration of retained components.

Microfiltration

Microfiltration designates a membrane separation process similar to UF but with even larger membrane pore size allowing particles in the range of 0.2 to 2 micrometers to pass through. The pressure used is generally lower than that of UF process. The membrane configuration is usually cross-flow. MF is used in the dairy industry for making low-heat sterile milk as proteins may pass through but bacteria do not. Please click above link for a schematic diagram of these membrane processes.

Hardware Design

Open Tubular: Tubes of membrane with a diameter of 1/2 to 1 inch and length to 12 ft. are encased in reinforced fibreglass or enclosed inside a rigid PVC or stainless steel shell. As the feed solution flows through the membrane core, the permeate passes through the membrane and is collected in the tubular housing. Imagine 12 ft long straws!

Hollow Fibre: Similar to open tubular, but the cartridges contain several hundred very small (1 mm diam) hollow membrane tubes or fibres. As the feed solution flows through the open cores of the fibres, the permeate is collected in the cartridge area surrounding the fibres.

Plate and Frame: This system is set up like a plate heat exchanger with the retentate on one side and the permeate on the other. The permeate is collected through a central collection tube.

Spiral Wound: This design tries to maximize surface area in a minimum amount of space. It consists of consecutive layers of large membrane and support material in an envelope type design rolled up around a perforated steel tube.

Electrodialysis

Electrodialysis is used for demineralization of milk products and whey for infant formula and special dietary products. Also used for desalination of water.

Principles of operation: Under the influence of an electric field, ions move in an aqueous solution. The ionic mobility is directly proportioned to specific conductivity and inversely proportioned to number of molecules in solution. ~3-6 x 102 mm/sec.

Charged ions can be removed from a solution by synthetic polymer membranes containing ion exchange groups. Anion exchange membranes carry cationic groups which repel cations and are permeable to anions, and cation exchange membranes contain anionic groups and are permeable only to cations.

Electrodialysis membranes are comprised of polymer chains - styrene-divinyl benzene made anionic with quaternary ammonium groups and made cationic with sulphonic groups. 1-2V is then applied across each pair of membranes.

Electrodialysis process: Amion and cation exchange membranes are arranged alternately in parallel between an anode and a cathode. The distance between the membranes is 1mm or less. A plate and frame arrangement similar to a plate heat exchanger or a plate filter is used. The solution to be demineralized flows through gaps between the two types of membranes. Each type of membrane is permeable to only one type of ion. Thus, the anions leave the gap in the direction of the anode and cations leave in the direction of the cathode. Both are then taken up by a concentrating stream.

Problems: Concentration polarization. Deposits on membrane surfaces, e.g. proteins - pH control is important. Prior concentration of whey, to 20% TS, is necessary before electrodialysis.

Ion Exchange

Ion exchange is not a membrane process but I have included it here anyway because it is used for product of protein isolates of higher concentration than obtainable by membrane concentration.

Fractionation may also be accomplished using ion exchange processing. It relies on inert resins (cellulose or silica based) that can adsorb charged particles at either end of the pH scale. The design can be a batch type, stirred tank or continuous column. The column is more suitable for selective fractionation. **Whey protein isolate (WPI)**, with a 95% protein content, can be produced by this method. Following adsorption and draining of the deproteined whey, the pH or charge properties are altered and proteins are eluted. Protein is recovered from the dilute stream through UF and drying. Selective resins may be used for fractionated protein products or enriched in fraction allow tailoring of ingredients.

Evaporation and Dehydration

The removal of water from foods provides microbiological stability, reduces deteriorative chemical reactions, and reduces transportation and storage costs. Both evaporation and dehydration are methods used in the dairy industry for this purpose. The following topics will be addressed here:

Evaporation: Evaporation refers to the process of heating liquid to the boiling point to remove water as vapour. Because milk is heat sensitive, heat damage can be minimized by evaporation under vacuum to reduce the boiling point. The basic components of this process consist of:

- heat-exchanger
- vacuum
- vapour separator
- condenser

The **heat exchanger** is enclosed in a large chamber and transfers heat from the heating medium, usually low pressure steam, to the product usually via indirect contact surfaces. The **vacuum** keeps the product temperature low and the difference in temperatures high. The **vapour separator** removes entrained solids from the vapours, channelling solids back to the heat exchanger and the vapours out to the **condenser**. It is sometimes a part of the actual heat exchanger, especially in older vacuum pans, but more likely a separate unit in newer installations. The condenser condenses the vapours from inside the heat exchanger and may act as the vacuum source.

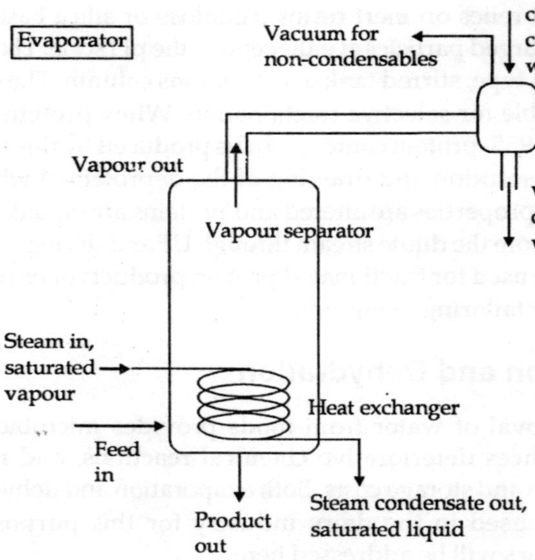

Principle of Operation

The driving force for heat transfer is the difference in temperature between the steam in the coils and the product in the pan. The steam is produced in large boilers, generally tube and chest heat exchangers. The steam temperature is a function of the steam pressure. Water boils at 100° C at 1 atm., but at other pressures the boiling point changes. At its boiling point, the steam condenses in the coils and gives up its latent heat. If the steam temperature is too high, burn-on/fouling increases so there are limits to how high steam temperatures can go. The product is also at its boiling point. The boiling point can be elevated with an increase in solute concentration. This boiling point elevation works on the same principles as freezing point depression.

Evaporator Designs:

- Types of single effect evaporators:
- Batch Pan
- Rising film
- Falling film

- Plate evaporators
- Scraped surface

Batch pan evaporators are the simplest and oldest. They consist of spherical shaped, steam jacketed vessels. The heat transfer per unit volume is small requiring long residence times. The heating is due only to natural convection, therefore, the heat transfer characteristics are poor. Batch plants are of historical significance; modern evaporation plants are far-removed from this basic idea. The vapours are a tremendous source of low pressure steam and must be reused.

Rising film evaporators consist of a heat exchanger isolated from the vapour separator. The heat exchanger, or calandria, consists of 10 to 15 meter long tubes in a tube chest which is heated with steam. The liquid rises by percolation from the vapours formed near the bottom of the heating tubes. The thin liquid film moves rapidly upwards. The product may be recycled if necessary to arrive at the desired final concentration. This development of this type of modern evaporator has given way to the falling film evaporator.

The **falling film** evaporators are the most widely used in the food industry. They are similar in components to the rising film type except that the thin liquid film moves downward under gravity in the tubes. A uniform film distribution at the feed inlet is much more difficult to obtain. This is the reason why this development came slowly and it is only within the last decade that falling film has superceded all other designs. Specially designed nozzels or spray distributors at the feed inlet permit it to handle more viscous products. The residence time is 20-30 sec. as opposed to 3-4 min. in the rising film type. The vapour separator is at the bottom which decreases the product hold-up during shut down. The tubes are 8-12 meters long and 30-50 mm in diameter.

Multiple Effect Evaporators

Two or more evaporator units can be run in sequence to produce a multiple effect evaporator. Each effect would consist a heat transfer surface, a vapour separator, as well as a vacuum source and a condenser. The vapours from the preceding effect are used as the heat source in the next effect. There are two advantages to multiple effect evaporators:

- Economy - they evaporate more water per kg steam by re-using vapours as heat sources in subsequent effects
- Improve heat transfer - due to the viscous effects of the products as they become more concentrated

Each effect operates at a lower pressure and temperature than the effect preceding it so as to maintain a temperature difference and continue the evaporation procedure. The vapours are removed from the preceding effect at the boiling temperature of the product at that effect so that no temperature difference would exist if the vacuum were not increased. The operating costs of evaporation are relative to the number of effects and the temperature at which they operate. The boiling milk creates vapours which can be recompressed for high steam econonmy. This can be done by adding energy to the vapour in the form of a steam jet, thermo compression or by a mechanical compressor, mechanical vapour recompression.

Thermo Compression (TC)

Involves the use of a steam-jet booster to recompress part of the exit vapours from the first effect. Through recompression, the pressure and temperature of the vapours are increased. As the vapours exit from the first effect, they are mixed with very high pressure steam. The steam entering the first effect calandria is at slightly less pressure than the supply steam. There is usually more vapours from the first effect than the second effect can use; usually only the first effect is coupled with multiple effect evaporators.

Mechanical Vapour Recompression (MVR)

Whereas only part of the vapour is recompressed using TC, all the vapour is recompressed in an MVR evaporator. Vapours are mechanically compressed by radial compressors or simple fans using electrical energy.

There are several variations; in single effect, all the vapours are recompressed therefore no condensing water is needed; in multiple effect, can have MVR on first effect, followed by two or more traditional effects; or can recompress vapours from all effects.

Dehydration

Dehydration refers to the nearly complete removal of water from foods to a level of less than 5%. Although there are many types of driers, spray driers are the most widely used type of air convection drier. It turns out more tonnage of dehydrated products than all other types of driers combined. It is limited to food that can be atomized, i.e. liquids, low viscosity pastes, and purees. Drying takes place within a matter of seconds at temperatures approximately 200° C. Evaporative cooling maintains low product temperatures, however, prompt removal of the product is still necessary.

Spray Drying - Process Summary

The liquid food is generally preconcentrated by evaporation to economically reduce the water content. The concentrate is then introduced as a fine spray or mist into a tower or chamber with heated air. As the small droplets make intimate contact with the heated air, they flash off their moisture, become small particles, and drop to the bottom of the tower and are removed. The advantages of spray drying include a low heat and short time combination which leads to a better quality product.

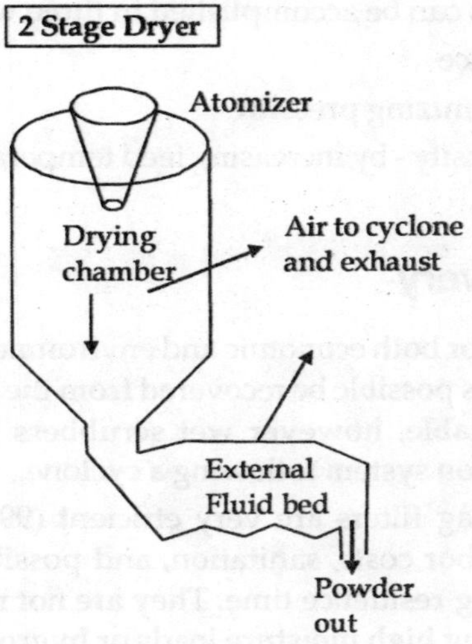

Principal components include:

- a high pressure pump for introducing liquid into the tower
- a device for atomizing the feed stream
- a heated air source with blower
- a secondary collection vessel for removing the dried food from the airstream
- means for exhausting the moist air
- usually includes a preconcentration step i.e. MVR evaporation

Atomizing devices are the distinguishing characteristic of spray drying. They provide a large surface area for exposure to drying forces:

1 litre = 12 billion particles = >300 ft^2 (30m^2)

The exit air temperature is an important parameter to monitor because it responds readily to changes in the process and reflects the quality of the product. Generally, we want it high enough to yield desired moisture without heat damage. There are two controls that may be used to adjust the exit air temperature:

- altering feed flow rate
- altering inlet temperature

If heat damage occurs before the product is dried, the particle size must be reduced; smaller particle dries faster, therefore, less heat damage. This can be accomplished in three ways:

- smaller orifice
- increase atomizing pressure
- reduce viscosity - by increasing feed temperature or reducing solids

Powder Recovery

It is essential for both economic and environmental reasons that as much powder as possible be recovered from the air stream. Three systems are available, however wet scrubbers usually act as a secondary collection system following a cyclone.

Bag filters: Bag filters are very efficient (99.9%), but not as popular due to labor costs, sanitation, and possible heat damage because of the long residence time. They are not recommended in the case of handling high moisture loads or hygroscopic particles.

Cyclone collector: Cyclones are not as efficient (99.5%) as bag filters but several can be placed in series. Air enters at tangent at high velocity into a cylinder or cone which has a much larger cross section. Air velocity is decreased in the cone permitting settling of solids by gravity. Centrifugal force is important in removing particles from the air stream. High air velocity is needed to separate small diameter and light materials from air; velocities may approach 100 ft/sec (70 MPH). Higher centrifugal force can be obtained by using small diameter cyclones, several of which may be placed in parallel; losses may range from 0.5-2%. A rotary airlock is used to remove powder from the cyclone. (An example of a rotary airlock is a revolving door at a hotel lobby which is intended to break the outside and inside environments).

Wet scrubber : Wet scrubbers are the most economical outlet air cleaner. The principle of a wet scrubber is to dissolve any dust powder left in the airstream into either water or the feed stream by spraying the wash stream through the air. This also recovers heat from the exiting air and evaporates some of the water in the feed stream (if used as the wash water).

Wet Scrubbers

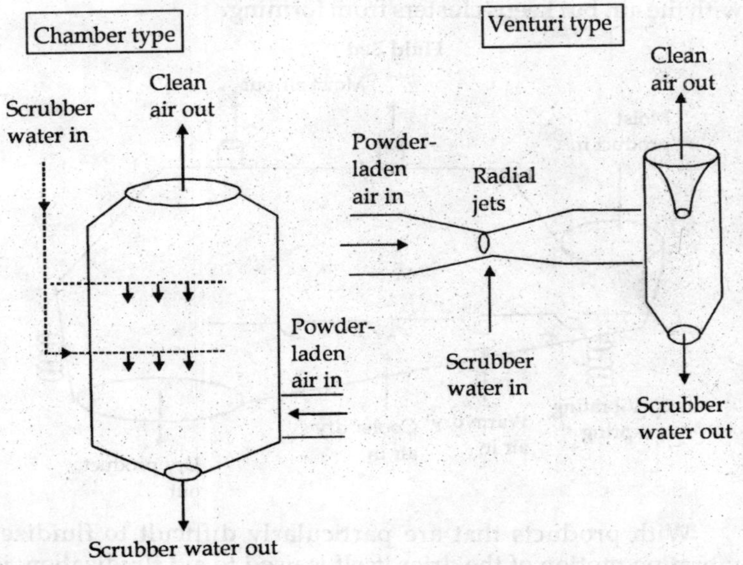

Wet scrubbers not only recover most of what would be lost product, but also recover approximately 90% of the potential drying energy normally lost in exit air. The exit air picks up moisture which increases evaporative capacity by 8% (concentration of feed). Cyclone separators are probably the best primary powder separator system because they are hygienic, easy to operate, and versatile, however, high losses may occur. Wet scrubbers are designed for a secondary air cleaning system in conjunction with the cyclone. Either feed stream or water can be used as scrubbing liquor. Also, there are heat recovery systems available.

Two and Three Stage Spray Drying With a Fluidized Bed

Principles of Fluid Beds

Air is blown up through a wire mesh belt on porous plate that supports and conveys the product. A slight vibration motion is imparted to the food particles. When the air velocity is increased to the point where it just exceeds the velocity of free fall (gravity) of the particles, fluidization occurs. The dancing/boiling motion subdivides the product and provides intimate contact of each particle with the air, but keeps clusters from forming.

Fluid Bed

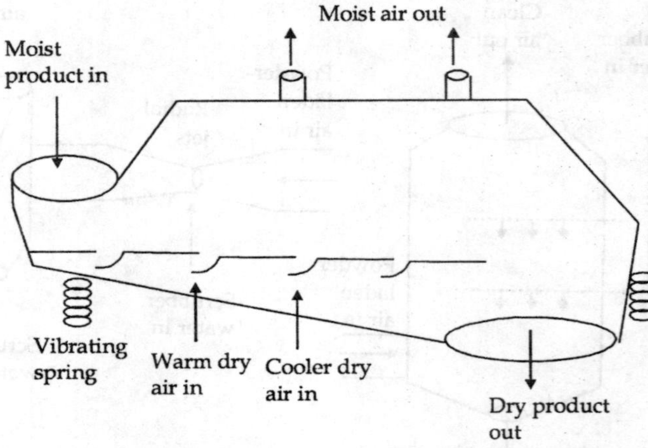

With products that are particularly difficult to fluidize, a vibrating motion of the drier itself is used to aid fluidization; it is called vibro-fluidizer which is on springs. The fluidized solid particles then behave in an analogous manner to a liquid., i.e. they can be conveyed. Air velocities will vary with particle size and density, but are in the range of 0.3 - 0.75 m/s. They can be used not only for drying but also for cooling. If the velocity is too high, the particles will be carried away in the gas stream, therefore, gravitational forces need to be only slightly exceeded.

Two and Three Stage Drying Processes

In standard, single stage spray drying, the rate of evaporation is particularly high in the first part of the process, and it gradually decreases because of the falling moisture content of the particle surfaces. In order to complete the drying in one stage, a relatively high outlet temperature is required during the final drying phase. Of course the outlet temperature is reflective of the particle temperature and thus heat damage.

Consequently the two stage drying process was introduced which proved to be superior to the traditional single stage drying in terms of product quality and cost of production.

The two stage drier consists of a spray drier with an external vibrating fluid bed placed below the drying chamber. The product can be removed from the drying chamber with a higher moisture content, and the final drying takes place in the external fluid bed where the residence time of the product is longer and the temperature of the drying air lower than in the spray dryer.

This principle forms the basis of the development of the three stage drier. The second stage is a fluid bed built into the cone of the spray drying chamber. Thus it is possible to achieve an even higher moisture content in the first drying stage and a lower outlet air temperature from the spray drier. This fluid bed is called the integrated fluid bed. The inlet air temperature can be raised resulting in a larger temperature difference and improved efficiency in the drying process. The exhaust heat from the chamber is used to preheat the feed stream. The third stage is again the external fluid bed, which can be static or vibrating, for final drying and/or cooling the powder. The results are as follows:

- higher quality powders with much better rehydrating properties directly from the drier

- lower energy consumption
- increased range of products which can be spray dried i.e., non density, non hygroscopic
- smaller space requirements

Agglomerating and Instantizing

These processes have allowed the manufacturing of milk powders with better reconstitution properties, such as instantized skim milk powder.

Agglomeration Mechanism: Powder is wetted with water or steam. The surface must be uniformly wetted but not excessively. The powder is held wet over a selected period of time to give moisture stability to the clusters which have formed. The clusters are dried to the desired moisture content and then cooled (e.g., fluid bed). Dried clusters are screened and sized to reduce excessively large particles and remove excessively small ones. The aggomeration process causes an increase in the amount of air incorporated between powder particles. More incorporated air is replaced with more water when the powder is reconstituted, which immediately wet the powder particles.

Agglomerating Techniques

Rewet Methods: This method uses powder as feed stock. An example is the ARCS Instantizer. Humidified air moistens powder which causes it to cluster. It is re-dried and wetted. The clustered powder is then exposed to heated, filtered, high-velocity air. The dried clusters are then exposed to cooled air on a vibrating belt. It is then sized (pelleted to uniform size) and the fines are removed.

Straight Thru Process: A multi-stage drying process produces powders with much better solubility characteristics similar to instantized powder. This method uses a low outlet temperature which allows higher moisture in powder as it is taken from spray drier with excess moisture removed in the fluid bed. The powder fines are reintroduced to the atomizing cloud in the drying chamber.

- Production and Utilization of Steam and Refrigeration
- Steam Production and Utilization
- Understanding steam

The diagram below helps to explain the various principles involved in the thermodynamics of steam. It shows the relationship between temperature and enthalpy (energy or heat content) of water as it passes through its phase change.

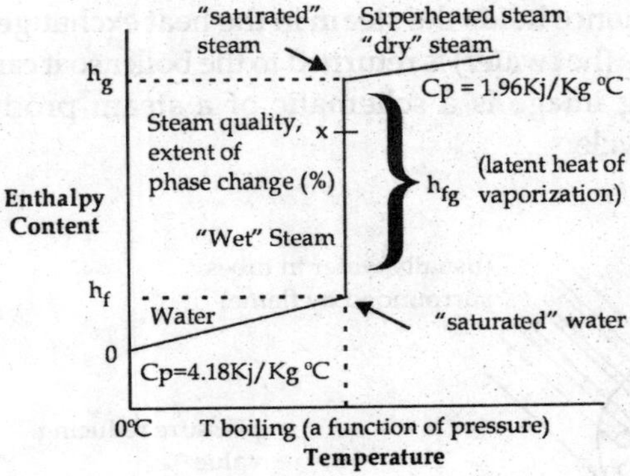

The reference point for enthalpy of water and steam is 0°C, at which point an enthalpy value of 0 kJ/kg is given to it (but of course water at 0o has alot of energy in it, which is given up as it freezes - it's not until 0K, absolute zero, when it truely has no enthalpy). As we increase the temperature of water, its enthalpy increases by 4.18 kJ/kg oC until we hit its boiling point (which is a function of its pressure - the boiling point of water is 100°C ONLY at 1 atm. pressure). At this point, a large input of enthalpy causes no temperature change but a phase change, latent heat is added and steam is produced. Once all the water has vaporized, the temperature again increases with the addition of heat (sensible heat of the vapour).

Steam Production and Distribution

Steam is produced in large tube and chest heat exchangers, called water tube boilers if the water is in the tubes, surrounded by the flame, or fire tube boilers if the opposite is true. The pressure inside a boiler is usually high, 300-800 kPa. The steam temperature is a function of this pressure. The steam, usually saturated or of very high quality, is then distributed to the heat exchanger where it is to be used, and it provides heat by condensing back to water (called condensate) and giving up its latent heat. The temperature desired at the heat exchanger can be adjusted by a pressure reducing valve, which lowers the pressure to that corresponding to the desired temperature. After the steam condenses in the heat exchanger, it passes through a steam trap (which only allows water to pass through and hence holds the steam in the heat exchanger) and then the condensate (hot water) is returned to the boiler so it can be reused. The following image is a schematic of a steam production and distribution cycle.

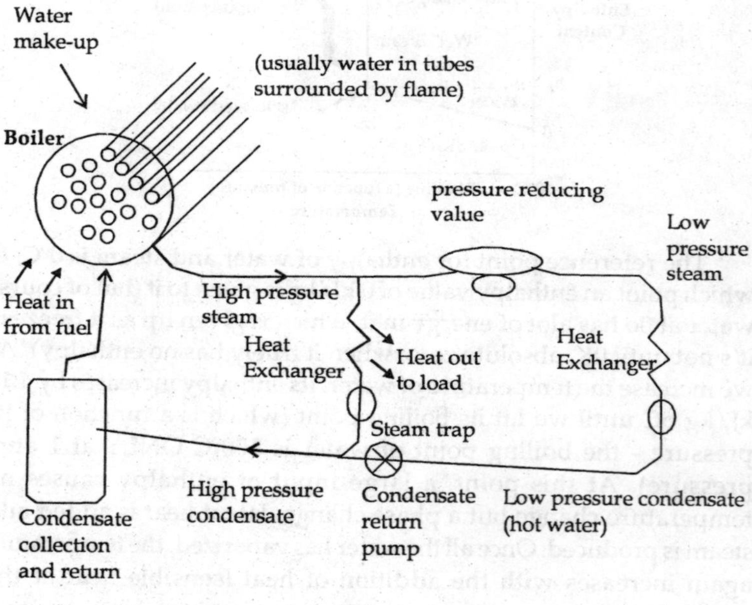

Refrigeration

The following image is a schematic of a refrigeration cycle. It is described in detail below, so you may want to go back and forth between the diagram and the description.

Mechanical refrigerators have four basic elements: an evaporator, a compressor, a condenser, and a refrigerant flow control (expansion valve). A refrigerant circulates among the four elements changing from liquid to gas and back to liquid.

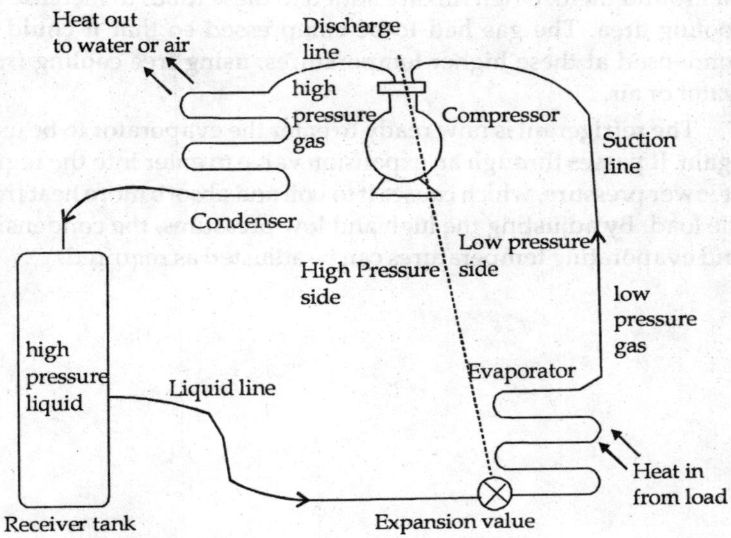

In the evaporator, the liquid refrigerant evaporates (boils) under reduced pressure and in doing so absorbs latent heat of vaporization and cools the surroundings. The evaporator is at the lowest temperature in the system and heat flows to it. This heat is used to vaporize the refrigerant. The temperature at which this occurs is a function of the pressure on the refrigerant: for example if ammonia is the refrigerant, at -18oC the ammonia pressure required is 1.1 kg/ sq. cm. The part of the process described thus far is the useful part of the refrigeration cycle; the remainder of the process is necessary only so that the refrigerant may be returned to the evaporator to continue the cycle.

The refrigerant vapour is sucked into a compressor, a pump that increases the pressure and then exhausts it at a higher pressure to the condenser. For ammonia, this is approx. 10 kg/sq. cm. To complete the cycle, the refrigerant must be condensed back to liquid and in doing this it gives up its latent heat of vaporization to some cooling medium such as water or air. The condensing temperature of ammonia is 29oC, so that cooling water at about 21oC could be used. In home refrigerators, the compressed gas (not ammonia) is sent through the pipes at the back, which are cooled by circulating air around them. Often fins are added to these tubes to increase the cooling area. The gas had to be compressed so that it could be condensed at these higher temperatures, using free cooling from water or air.

The refrigerant is now ready to enter the evaporator to be used again. It passes through an expansion valve to enter into the region of lower pressure, which causes it to boil and absorb more heat from the load. By adjusting the high and low pressures, the condensing and evaporating temperatures can be adjusted as required.

16

PROCESS CONTROL

Objectives of Cheese Manufacturing

To maximize returns, the cheese maker must obtain the maximum yields which are consistent with good cheese quality. For example, water and salt are cheaper than milk fat and protein, but you can only have so much cheese moisture and salt. With respect to consistent production of high quality cheese the objectives of the cheese maker are to:

(1) Develop the basic structure of the cheese.

(2) Obtain cheese composition required for optimum microbial and enzyme activity during curing. Optimum composition mainly means optimum levels of moisture, fat, pH (lactic acid), minerals, and salt.

For example, the characteristic texture of Swiss cheese is largely determined at the time when the curd and whey are transferred to the press table. At this time the basic structure (i.e., the manner in which the casein micelles and fat globules are arranged) and chemical composition (especially mineral content) is already determined. You can not take Swiss curd at this stage and make Cheddar cheese. On the other hand it is possible to produce both Feta and a Brie type cheese from the same curd.

Moisture Control

Cheese making is a process of removing moisture from a rennet coagulum or an acid coagulum consisting of fat globules (unless the milk is skimmed) and water droplets trapped in a matrix of casein micelles

- cheese is, therefore, a concentrate of milk protein and fat.
- most cheese making operations are related to this process of removing water from the milk gel by the process of syneresis
- syneresis = to contract; refers to contraction of the protein network with the resulting expulsion of water from the curd
- the water and water soluble components are literally squeezed out of the curd this liquid, (whey) contains water, sugar, whey proteins, lactic acid and some of the milk minerals the final moisture content, therefore, to a large extent determines the final pH of the cheese because it determines the residual amount of fermentable lactose in the cheese at the same time other factors such as the amount and rate of acid development and the temperature and time of cooking, determine the amount and the rate of syneresis.

pH Control

With respect to cheese quality and safety, the most important process control factor is the development of acidity increasing acidity causes:

- syneresis (due to reduced charge repulsion on casein micelles) and moisture expulsion solubilization of calcium phosphates
- disruption of casein micelle structure with alterations in curd texture reduced lactose content by fermentation to lactic acid
- acid development occurs mainly within the curd because most bacteria are trapped in the gel matrix during coagulation final pH (acidity) is dependent on the amount of acid developed during manufacture and the residual lactose which will ferment during early curing and cause further acid development the residual lactose content is mainly determined by the moisture content, washing which removes lactose by

leaching, and the extent of fermentation ability of culture to ferment galactose is also important both the rate of acid development and the amount of acid development (as measured by final pH) are important eg., final pH of Swiss is the same as Cheddar but Cheddar cheese reaches pH 5.2 after about 5 hours while Swiss cheese requires about 15 h to reach this pH it is important to maintain uniform rate of acid development; if acidity develops too slow or too fast, adjust the amount of culture rather than changing cooking time or temperature pH at draining largely determines the mineral and residual sugar contents of the cheese and from the sugar, the final pH salting reduces the rate of acid development, and, therefore, the time and amount of salting is important to the pH at 1 day and 7 days following manufacture.

Mineral Control

Loss of calcium phosphate determines extent of casein micelle disruption—hence it determines basic cheese structure; the important parameter is the ratio of Ca to casein or Ca to SNF which is easier to measure in Swiss (high Ca, about 750 mM Ca/kg SNF) micelle globular structure is intact while extensive dissociation and disruption of submicelles is evident in Feta types (low Ca, about 400 mM Ca/kg SNF)) retention of calcium phosphate in the cheese also increases the buffer capacity of the cheese pH at draining determines the solubility of calcium and phosphate when the curd is separated from the whey more Ca is retained at high draining pH as in Swiss cheese (pH 6.4 - 6.5) versus Cheddar 6.1 - 6.3 little. Ca retained in Feta cheese which needs some explanation:

- Feta is dipped into the forms early while the pH is still quite high. However, the moisture is also high because no cooking has taken place. Therefore, the moisture is removed by syneresis as the pH decreases while the cheese is in the forms. The net result is that a great deal of moisture (whey) is removed at low pH and most of the calcium phosphate is removed with it. This is also true for other soft ripened cheese like blue and camembert.

Texture Control

Untypical texture in a young cheese is a strong indication of probable flavour defects later; therefore, a primary objective of cheese making is to develop the ultrastructure which will determine the proper texture conformation of the protein matrix is also influenced by pH—at lower pH micelles are disrupted, but the proteins are tightly packed because of reduced charge repulsion; therefore, Feta is brittle while Camembert is soft and smooth due to alkalinity contributed by ammonia during ripening cheese drained at higher pH has higher calcium content and is firmer and more elastic firmness is also affected by ripening agents other factors also play a role—salt, moisture, and fat, but none of these will alter the basic structure of the protein matrix at the submicellar level.

Flavour Control

Milk heating and clarification treatments which determine non-starter bacteria present in the milk types of cultures and coagulating enzymes all cooking and curd handling procedures have specific effects on the types of ripening agents (bacteria and enzymes) which remain to ripen the cheese; especially in cheese such as Swiss where the composition and functions of the culture are more complex pH at draining again important because it determines the distribution of plasmin and rennin between the curd and the whey plasmin is the principal milk protease: it prefers neutral to slightly alkaline pH and is more soluble at low pH; therefore, cheese which are dipped at high pH have higher retention and activity of plasmin (eg., in Swiss protein breakdown during ripening is due to plasmin) calf rennet is more soluble at higher pH but more active at lower pH; therefore, an acid cheese such as Feta or Cheshire, has more rennet activity than Cheddar the solubility of microbial rennets is independent of pH.

The following charts illustrate how a cheese maker may adjust process parameters to make cheese with different moisture and ripening targets.

Table 11.1a. Pasteurized Milk Cheddar Cheese (also for Heat Treated Milk) Record of Manufacture.

Maker:	Joe Cheesehead	**Vat**	100	**Date:** March 7, 2000
Milk:	10,000 Kg	**Starter acid**	0.70% Age 15 h	
Starter:	100 Kg	**Whey Fat**	0.32 kg/100 Kg	
Total:	10,100 Kg	**Cheese milk with culture:**	Fat 3.50%	Protein 3.30%

Operation	Time	Tempearture °F	Tempearture °C	Acid%	pH	Comments
Pasteurization	16 sec	161-163	72-73	–	–	Pasteurized March 7, 7:00 h
Added starter	8:00	86	30	0.155	6.60	1% bulk set, mesophilic
Added color	8:45	86	30	0.16	–	425g
Added rennet	9.00	86	30	0.165	6.55	850g
Coagulation	9:15	86	30	–	–	
Cutting	9:30	86	30	0.10	6.50	Knives 1/4 × 1/4 in. (6.4 mm)
Steam on	9:45	86	30	0.105	6.45	Cook slowly, follow schedule
Steam off	10:15	102	39	0.11	6.40	Slow agiators
Draining	11:30	102	39	0.14	6.20	Stir out once
Packing	11:45	101	38	0.17	6.10	pH of curd
Milling	14:00	90	32	0.6-0.7	5.40	
Salting	14:20	88	31	–	–	11.3 kg
Pressing	15:00	70	20	No Test	–	press slowly at first

Cheese	Kg	% Fat	% Moist	%Salt	pH	Yield kg/100 kg milk Actual	Yield kg/100 kg milk Adjusted 37% M, 1.7% Salt
Hooping	1037.1	33.1	38.2	–	5.4	–	–
Pressing	979.7	34.6	35.0	1.7	5.15	9.70	9.87

Table 11.1b. Raw Milk Cheddar Cheese Record of Manufacture

Maker: Joe Cheesehead	**Vat**	101	Date: March 7, 2000
Milk: 10,000 Kg	**Starter acid**	0.70% Age 15 h	
Starter: 200 Kg	**Whey Fat**	0.32 kg/100 Kg	
Total: 10,200 Kg	**Cheese milk with culture:**	Fat 3.50%	Protein 3.30%

Operation	Time	Tempearture °F	°C	Acid%	pH	Comments
Pasteurization		Not pasteurized				
Added starter	8:00	86	30	0.17	6.60	2% bulk set, mesophilic
Added color	–	86	30	0.175	–	359g
Added rennet	9.00	86	30	0.18	6.50	850g
Coagulation	9:15	86	30	–	–	
Cutting	9:30	86	30	0.12	6.45	Knives 1/4 × 1/4 in. (6.4 mm)
Steam on	9:40	86	30	0.125	6.40	follow cooking schedule
Steam off	10:10	102	39	0.125	6.35	
Draining	11:40	102	39	0.19	6.10	Stir out twice
Packing	12:00	101	38	0.24	6.00	pH of curd
Milling	14:45	90	32	0.80	5.30	
Salting	15:00	88	31	0.85	–	11.3 kg
Pressing	15:40	70	20	–	–	press slowly at first

Cheese	Kg	% Fat	% Moist	%Salt	pH	Yield kg/100 kg milk Actual	Adjusted 37% M, 1.7% Salt
Hooping	1018.3	33.3	37.4	–	5.30	–	–
Pressing	969.0	35.0	34.5	1.7	5.05	9.50	9.89

Table 11.1c. High Moisture Cheddar Record of Manufacture

Maker: Joe Cheesehead	**Vat**	102	**Date:** March 7, 2000
Milk: 10,000 Kg	**Starter acid**	0.70% Age 15 h	
Starter: 70 Kg	**Whey Fat**	0.32 kg/100 Kg	
Total: 10,070 Kg	**Cheese milk with culture:**	Fat 3.50%	Protein 3.30%

Operation	Time	Tempearture °F	°C	Acid%	pH	Comments
Pasteurization	16 sec	161-163	72-73	–	–	Pasteurized march 7, 7:00 h
Added starter	8:00	86	30	0.16	6.6	0.7% bulk set, mesophilic
Added color	8:30	86	30	0.16	–	425g
Added rennet	8:45	86	30	0.165	6.55	850g
Cutting	9:15	86	30	0.10	6.50	Knives 3/8 × 3/8 in. (8.3 mm)
Steam on	9:30	86	30	0.10	6.45	slowly, follow schedule
Steam off	10:00	102	39	0.105	6.40	slow agitators
Draining	11:15	102	39	0.14	6.30	do not stir out curd
Packing	11:45	101	38	0.17	6.25	pH of curd
Milling	13:15	91	32	0.50	5.45	
Salting	14:15	89	31.5	–	–	11.3 kg
Hooping	14:15	88	31	–	–	
Pressing	14:35	70	20	–	–	

Cheese	Kg	% Fat	% Moist	%Salt	pH	Yield kg/100 kg milk Actual	Adjusted 37% M, 1.7% Salt
Hooping	1086.6	30.2	41.0	–	5.45	–	–
Pressing	1026.3	33.6	38.0	1.8	5.15	10.19	10.02

Yield Efficiency

Distribution of Components During Cheese Making

Table 16.2. Distribution of milk components during cheese making (% by weight) and percent transfer from milk to cheese.

	Fat	Protein	CHO	Ash	Solids
Milk composition %	3.3	3.2	5.0	0.7	12.4
Cheese composition %	31	25	2.0	2.1	60
Whey Composition %	0.22	0.61	5.3	0.58	7.0
% Transfer	93	78	4	30	49

Factors Affecting Yield

Milk casein is the principal yield determining factor. Casein contributes absorbed water and minerals as well as its own weight. Cheese quality limits the ratio of moisture/casein, a ratio which corresponding to MNFS.

Fat is also a principal yield component. Fat interferes with syneresis and, therefore, also contributes more than its own weight, but if other conditions are adjusted to maintain constant MNFS, then fat contribution to yield is dependent only on the conversion factor of fat from milk to cheese (i.e., fraction of milk fat recovered in the cheese).

Cheese moisture. A 1% increase in Cheddar cheese moisture causes about 1.8% increase in cheese yield, partly because more moisture means more whey solids and salt are recovered in the cheese (eg., given 90 kg cheese/1000 kg milk, a moisture adjustment to 36% would result in 91.6 kg cheese/1000 kg milk)

Cheese salt. An extra 0.1% salt means an extra 0.14% yield of Cheddar cheese if the moisture content is increased accordingly.

Milk quality factors: somatic cell counts, psychrotrophic bacteria, protein quality etc.

Increasing time and temperature of milk pasteurization increases cheese moisture retention and the recovery of whey proteins and soluble solids. There doesn't seem to be any consensus on how much is desirable but it's safe to say that it depends on the type of cheese and the quality standards of the manufacturer.

- Process control parameters
- Careless cutting.
- Heating too fast at early stages of cooking.
- Salting too soon after milling of Cheddar allows rapid salt uptake which in turn causes rapid synerisis and increased solubility of casein. Yield is, therefore, reduced by losses of protein, fat and soluble solids.
- High temperatures during pressing cause loss of fat.
- Proteolytic cultures or coagulating enzymes cause protein losses before and after cutting.
- Washing removes soluble solids.
- Working as in Mozzarella removes fat and soluble solids. Loss of soluble solids is minimized by equilibration of the wash water with the cheese moisture.

Principles of Yield Optimization

With respect to yield the cheese maker's objectives are to:

(1) Obtain highest MNFS (moisture in non-fat substance) consistent with good quality to maximize moisture and the recovery of whey solids

(2) Standardize milk to obtain maximum value for milk components consistent with good quality (eg., adjust P/F to maximize cost efficiency).

(3) Minimize losses of fat and casein in the whey

Yield Control

It is absolutely vital to be able to measure and maximize yield efficiency. This means maximizing the return (or minimizing the loss in the case of lactose) from all milk components entering the plant. This includes obtaining maximum returns for whey non-fat-solids, whey cream and cream skimmed during standardization. In general the highest return for all milk components, is obtained by keeping them in the cheese, but this may not always be the case.

Recovery of Milk Components

Yield efficiency can be determined by monitoring recovery of milk components and losses in the whey as recommended by Gilles and Lawerence N.Z.J. Dairy Sci. Technol. 20(1985):205. By keeping accurate records of all incoming milk components and their distribution between cream, cheese, whey cream and defatted whey it is possible to determine the plant mass balance.

Yield Prediction

Purposes of Calculating Predicted Yields:

(1) Provide a target against which to judge actual yields and determine mass balance within the plant

(2) Flag errors in measurement: eg. weights of milk or improper standardization etc.

(3) Early signal of high or low moisture content which allows adjustment on the following vats. This can be met by rapid moisture tests (microwave) which is sufficiently accurate for this purpose

The Van Slyke and Price Formula:

The formula most often used for Cheddar cheese is the Van Slyke formula which was published in 1908 and has been used successfully ever since. The Van Slyke formula is based on the premise that yield is proportional to the recovery of total solids (fat, protein, other solids) and the moisture content of the cheese.

$$Yield = \frac{(0.93F + C - 0.1)1.09}{1 - M} = 9.945\%$$

F = Fat content of milk (3.6 kg/100 kg)

C = Casein content of milk (2.5 kg/100 kg)

0.1 = Casein lost in whey due to hydrolysis of -casein and fines losses

1.09 = a factor which accounts for other solids included in the cheese; this represents calcium phosphate/citrate salts associated with the casein and whey solids

M = moisture fraction (0.37)

This formula has several important limitations:

First, it's difficult to measure casein. Many plants use total protein in the predictive formula and multiple by a factor to estimate casein. The classical procedure for casein determination is Rowland Fractionation which is too involved for most cheese plants. I recommend that two or three silo samples be sent to a private lab every 4 weeks to monitor seasonal variation in the casein fraction of protein. A second difficulty is that the formula fails to consider important variables such as variation in salt content and whey solids.

Third difficulty is that the equation is quite specific to Cheddar.

Many other formulae have been developed and used. Probably the best proven formulae are those developed in Holland where commercial cheese manufacturers have been making good use of predictive yield equations for many years.

17

DEFECTS AND GRADING

Common Cheese Defects

In the context of modern sensory analysis body refers to texture, which is confusing because cheese graders use the term 'texture' to refer to cheese openness. Here, we will use the traditional cheese grading terms. Some descriptors for body defects are:

- **Crumbly/short:** often due to excess salt or acid
- **Corky:** due to overcooking, low fat, low moisture, or excess salt.
- **Mealy:** this defect can be detected on the palate or by massaging the cheese between the thumb and forefinger. It is usually associated with excess acidity.
- **Pasty:** sticks to the palate and fingers; due to excess moisture.
- **Weak:** breaks down too quickly when worked by hand; due excess fat or moisture.

Texture relates to openness in the cheese which may or may not be desirable depending on the type of cheese and the cause of openness. Openness can be due to:

Mechanical openings which are holes of irregular shape caused by trapped whey. Trapped whey makes the impression in the cheese during pressing, but during ripening the moisture is dispersed through out the cheese leaving the hole behind. Openness is desirable in Colby, but is considered a defect in Cheddar. Mechanical openings can lead to discolouration around the opening due to local acid development. Usually mechanical openings are closed by vacuum packaging.

Gas holes are, of course, desirable in many types of cheese. Gas hole defects include:

Early gas defects due to coliforms. These appear as small, sphericle, shiny holes. The defect is often associated with unclean flavour.

Late gas due to *Clostridium. tyrobutryricum* or *perfringens,* especially in some European made cheese. *Clostridia* spores are often present in American cheese as well but do not normally cause problems. However, they may be activated by the heat treatment and, therefore, sometimes cause gas defect in processed cheese.

A third gas defect occurs in Cheddar and American types. The defect is distinctive in that the gas (mainly $C0_2$ with some hydrogen sulfide) blows the package but not the cheese. The defect occurs at 6 - 9 months in Cheddar but a similar defect is sometimes observed earlier in American Mozzarella and Colby. The causative anaerobic organism is not fully identified, however, experiments have demonstrated that the defect does not occur in cheese aged at < 10C.

Yeast slits due to yeast growth.

Flavour: Most grading systems assign the greatest weight to flavour defects. A few common descriptors are:

Acid flavour is often associated with acid body defects noted above. The common causes all relate to process control:

- Too much moisture (i.e., too much lactose).
- Too much starter (i.e., too much acid development before dipping).
- Salting too late or too little.
- Too warm during or immediately after pressing.

Bitter flavours are common defects in American but also other cheese, including fresh cheese. Some causes include:

- High moisture
- Excess rennet
- Bitter cultures
- High ripening temperatures

- Fruity/Yeasty flavours are usually associated with high pH and bitterness, and sometimes with yeast slits.
- Unclean flavours are reminiscent of the barn yard, and may be associated with coliforms.

Whey taint is due to high moisture and is usually associated with acid defects including bitterness.

Colour. Other than traditional colour preferences such as orange cheddar and white goats' cheese, the most important colour parameter is uniformity. Even for cheese such as Colby which is coloured with annatto, graders do not evaluate colour intensity. Rather, they look for nonuniformity which may signal a manufacturing defect. Here are some common descriptors:

- Acid cut (pink or bleached): low pH, oxidation of annatto.
- Mottled: may be an acid defect or caused by mixing cheese from different vats.
- Seamy: this is Cheddar defect where the curd particles fail to knit properly. Causes are:
    - Greasy curd from too much vat or high temperature during pressing
    - Improper salting, too soon after milling or pH at salting is too high or too low
    - Hooped too soon after salting.
- Finish. There is a lot of art and patience required to produce cheese with a good finish. Common defects are:
    - Checked/Cracked: too dry on surface
    - Greasy: temperature too high during pressing or curing
    - Huffed: gassy
    - Mineral Deposits due to calcium lactate
    - Common on Cheddar cheese and sometimes on American varieties
    - Encouraged by certain non-starter Lactobacilli and Pediococci which favour formation of D-lactate which in turn encourages crystallization of DL-calcium lactate.

- Control measures are:
  - Decrease numbers of non-starter bacteria (eg., pasteurize versus heat treat and/or bactofuge the milk)
  - Use tight packaging. Calcium lactate crystals tends to form in areas where the package is loose or in depressions on the cheese surface.
  - Avoid temperature fluctuations. Calcium lactate crystals often form in the dairy case where temperatures are not constant.
  - Encourage rapid turn over in the dairy case.
  - Rind rot caused by mites or mould. Mites are almost unheard of in modern cheese making practice, but I have some great pictures
  - Surface mould is definitely one of the most common defects. Indeed a frequent question to me, is about the safety of eating mouldy cheese.
  - Unsymmetrical/Rough: poor workmanship.

Grading

The following grading description and score sheets are included as examples only. The Agriculture and Agri-Food Canada official scoring system for export Cheddar is described below. Also included is a typical score sheet used by the Canadian scoring system, and a general score card entitled "Cheese Judging Score Card" which can be used for any cheese variety.

Agriculture and Agri-Food Guidelines for Grading Cheddar Cheese

Standards - Canada Dairy Products Act.

- Flavour 45
- Texture 25
- Closeness 15
- Colour 10
- Finish 5

Flavour: An ideal cheddar cheese should have a clean, mildly salty, nutty flavour and a pleasing aroma. The intensity of flavour varies with age.

Body: The desirable body should be firm and springy, slightly elastic. The cheese should be smooth and waxy when crushed between the fingers. A slight weakness or coarseness may be permitted in first grade.

Closeness: The ideal cheese should be continuous and free from openings, cracks, breaks or fissures. A slight openness may be permitted in 1st grade. Slight gas holes in second grade and gas holes or Swiss holes are third grade defects.

Colour: The colour should be uniform and translucent whether white or coloured. A slight seaminess may be allowed in 1st grade.

Finish: The cheese should present an unbroken rind or symmetrical shape and a clean neat attractive appearance.

Notes:

1. Cheese should be held overnight at 14.5 - 15.58C before grading.
2. Cheese samples should be 9 kg in weight.
3. Cheese should be at least 21 days old before grading.
4. Early evaluation of aging potential can be obtained by grading a sample stored at 158C for 21 days.

Common Descriptors used in Grading Canadian Cheddar Cheese

Code - Total Score, Maximum 94

1. Sl. open, sl. stiff, sl. coarse, blurred branding, sl. damp end, sl mouldy surface.
2. As above plus slight acid tendency.
3. Weak, open, coarse, wet ends, sl. acid, sl. gas or pin holes, mottled colour etc.
4. Checked rinds with mould penetration. Sl. gas or pin holes. Any above defect plus a second defect except weak and open.
5. Very weak, very acidy, very stiff, very open, gas or Swiss holes (always 3rd), very uneven colour, very mottled.
6. Checked rinds, mould penetration, gas or Swiss holes (always 3rd).

Code - Flavour Score, Maximum 40

- F_1 Sl. unclean, sl. off, sl. fruity, sl. weak. sl. musty, sl. bitter, sl. sour.

- F_2 Sl. rancid, fruity, off, bitter, weed, sour, musty.
- F_3 Very fruity, rancid, badly off, very bitter, very unclean, very weedy.

Typical examples: Cheese Score

- $40 - 92^1$ - A 1st grade cheese with no flavour defects but which has objectionable body defects such as (1) sl. open, sl. stiff, or blurred branding.
- $39 - 88^5$ - A 2nd grade cheese with no flavour defects but which has objectionable body defects such as (5) checked rinds with mould penetration very weak or very acidy etc.
- $38^{(F1)}-88^3$ - A 2nd grade cheese with (F^1) a sl. unclean, sl. off, sl. fruity, sl. weed, etc., flavour and with defective body characteristics (2) open, weak or sl. acid.
- $36^{(F3)}-86^{5or6}$ - A 3rd grade cheese with (F3) very fruity, rancid flavour, etc. and has objectionable body characteristics (5 or 6) such as checked rinds with mould penetration or large gas holes, etc.
- sl. - slight

Table 17.1. Cheddar Cheese Judging Score Card - Agriculture Canada Grading System

Name: .... Date: ....

Sample No.	1	2	3	4	5	6	7	8	9	10
45–Flavour										
Acid										
Bitter										
Flat										
Fruity										
Yeasty										
Heated										
Moldy										
Unclean										
Weedy										
Whey-taint										

(Contd.)

Sample No.	1	2	3	4	5	6	7	8	9	10
25–Texture (body)										
Corky										
Crumbly										
Curdy										
Mealy										
Pasty										
Short										
Weak										
15–Closeness										
Gassy										
Open										
Sweet holes										
Yeast holes										
Swiss holes										
10–Colour										
Acid Cut										
Mottled										
Seamy										
Wavy										
5–Finish (allowed perfect in contest)										
Normal Range	**Scrore**									
35-42	Flavour									
85-94	Total Grade									

18

Insemination of Dairy Cows

Reproductive efficiency of the dairy herd is important to the economic success of the dairy operation. One of the most important reproductive technologies of the dairy industry is artificial insemination (AI). Artificial insemination reduces the incidence of sexually transmitted diseases among cattle and increases the use of genetically superior sires to improve performance of the herd.

Standing estrus, or "heat," is the most reliable indication that a cow is going to ovulate and release an ovum or "egg." Estrous behavior is used to determine when a cow should be inseminated. A brief window of opportunity exists for fertilization of the ovum and pregnancy of the cow to occur. Senger estimated that the U.S. dairy industry loses more than $300 million annually due to failure and/or misdiagnosis of estrus. Thus, the efficient and accurate detection of estrus and the proper time of insemination are of utmost importance if dairy producers want to increase reproductive efficiency of the herd.

Estrus or "Heat"

Estrous behavior, or heat, is due to the actions of the steroid hormone estrogen (E2) on the brain of cattle. Early research by Trimberger found the duration of estrus in dairy cows ranged from 2.5 to 28 hours with a mean of 18 hours in cows visually observed three times daily. With the recent advent of continuous observation of estrous behavior by radiotelemetric systems, duration of estrus averaged 7 hours.

Several factors related to dairy management affect estrous behavior in dairy cattle. Increasing the number of cows penned together increases the intensity (number of mounts) and duration of estrus. Dairy cows observed for estrus on a dirt surface had greater intensity and duration of estrus compared with cows on concrete surfaces. Environmental factors such as high temperatures decrease estrous activity. Estrous behavior was greatest in dairy cows observed twice daily when ambient temperatures were less than 77°F (25°C) compared with temperatures above 86°F (30°C).

Proper estrus detection is critical to the success of AI. Approximately 75 to 80 percent of cows in estrus will be identified when the herd is visually observed twice daily (30 minutes each time). When estrous detection is increased to three times daily, 85 percent of cows in estrus may be detected, while four daily observations identify more than 90 percent of estrual cows. Several aides have been developed to assist producers in estrous detection, including pedometers, Kamar patches, tail paint, chin-ball markers, and radiotelemetric systems. A combination of both visual observation and one or more of the detection aides increases the efficiency of estrous detection compared with visual observation or detection aides alone.

Ovulation in Dairy Cows

Ovulation is initiated by a surge of luteinizing hormone (LH) from the brain of cattle. This surge of LH results in the rupture of the follicle and the release of the ovum from the ovary. Ovulation usually occurs approximately 28 to 32 hours after the onset of estrus in dairy cows. After ovulation, there is only a short period when ova can be fertilized. Optimal fertility of ova is projected to be between 6 and 12 hours after ovulation. The viable life span of sperm in the reproductive tract is estimated at 24 to 30 hours.

Artificial Insemination Relative to Estrus

For the past 50 years, researchers have investigated the optimal time at which to inseminate cows relative to the stage of estrus.

Trimberger found that conception rates were highest when cows were inseminated between 6 and 24 hours before ovulation. This early work led to the establishment of the "a.m.-p.m." recommendation. This guideline suggests that cows in estrus during a.m. hours should be inseminated during the p.m. hours, and cows in estrus in the p.m. should be bred the following a.m. However, research with large numbers of cows indicates that maximum conception rates may not be achieved using the a.m.-p.m. rule.

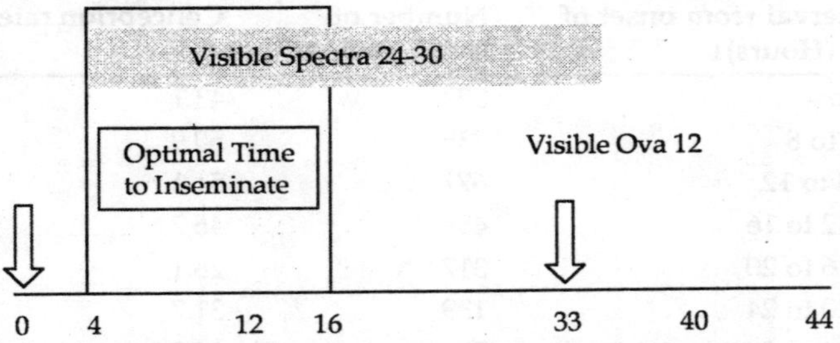

Fig. 18.1. Optimal Time in Inseminate Diary Cows.

A large field trial (44,707 cows) found no difference in the percentage of non return rates at 150 and 180 days (which would indicate pregnancy) between cows bred either the same morning as observed estrus, between noon and 6 p.m. on the day of observed estrus, or cows bred the following morning after observed estrus the previous evening. This indicates that a single mid-morning insemination for all cows observed in estrus the night before or the same morning should give near maximum conception. Also, cows bred once daily (between 8 a.m. and 11 a.m.) had similar non-return rates as cows bred according to the a.m.-p.m. rule. Research from Virginia suggests that cows be bred earlier than the a.m.-p.m. rule guidelines. Highest conception rates for AI occurred between 4 and 12 hours after the onset of estrus. Cows inseminated 16 hours after the onset of estrus had lower conception rates than cows bred between 4 and 12 hours after the onset of estrus.

When Should Dairy Cows Be Inseminated?

Use of the traditional a.m.-p.m. rule may not provide the best conception rates because cows probably will be bred too long after the onset of estrus, so the chance for successful fertilization may be missed. The exact onset of estrus is usually unknown. For example, according to the a.m.-p.m. rule, a cow beginning estrus at 1 a.m. and observed in estrus at 6 a.m. would be bred approximately 17 to 18 hours after the onset of estrus. Breeding cows at this time would limit the number of cows that become pregnant.

Table 18.1. Conception rates of dairy cows inseminated at different times after the onset of estrus, or "heat".

Interval from onset of AI (Hours)1	Number of inseminations	Conception rate (%)
0 to 4	327	43.1
>4 to 8	735	50.9
> 8 to 12	677	51.1
> 12 to 16	459	46.2
> 16 to 20	317	28.1
> 20 to 24	139	31.7
> 24 to 26	7	14.3

1Onset of estrus determined by HeatWatch system.

The herd should be observed twice daily, usually 30 minutes each time, to identify a majority (75-80 percent) of cows in estrus. Influences of the environment and managerial practices on behavioral estrus must be recognized so that failure or misdiagnosis of estrus is minimized. Cows should be inseminated within 4 to 16 hours of observed estrus when the precise onset of estrus is unknown. If estrous detection is conducted twice daily, most cows should be within this time period. A single mid-morning insemination of cows that have been observed in estrus the same morning or the previous evening should provide the best conception rates.

19

Management Considerations in Holstein Heifer Development

The purpose of the heifer herd is to provide replacements for cows leaving the herd and to improve genetic progress. First-lactation cows significantly contribute to herd production and profit. A recommended goal for dairy replacement heifers is to calve at 24 months of age with a targeted post calving body weight of 1250 pounds. A common misconception is that this goal is either unattainable or uneconomical. Feeding heifers for rapid gains costs more per day than feeding for low gains, but development of replacement heifers is an investment in the future. The replacement heifer program should rear heifers to reach a desired age and body weight at a minimum cost.

Why 1250 Pounds?

Why should producers strive for a target weight of 1250 pounds after calving? A large field study conducted from 1980 to 1984 involving DHIA records found that Holstein heifers calving between 1195 and 1250 pounds had the greatest first-lactation milk yield. The importance of achieving calving weight goals is illustrated by the dramatic decline in milk yields when post calving weights were below 1100 pounds. A first-lactation cow that weighs 1250 pounds produces 1775 pounds more milk than a first-lactation cow calving with a weight of 900 pounds or less. Calving weight had a greater impact on first-lactation performance than did calving age, suggesting heifers should be bred by weight, not age.

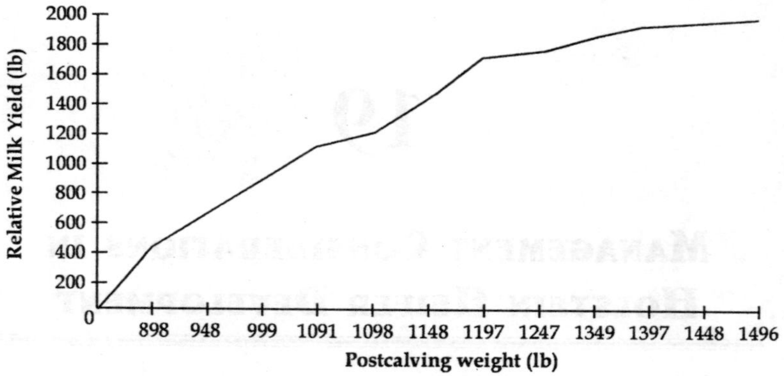

Fig. 19.1. Effect of postcalving body weight on relative milk yield during first lactation.

Over 50,000 DHIA records from Virginia were evaluated to determine the relationships between age at first calving, post calving body weight, and first-lactation milk yield. Optimum first-lactation milk yield occurred when post calving body weight was approximately 1200 to 1300 pounds, independent of calving age. However, milk yields declined when post calving body weight exceeded 1300 pounds, suggesting that over conditioned heifers have lower milk yields than well-conditioned heifers.

These results support the recommended 1200- to 1250-pound post calving target weight. It is important to remember that a 1200- to 1250-pound post calving weight translates to a 1300- to 1350-pound pre-calving weight.

Heavier heifers produce more milk than smaller heifers because they have less growth remaining to reach mature body size, so nutrients can be used for milk production instead of growth. Smaller heifers also may take in less feed at the feed bunk due to competition from heavier, more aggressive heifers.

Over conditioned heifers also perform poorly. Fat heifers can be predisposed to fatty liver, which can lead to ketosis and reduced feed intake. Over conditioned heifers have low lactation performance and a high incidence of dystocia, or difficult labor.

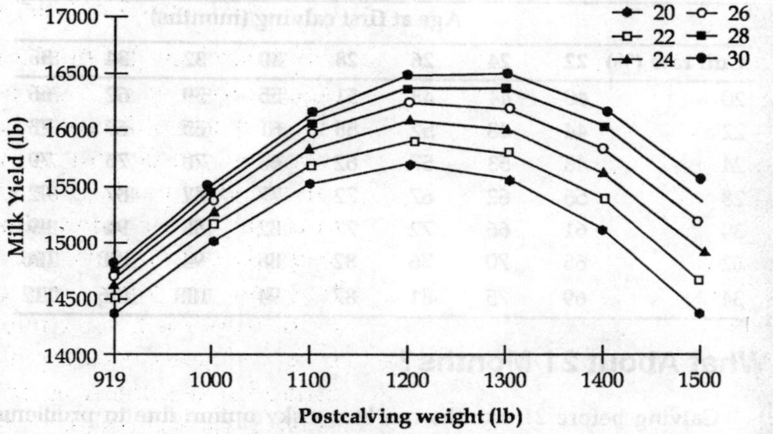

Fig. 19.2. Prediction of first-lactation milk yield for Holstein heifers at varied body weights for 20, 22, 24, 26, 28, and 30 month calving ages.

Why 24 Months?

It is well established that heifers should be between 23 and 26 months of age at first calving. Heifers that calve early spend more of their life producing milk than heifers that calve late. A large investment ($1150 to $1200) is required to rear heifers from birth to calving, and monthly cost thereafter is $55 to $65. The earlier heifers enter the milking herd, the sooner the return on the initial investment. Greater age at first calving dramatically increases herd costs. An extra day to first calving is estimated to cost 13 times as much as an extra day open. Delayed calving can increase rearing costs $50 per heifer for each month beyond 24 months.

The number of replacements needed to maintain herd size increases when calving is delayed. Assuming a 30 percent cull rate, increasing age at first calving from 24 to 28 months requires 11 percent more heifers to maintain herd size, or 110 more heifers on a 1000 cow dairy. Alternatively, decreasing age at first calving from 28 to 24 months results in 110 surplus heifers that can be sold. Heifers should calve between 22.5 and 23.5 months of age to maximize lifetime performance.

Table 19.1. Effect of First Calving and Culling rate on numbers of replacements needed to maintain a herd size of 100.

	Age at first calving (months)							
Cull rate (%)	22	24	26	28	30	32	34	36
20	40	44	48	51	55	59	62	66
22	44	48	52	56	61	65	69	73
24	48	53	57	62	66	70	75	79
28	56	62	67	72	77	82	87	92
30	61	66	72	77	82	88	94	99
32	65	70	76	82	88	94	100	106
34	69	75	81	87	94	100	106	112

What About 21 Months?

Calving before 21 months can be a risky option due to problems associated with rapid growth. Since calving weight, not calving age, is the major factor affecting first-lactation milk yield, successfully calving heifers at 21 months would require daily gains near 2.0 pounds/day from birth to calving for large-breed heifers. To reduce calving age to 21 months, age at first breeding must be reduced to 11 to 12 months, which would require excessive prepubertal gains to achieve breeding weight goals. Body weight gains in excess of 2.0 pounds/day can be detrimental to mammary development in heifers under 12 months of age.

Attaining 1250 Pounds in 24 Months

Heifers must gain an average of 1.7 to 1.8 pounds daily from birth to calving to achieve a precalving weight of 1350 pounds. Overall feeding cost from weaning to calving is less when heifers are fed to gain 1.7 pounds/day than when they are fed to gain 1.3 or 1.5 pounds/day. Remember, a 1250-pound post calving weight translates to about a 1350-pound pre calving weight. This goal is attainable with intensive management, even with less than optimal facilities and feed quality.

Weaning to Breeding

Age at onset of puberty is positively related to body weight. Sexual maturity of Holstein heifers begins at approximately 550 to

650 pounds, independent of age. Consequently, nutrition has a dramatic effect on age at puberty and first breeding. Too little or too much body weight gain during this growth period is a problem.

Table 19.2. Feed Costs for heifers on a corn silage, grass hay, and soybean diet from birth to calving fed to gain 1.3, 1.5 and 1.7 pounds/day.

Body weight (lb)	Gain	Age (mo)	Feed cost/ day	Feed cost/ period	Cumulative feed cost	% period[1]
100-150	1.2	1.4	$0.96	$40.00	$40.00	1.7
150-200	1.8	2.3	$0.45	$12.50	$52.50	2.2
200-400	1.3	7.4	$0.36	$55.38	$107.88	4.5
400-600	1.3	12.6	$0.59	$90.77	$198.65	8.3
600-800	1.3	17.7	$0.75	$115.38	$314.04	13.1
800-1000	1.3	22.8	$0.72	$110.77	$424.81	17.8
1000-1200	1.3	28.0	$0.91	$140.00	$564.81	23.6
1200-1350	1.3	31.8	$1.06	$122.43	$687.24	28.8
100-150	1.2	1.4	$0.96	$40.00	$40.00	1.8
150-200	1.8	2.3	$0.45	$12.50	$52.50	2.3
200-400	1.5	6.8	$0.40	$55.33	$105.83	4.7
400-600	1.5	11.2	$0.63	$84.00	$189.83	8.5
600-800	1.5	15.6	$0.78	$104.00	$293.83	13.1
800-1000	1.5	20.1	$0.77	$102.67	$396.50	17.7
1000-1200	1.3	24.5	$0.93	$124.00	$520.50	23.3
1200-1350	1.5	27.8	$1.15	$115.00	$635.50	28.4
100-150	1.2	1.4	$0.96	$40.00	$40.00	1.9
150-200	1.8	2.3	$0.45	$12.50	$52.50	2.5
200-400	1.7	6.2	$0.43	$50.59	$103.09	4.9
400-600	1.7	10.2	$0.67	$78.82	$181.91	8.6
600-800	1.7	14.1	$0.83	$97.65	$279.56	13.2
800-1000	1.7	18	$0.81	$95.29	$374.85	17.7
1000-1200	1.7	21.9	$0.99	$166.47	$491.32	23.2
1200-1350	1.7	24.8	$1.21	$106.72	$598.04	28.2

[1]Percent of feed costs incurred during each period

Low body weight gains pose a problem. Low weight gain before breeding is an obvious problem because it delays puberty, breeding, and calving. Average daily gains between 1.5 and 1.7 pounds are necessary to achieve a breeding weight goal of 800 pounds at 14 months of age for large-breed heifers. Therefore, an average daily gain below 1.5 pounds for large-breed heifers is unacceptable and costly because it delays sexual maturity.

Rapid body weight gains are risky. Gains greater than 2.0 pounds/day for large-breed heifers prior to puberty are risky. Holstein heifers fed diets to gain 2.8 pounds/day had larger mammary glands, but less total secretary tissue due to increased mammary adipose (fat) tissue than heifers gaining 1.4 pounds/day. Growth rate did not influence mammary composition when similar treatments were applied to post pubertal heifers. Pre-pubertal heifers gaining 2.2 pounds/day between 19 and 39 weeks of age had less (7.1 percent) first-lactation fat-corrected milk than heifers gaining 0.9 pounds/day.

Excessive pre-pubertal gains can reduce milk yield during the first and later lactations due to a lack of secretary tissue in the mammary gland. However, critics argue that heifers in these studies were fed for an unusually high rate of gain approaching that of feedlot cattle. Research consistently supports the theory that rapid pre-pubertal gains impair mammary development, although gains are greater than the normal range in many studies. Sejrsen and Purup suggest further research is needed to understand the relationship between nutrition and mammary development. Limited research suggests no correlation between rapid prepubertal weight gains and impaired mammary development when high-crude-protein diets are fed. Further research is needed to recommend rates of gain exceeding 1.8 pounds/day for prepubertal dairy heifers. The recommendation for average daily gains for growing dairy heifers prior to puberty is between 1.5 and 1.8 pounds/day.

Breeding-Age Heifers

An ideal time to evaluate heifers for body weight, wither height, and body condition is at breeding. Other than the preweaning period, this is one of the few times when heifers are observed closely. Heifers need to be bred in a timely fashion (14 to 15 month average age at first breeding) to achieve a successful replacement program.

Conception by 14 to 15 months is necessary if heifers are to calve by 23 to 26 months of age. Heifers need to gain weight (1.5 to 2.0 pounds/day) and have adequate body condition to achieve high conception rates. Rations should be balanced in energy (64 to 68 percent TDN, or total digestible nutrients) and protein (13 to 15 percent).

Conception problems occur when heifers experience weight loss or are in poor body condition. Balancing rations is critical to avoid these problems. Heifers leaving confinement also can experience weight loss and low conception rates. Researchers at Virginia Tech found heifers experience a body weight loss of up to 60 pounds for a 1- to 2-month period after leaving a confinement facility and moving to pasture. It may be that the increased exercise on pasture reduces the amount of energy available for growth. Therefore, to avoid breeding problems, breeding should occur either before leaving confinement or 2 months after entering pasture.

Breeding to Calving

Animals with the lowest priority on a dairy farm are usually the bred heifers. This group does not require the intensive management that younger heifers do. Calving dates have already been set, so the major goal is for heifers to gain sufficient body weight to achieve desired calving weight and body condition. Average daily gain must be 1.7 to 2.1 pounds during gestation if heifers were bred at 750 to 850 pounds. Body weight gains above 2.0 pounds/day are acceptable for bred heifers during the first 6 to 7 months of gestation. Body weight gains in excess of 2.0 pounds/day should be avoided 1 to 2 months prepartum to prevent calving and postpartum problems because fetal and mammary growth accelerate during this time. Also, excessive body condition (> 4.0 on a 5-point scale) at calving can lead to postpartum health problems.

Table 19.3. Recommended ranges of body weight, wither height, and wither height index for Holstein heifers.

Age (mo)	Body weight (lb)	Wither height (in)	Wither height index[1] (lb/in)
1	130-135	31.7-33.2	4.1-4.2
2	177-189	33.5-35.2	5.3-5.4
3	226-244	35.2-37.1	6.4-6.6

(Contd.)

Age (mo)	Body weight (lb)	Wither height (in)	Wither height index[1] (lb/in)
4	275-299	36.9-38.8	7.4-7.7
5	323-354	38.4-40.4	8.4-8.8
6	372-408	39.8-42.0	9.3-9.7
7	420-463	41.1-43.3	10.2-10.7
8	469-518	42.3-44.5	11.1-11.6
9	518-572	43.4-45.7	11.9-12.5
10	566-627	44.0-46.7	12.9-13.4
11	615-682	45.4-47.6	13.5-14.3
12	664-737	46.3-48.5	14.3-15.2
13	712-791	47.1-49.3	15.1-16.1
14	761-846	47.8-50.0	15.9-16.9
16	858-956	49.0-51.2	17.5-18.7
18	956-1065	50.2-52.1	19.0-20.4
20	1053-1174	51.0-53.0	20.6-22.2
22	1150-1284	51.7-55.0	22.2-23.3
24	1247-1393	52.2-56.5	23.9-24.7

[1]Pounds of body weight/inches of wither height.

Monitor Gains

It is essential that body weight gains and wither heights of heifers are monitored due to the narrow window of recommended gains (1.5 to 1.8 pounds/day). A scale or weight tape and a wither height stick should be available to periodically monitor heifer performance at all ages. At a minimum, heifers should be weighed every time they are worked (such as for deworming, vaccination, and breeding). Recommended body weights and wither heights for growing Holstein heifers at various ages are indicated in table 3. Heifers that achieve body weight goals but are lacking in wither height likely have excessive body condition. Body condition may be difficult to measure objectively, particularly in younger heifers.

An alternative to visual scoring is to calculate a wither height index (pounds body weight/inches of wither height) to estimate body condition. The subjectivity and bias of body condition scoring are avoided with wither height indices. Average wither height indices for a group of heifers should be similar to those in table 3.

Due to the large variation among heifers, producers should monitor groups, not individuals. If wither height indices are low, indicating poor body condition, rations should be evaluated to assure nutrient intake is adequate. A common cause of high wither height indices (excessive body condition) is a diet deficient in protein but excessive in energy.

Rations

Rations formulated to attain a 1.8 pound gain/day are adequate to achieve the precalving target of 1350 pounds at 24 months. Three sample heifer rations are shown in table 4. These rations assume that forage quality is average and grain supplementation does not exceed 3.7 pounds/day. High-quality forages require less grain supplementation. Large quantities of grain are not necessary to achieve high rates of gain. The important component is ration balancing, or supplying nutrients in the proper proportions. A ration balanced in energy and protein promotes high rates of lean gain. However, a ration high in energy but deficient in protein can result in high gains, but with excessive condition. Therefore, rations need to be evaluated periodically, as are rations for lactating cows.

Table 19.4. Rations for 600-, 800-, 1000-pound Holstein heifers gaining 1.8 pounds/day.

	Heifer weight (lb)		
Ration component	**600**	**800**	**1000**
Corn silage,[a] lb (as fed)	15.0	18.0	20.0
Grass hay,[b] lb (as fed)	8.0	10.0	12.0
Shelled corn, lb (as fed)	1.0	1.5	1.5
48% Soybean mean, lb (as fed)	2.0	2.0	2.2
2:1 mineal, lb (as fed)	0.1	0.1	0.1
CP, % of DM	14.4	13.5	13.4
TDN, % of DM	64.7	64.5	64.0
ADF, % of DM	31.6	32.0	32.7

[a]Corn Silage: 67% TDN, 7.5% CP, 28% ADF, 38% DM

[b]Grass hay: 55% TDN, 10.4% CP, 45% ADF, 87% DM

ADF: Acid detergent fiber CP: Crude protien

DM: Dry matter TDN: Total digestible nutrients

All three of the sample rations contain a mineral with ionophores, either BovatecTM or RumensinTM. Ionophores improve energy metabolism and protein use in the rumen, resulting in improved gains and/or feed efficiency. Additionally, ionophores have coccidiostat properties (they reduce and control coccidia) when fed at recommended dosages (200 mg/day) and are inexpensive to supplement (about 1.2 cents/day).

Some producers have an interest in rearing heifers on pasture. Feed costs can be reduced with pasture without decreasing daily gains. To achieve high rates of gain, pastures must be managed intensively. Rotational grazing can allow heifers to continually consume immature, high-quality forage. Mature grasses are lower in quality and will result in lower gains. Holstein heifers (400 to 1000 pounds) grazing orchardgrass pasture at the Virginia Tech Dairy Center gained over 2.0 pounds/day while receiving 2 pounds of a 16 percent crude protein corn and soybean meal mix. Gains were improved by feeding RumensinTM in the grain. Researchers at New Mexico State University found dairy heifers can gain 1.75 pounds/day grazing a Kleingrass-alfalfa mixture (no supplementation) during the summer months (June, July, and August).

Economics of 1250 Pounds at 24 Months

The bottom line for the heifer replacement enterprise is profitability. The benefits of a 1250-pound postcalving weight at 24 months must outweigh the production costs to be profitable. Two questions must be answered: 1) Is it profitable to feed for a 1250-pound postcalving weight?, and 2) For a target calving weight, is it profitable to decrease calving age to 24 months or less?

Is it profitable to feed for a 1250 pounds postcalving weight? The benefit of achieving a 1250-pound postcalving weight is increased first-lactation milk yield. The increased milk yield should pay for the increased feed costs. Body weight and total feed cost increase as average daily gain increases. Heifers that averaged 1.7 pounds/day had higher feed costs ($103.44 increase) and precalving weights (261 pounds heavier) than heifers that gained 1.3 pounds/day. Heifers with a postcalving body weight of 1250 pounds produced approximately 1000 pounds more in first-lactation milk yield than heifers with a postcalving weight of less than 950 pounds. At $12/cwt for milk, the additional revenue from milk would be $120. Therefore, it would be profitable to achieve a postcalving weight of 1200 to 1250 pounds. However, there is little benefit, and possibly harm, in postcalving weights exceeding 1300 pounds.

Table 19.5. Extrapolated feed costs from table 2 for heifers at 24 months of age or 1350-pound precalving body weight under three feeding regimes.[1]

		Average daily gain (lb/day)		
		1.3	**1.5**	**1.7**
24 months of age	Total feed costs[2]	$451.08	$487.79	$554.52
	Body weight[3], lb	1047	1178	1308
1350 lb body weight[3]	Total feed cost[2]	$687.24	$635.50	$598.04
	Age, months	31.8	27.8	24.8

[1]Three feeding regimes are 1.3 lb/day, 1.5 lb/day, and 1.7 lb/day gain from weaning until calving.

[2]Total feed costs from birth until calving.

[3]Precalving body weight.

Is it profitable to decrease calving age to 24 months or less? Decreasing age at first calving decreases total feed costs from birth until calving, assuming a similar precalving weight. Heifers gaining 1.7 pounds/day were seven months younger at first calving and cost $89.20 less to feed than heifers gaining 1.3 pounds/day. Although early calving heifers had a higher daily feed cost, the total feed cost until calving was lower. This alone is an economic incentive to decrease age at first calving, because milk yields should be similar if body weights are similar. Decreasing first-calving age also increases the number of surplus heifers available to sell. Heifers that calve early return income (milk sales) sooner than later calving heifers. Considering all the advantages, there is little doubt that reducing age at first calving is profitable. However, calving ages less than 22 months may not be feasible due to the excessive prepubertal gains required.

Summary

Development of replacement heifers is critical because first-lactation cows account for between 30 (DRMS, Raleigh, NC) and 38 percent (DHI Computing Service, Provo, Utah) of all milking cows. Research indicates that the goal of dairy replacement heifers calving at 1250 pounds and 23 to 24 months of age is attainable and economically viable. To achieve this goal, heifer growers must monitor gains and routinely evaluate rations. Monitoring performance and balancing rations to provide adequate but not excessive nutrient intake will help ensure well-grown heifers that perform to their potential. Proper management of the heifer herd is one area on most dairy operations in which production costs can be reduced and herd productivity and profitability increased.

20

MANAGING MILK COMPOSITION: NORMAL SOURCES OF VARIATION

Many factors influence the composition of milk, the major components of which are water, fat, protein, lactose and minerals.

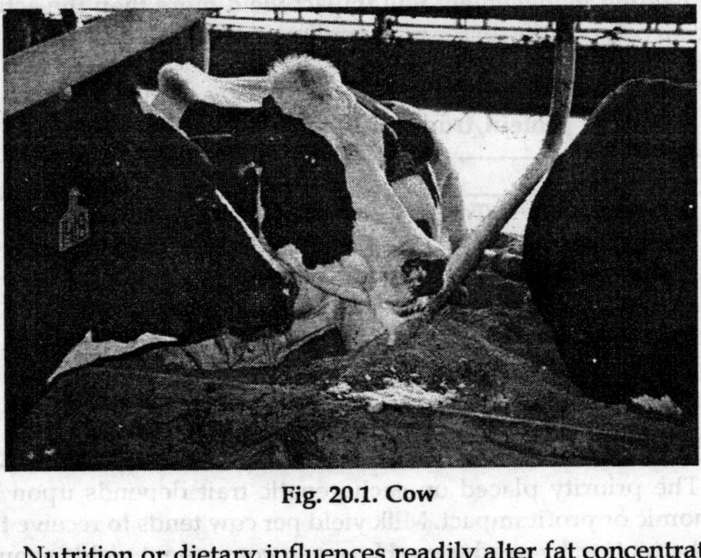

Fig. 20.1. Cow

Nutrition or dietary influences readily alter fat concentration and milk protein concentration. Fat concentration is the most sensitive to dietary changes and can vary over a range of nearly 3.0 percentage units. Dietary manipulation results in milk protein concentration changing approximately 0.60 percentage units. The concentrations of lactose and minerals, the other solids constituents of milk, do not respond predictably to adjustments in diet.

Milk composition and component yields also can be affected by genetics and environment, level of milk production, stage of lactation, disease (mastitis), season and age of cow.

Normal Sources of Variation in Composition

Genetics and Environment: Table 20.1 contains the breed averages for percentage of milk fat, total protein, true protein and total solids. A change in milk composition using traditional breeding techniques occurs slowly, although new techniques of genetic manipulation may allow faster progress in the future. Yields of milk, fat, protein and total solids are not easily impacted by genetics; heritability estimates for yield are relatively low at about 0.25. Meanwhile, heritability estimates for milk composition are fairly high at 0.50. Conversely, environmental factors such as nutrition and feeding management will impact yield more than the actual percent composition of the major milk constituents.

Table 20.1. Breed averages for percentages of milk fat, total protein, true protein and total solids.

	Percent			
Breed	**Total Fat**	**Total Protein**	**True Protein**	**Total Solids**
Ayrshire	3.88	3.31	3.12	12.69
Brown Swiss	3.98	3.52	3.33	12.64
Guernsey	4.46	3.47	3.28	13.76
Holstein	3.64	3.16	2.97	12.24
Jersey	4.64	3.73	3.54	14.04
Milking Shorthorn	3.59	3.26	3.07	12.46

The priority placed on each genetic trait depends upon its economic or profit impact. Milk yield per cow tends to receive the most attention by producers. However, component yields should not be overlooked. Genetic selection should be directed toward increasing fat, protein and nonfat solids yields. But, because component percentages tend to have negative genetic associations with yield traits, a change in these percentages is not likely to be achieved through genetic selection alone.

Level of Production: Yields of fat, protein, nonfat solids and total solids are highly and positively correlated with milk yield. Under selection programs that emphasize milk yield, fat and protein yields also increase. However, the percentages of fat and protein in the total composition decrease.

The concept of milk component yield versus milk composition can be illustrated by comparing different bulk tank production averages with similar protein composition. If the tank average increases from 65 pounds to 70 pounds while protein composition remains constant at 3.1 percent, an additional 0.16 pounds of protein is produced per cow per day. However, if the percentage of protein increases from 3.1 to 3.2 percent while the bulk tank average production remains at 65 pounds, protein production (yield) increases by only 0.07 pounds per cow per day.

Stage of Lactation: The concentration of milk fat and protein is highest in early and late lactation and lowest during peak milk production through mid-lactation (Fig. 20.1). Normally, an increase in milk yield is followed by a decrease in the percentages of milk fat and protein while the yields of these constituents remain unchanged or increase.

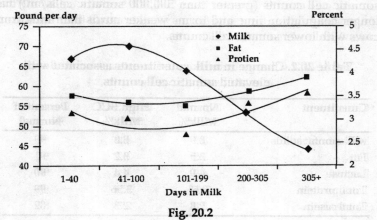

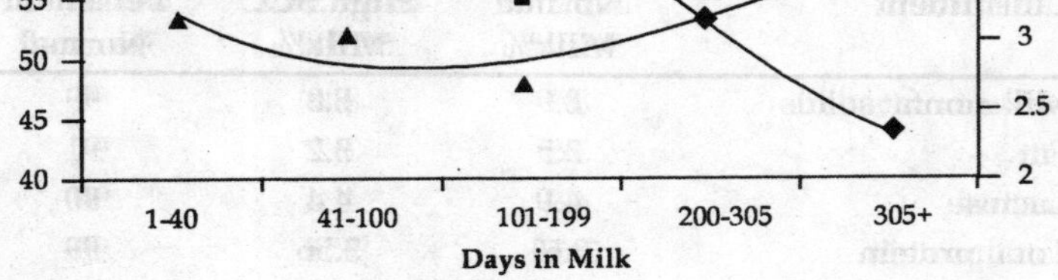

Fig. 20.2

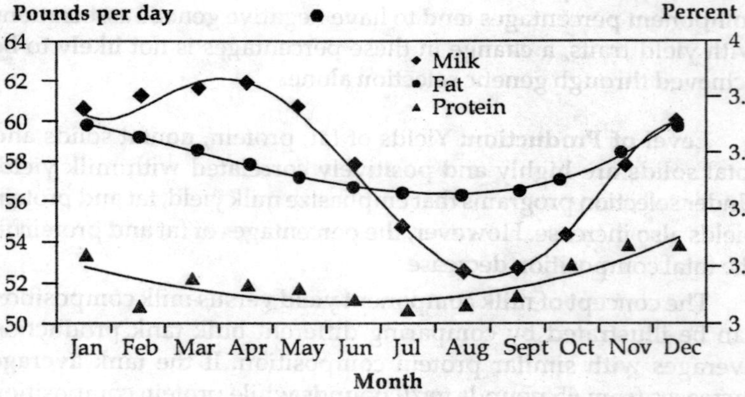

Fig. 20.3.

Disease: Although other diseases can affect milk component content and distribution, mastitis has been the predominate disease studied. Table 20.2 shows the compositional changes in milk constituents associated with elevated somatic cell counts (a measure of severity of the disease). Mastitis results in a reduction in fat and casein content and an increase in whey content of milk. These changes in the milk proteins, in conjunction with alterations in lactose, mineral content and milk pH, result in lower cheese yields and altered manufacturing properties. Milk from cows with elevated somatic cell counts (greater than 500,000 somatic cells/ml) has longer coagulation time and forms weaker curds than milk from cows with lower somatic cell counts.

Table 20.2. Change in milk constituents associated with elevated somatic cell counts.

Constituent	Normal Milk%	High SCC Milk%	Percent of Normal
Milk nonfat solids	8.9	8.8	99
Fat	3.5	3.2	91
Lactose	4.9	4.4	90
Total protein	3.61	3.56	99
Total casein	2.8	2.3	82

Constituent	Normal Milk%	High SCC Milk%	Percent of Normal
Whey protein	0.8	1.3	162
Sodium	0.057	0.105	184
Chloride	0.091	0.147	161
Potassium	0.173	0.157	91
Calcium	0.12	0.04	33

Season: Milk fat and protein percentages are highest during the fall and winter and lowest during the spring and summer. This variation is related to changes in both the types of feed available and climatic conditions. Lush spring pastures low in fiber depress milk fat. Hot weather and high humidity decrease dry matter intake and increase feed sorting, resulting in lower forage and fiber intake.

Age (Parity): While milk fat content remains relatively constant, milk protein content gradually decreases with advancing age. A survey of Holstein DHIA (Dairy Herd Improvement Association) lactation records indicates that milk protein content typically decreases 0.10 to 0.15 units over a period of five or more lactations or approximately 0.02 to 0.05 units per lactation.

Summary

Many factors besides nutrition management can influence milk composition. This is an important point to remember when evaluating the potential to improve a herd's milk composition and component yields. Certainly, genetics plays an important role, but changes here are slow. Producers who pay attention to detail, keep disease to a minimum and adjust their management program as the seasons dictate will be in the best position to take advantage of nutrition management changes to alter milk composition and improve their bottom line.

21

Managing Milk Composition: Evaluating Herd Potential

The major components of raw milk are water, fat, protein, lactose and minerals. These components can be influenced by many factors, including genetics and nutrition.

Nutrition or dietary influences readily alter the principle solids constituents of fat concentration and milk protein concentration. Fat concentration is the most sensitive to dietary changes and can be altered over a range of nearly 3.0 percentage units. Milk protein concentration can also be altered by dietary manipulation. However, compared to the alterations possible in fat concentration, the range is much smaller at approximately 0.60 percentage units. The concentrations of lactose and minerals, the other solids constituents of milk, do not respond predictably to dietary alterations.

Before attempting to alter and improve milk fat and protein production, however, it is important to evaluate the potential of a herd to respond to feed management changes. Following are some key points that can help determine your herd's potential.

Evaluating Potential

Fat and Protein Tests: Milk protein percent generally follows changes in milk fat content, except when milk fat depression occurs and when high levels of fat are fed. If the milk protein-to-milk fat ratio is less than 0.80 for Holsteins, milk protein depression may be a problem. When the ratio is greater than 0.95, the herd suffers from milk fat depression (low milk fat test). In general, if results of the fats test are below the protein test by 0.2 points (e.g., 2.8 percent fat and 3.0 percent protein), rumen acidosis can be a problem. If greater than 20 percent of the cows exhibit fat:protein inversions, examine the feeding management program. Also, if protein tests below breed average or greater than 20 percent of cows have fats tests below 3.0 percent, reevaluate the feeding program.

Table 21.1. Recommended range of protein-to-fat ratios for the various breeds.*

Breed	Protein-to-Fat Ratio Range
Ayrshire	0.80 - 0.83
Brown Swiss	0.83 - 0.85
Guernsey	0.73 - 0.75
Holstein	0.80 - 0.83
Jersey	0.73 - 0.75
Milking Shorthorn	0.83 - 0.85

*Ratios calculated using true protein.

Feed Intake and Peak Milk Production: Feed intake is controlled by the animal's brain and is determined by meal frequency and size. However, the individual animal, type of ration and environmental factors influence intake.

Maximum feed intake minimizes negative energy balance during early lactation. As cows move into positive energy balance by consuming more energy than they are using, body weight is regained, losses in body condition are minimized and cows produce milk of normal fat and protein content. Increasing feed intake can improve milk protein by 0.2 to 0.3 units. This increase in milk protein percent may be caused by an overall increase in energy intake.

Cows should reach peak milk production between 4 to 8 weeks postpartum, followed closely by peak dry matter intake between 10 to 14 weeks postpartum. High producing cows eat 3.5 to 4.0 percent of their body weight daily as dry matter. If a herd is consuming less than 3.5 to 4.0 percent of body weight as dry matter, production of solids-corrected milk may be limited.

A slow rise in postpartum feed intake lengthens the days to peak milk production and may reflect metabolic problems or obese cows. Research has demonstrated that fat cows have depressed appetites at calving compared to thin cows. This results in longer delays to peak milk yield.

Cows with body condition scores greater than 3.75 at calving (obese) suffer from dry matter intake depressions of 1.5 to 2.0 percent for every 0.25 body condition score over 3.75. Therefore, monitor feed intake and days to peak milk production to determine if cows are managed properly with adequate, but not excessive, body condition.

Rumen pH: Evaluating rumen pH can be a useful tool in determining if acidosis is a potential problem in a herd and a cause for low fat tests or fat:protein inversions. The pH within the rumen can vary from 5.5 to 6.8, with 6.0 to 6.3 being optimal. The critical pH threshold is less than 5.0 for acute acidosis and less than 5.5 for subacute acidosis. In many dairy operations, subacute acidosis is a frequent challenge. Daily episodes of pH less than 5.5 ultimately predispose cattle to low-grade acidosis. Symptoms include erratic appetite, body weight loss, diarrhea and lameness.

Historically, stomach tubing has been used to collect samples of rumen fluid for pH determination. However, this procedure can lead to false interpretation because saliva contamination causes pH values higher than the actual rumen environment. Recently, rumenocentesis has been promoted as a means of collecting rumen fluid for diagnosis of low-grade acidosis. However, research indicates the rumenocentesis procedure can result in the development of abdominal abscesses accompanied by a temporary loss in milk production.

Cannulation of the rumen by a veterinarian is probably the preferred method for obtaining representative samples of rumen fluid. Cannulation has traditionally been used for research purposes and is not particularly suited for use on commercial dairy operations. In comparing results from the two methods, pH values from cannula collections will be approximately 0.35 points higher than those obtained by rumenocentesis.

Take rumen samples for pH determination 5 to 8 hours after feeding for herds receiving total mixed rations and 2 to 5 hours after concentrate feeding when forage and concentrate are fed separately.

To obtain the best results and reduce variations, collect samples from a minimum of 10 to 12 animals per affected herd. If more than 30 percent of the cows within this subgroup have a pH less than 5.5, consider the entire group abnormal. Evaluate feeding management practices and adjust as needed.

Ration Particle Size: Adequate particle size in the ration is necessary to avoid digestive upset and low milk fat production. Cows require fiber and forage to stimulate chewing activity and saliva production, both of which are necessary for maintenance of rumen pH and rumen health.

Particle size separators have been developed to measure particle size distribution in feeds. Separators consist of a series of stacked screens that separate a ration sample into various sized particles. This provides a visual, quantitative assessment of particle size distribution as it occurs in the rumen.

Use of a separator, such as the Penn State Particle Size Separator, is simple and can be used on-farm to monitor changes in forage harvesting procedures or feed mixing protocols. This tool separates particles into three groups: particles greater than 0.75 inches, between 0.31 and 0.75 inches, and less than 0.31 inches. The upper screen identifies particles that will be included in the rumen mat and will stimulate cud chewing and saliva production. The middle screen identifies the portion of the total mixed ration (TMR) that is moderately digestible. The bottom pan collects particles that are readily digestible or rapidly removed from the rumen. Table 21.2 contains particle size distribution recommendations from Penn State University for forages and total mixed rations.

Use caution when applying these recommendations to southern dairies because both forage base and feeding management practices differ from the Northeast U.S. A Texas study evaluated particle size of lactation rations on 20 commercial dairies in Central Texas. Samples were evaluated using the Penn State Separator and compared to the Northeast recommendations. Results from this study (Table 21.2) show that Texas rations are considerably different and suggest that Northeast recommendations may not apply to rations fed in the South. Particle size analysis needs to be compared with other information about ration formulation, feeding management practices and, most importantly, responses from the cows to changes.

Table 21.2 Forage particle size distribution in Texas rations1.

	Top(>0.75") Screen 2	Middle (0.75 - 0.31") Screen 2	Bottom (<0.31") Screen 2
Silage-based TMR		18	43
Hay-based TMR		22	32

2Portion remaining on screen (%).

Chewing Activity: The level of fiber feeding and the physical size of the fiber particles contribute to the effectiveness of a fiber source for stimulating rumination (cud chewing), buffer production (salivation) and maintenance of milk with normal fat and composition. Feeding diets low in forage (less than 40 percent on total ration dry matter) or forages that are finely ground results in inadequate stimulation of chewing activity (less than 8 to 10 hours per day) and lower saliva production. As a general rule, approximately 40 percent of the cows not eating or drinking should be chewing their cuds during daylight hours.

Manure Evaluation: Manure that contains large amounts of undigested corn or with a pH less than 6.0 indicates that too much grain or nonfiber carbohydrates are being fed. It also indicates that acidosis may be a potential problem, resulting in low fat tests or protein: fat inversions.

Manure also can be evaluated and scored based on its consistency, which may indicate ration imbalances and signal potential problems. Table 21.3 lists fecal consistency scores and descriptions as well as example situations when certain fecal consistencies may occur. Various stages of production in a cow correlate to suggested fecal scores:

dry cows	3.5
close-up dry cows	3.0
fresh cows	2.5
high producing cows	3.0
late lactation cows	3.5

Manure scoring is not likely to become a popular management tool because considerable cow-to-cow variation exists. However, abrupt changes in appearance of feces can indicate changes in ration composition and alert managers to potential problems.

Table 21.3. Fecal consistency scores, descriptions and examples.

Score	Description	Example
1	Thin, fluid, green	Sick cows, off feed, cows on pasture
2	Loose, splatters, little form	Fresh cows, cows on pasture
3	Stacks 1 to 1.5" high, dimples, 2 to 4 concentric rings	Recommended for high producing cows
4	Stacks 2 to 3"	Dry cows, low protein, high fiber
5	Stacks over 3"	All forage, sick cows

Fig. 21.1

A separator is simple to use and can be used on-farm to monitor changes in forage harvesting procedures or feed mixing protocols.

The separator divides forage particles into three groups: particles greater than 0.75 inches, betwen 0.31 and 0.75 inches, and less than 0.31 inches.

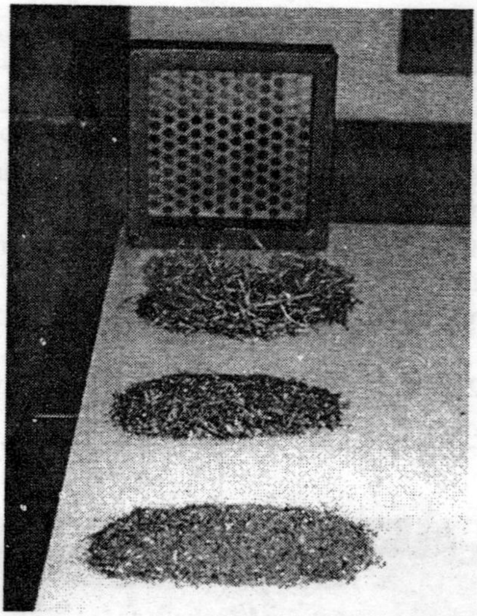

Fig. 21.2.

Summary

Producers using DHIA (Dairy Herd Improvement Association) records are in the best position to critically evaluate their nutrition and feeding management programs. They are encouraged to work with their management teams to consider the above points in determining if their herds will respond to feed management changes to improve milk component composition. Refer to the publication "Managing Milk Composition: Maximizing Rumen Function" for more information.

22

Managing Milk Composition: Maximizing Rumen Function

Various feeding management practices impact the levels of milk fat and protein concentration in raw milk. Feeding strategies that optimize rumen function also maximize milk production and milk component percentages and yield. There are several strategies that producers can use to enhance rumen function and the resulting milk components. Producers who use records, such as those provided by DHIA (Dairy Herd Improvement Association), can critically evaluate their nutrition and feeding management programs.

Feed Intake: Feed provides the nutrients that are the precursors, either directly or indirectly, of the principal milk solids. Thus, an increase in feed intake usually results in the production of a greater volume of milk. In general, the proportional increases in fat, protein and lactose yields are approximately the same as the proportional increase in milk volume. Milk composition changes little.

It is critical to maximize feed intake of cattle so that negative energy balance is minimized during early lactation. As cows consume more energy than they use, body weight is regained, losses in body condition are minimized and cows produce milk of normal fat and protein content. Increasing feed intake, and the resulting overall increase in energy, can increase milk protein content by 0.2 to 0.3 percent.

High producing cows should eat 3.5 to 4.0 percent of their body weight daily as dry matter. If a herd is consuming less than this, production of solids-corrected milk may be limited. Major factors that can affect feed intake include:

- Feed bunk management (keep feed bunks clean, not empty)
- Feeding frequency
- Feed sequencing
- Ration moisture between 25 and 50 percent (to optimize dry matter intake)
- Social interactions and grouping strategy of the herd
- Abrupt ration changes
- Physical facilities
- Environmental temperature.

Increased feeding frequency of low fiber, high grain diets increases milk fat levels. The greatest increase occurs in diets of less than 45 percent forage and when grain is fed separately as in parlor feeding. When diets are fed as a total mixed ration, feeding frequency becomes less important as long as the feed remains palatable and is fed and mixed a minimum of once a day. During hot weather, more frequent feeding helps keep feed fresh and palatable.

Forage to Concentrate Ratio: On a DM (dry matter) basis, the minimum ratio of forage to concentrate required to maintain normal milk fat percentage is approximately 40-to-60. This ratio should serve only as a guide; other dietary factors influence the general effects that a decreased ratio has upon rumen fermentation. These effects include decreased rumen pH, increased propionic acid production and reduced fiber digestion. Obviously, type and physical form of ingredients that contribute to the forage or concentrate portion of this ratio must be considered.

Grain Feeding: The proper feeding of concentrates involves maintaining proper forage-to-concentrate ratios and non fiber carbohydrate levels. Feeding appropriate non fiber carbohydrate levels can improve both milk fat and protein levels, while overfeeding leads to milk fat depression of one unit or more and often increases milk protein percent by 0.2 to 0.3 units.

Nonfiber carbohydrates include starch, sugars and pectin. The percentage of nonfiber carbohydrate is calculated as NFC = 100 - (% Protein + % NDF + % Fat + % Ash). Depending on the digestibility of the neutral detergent fiber (NDF) present, nonfiber carbohydrates should range from 34 to 40 percent of the total ration dry matter. In most instances, a nonfiber carbohydrate level between 36 to 38 percent is considered ideal. This level is typical of diets with less than 60 percent forage. Diets with greater than 60 percent forage may be deficient in nonfiber carbohydrates.

When feeding for component changes, limit the amount of grain consumed during one feeding to 5 to 7 pounds to avoid rumen acidosis and off-feed problems that result in reduced fat content of milk. Grain feeding guidelines to maximize milk fat and protein production are provided in Table 22.1. Limit grain consumption to a maximum of 30 to 35 pounds per cow daily.

Table 22.1. Grain feeding guidelines.

Breed	Milk Production	Grain Feeding Guideline
Holstein and Brown Swiss	Less than 40 lbs.	1 lb. per 4 lbs. of milk
	40 to 70 lbs.	1 lb. per 3 lbs. of milk
	Greater than 70 lbs.	1 lb. per 2.5 lbs. of milk
Jersey, Ayrshire & Guernsey	Less than 30 lbs.	1 lb. per 3 lbs. of milk
	30 to 60 lbs.	1 lb. per 2.5 lbs. of milk
	Greater than 60 lbs.	1 lb. per 2 lbs. of milk

Manure containing large amounts of undigested corn or with a pH less than 6.0 can indicate too much grain or an imbalance of nonfiber carbohydrates in the diet. Fibrous byproducts such as soybean hulls can replace starchy grain and reduce the severity of milk fat depression in rations high in nonfiber carbohydrate.

Grain Processing: The type of grain and processing method can have a significant impact on the site and extent of starch digestion of a particular diet and resulting milk component composition and yield. Generally, ground, rolled, heated, steam flaked or pelletized grain increases starch digestibilities and propionic acid production in the rumen. Steam flaked corn or sorghum compared to steam rolled corn or dry rolled corn or sorghum consistently improves milk production and milk protein yield. In six comparisons, steam flaked corn increased milk protein percentage and yield and decreased milk fat percentage compared to steam rolled corn. Milk fat yield remained unchanged in these trials. Twenty-four (24) comparisons of dry rolled and steam flaked sorghum have produced similar results. These results are attributed to increased total tract starch digestibility, increased recycling of urea to the intestinal tract and increased microbial protein flow to the small intestine.

Table 2. Rate of rumen starch digestion as impacted by grain type and processing method.

Rate	Grain Type/Processing Method
Fast	Diy rolled wheat
	Dry rolled barley
	High moisture corn (ground)
Intermediate	Steam flaked corn
	High moisture corn (whole)
	Steam flaked sorghum
	Dry rolled corn
	Whole corn
Slow	Dry rolled sorghm

Extensive use of grains, such as wheat, that consist of a rapidly fermentable carbohydrate and over-processing of grains can result in severe milk fat depression, off-feed problems and reduced milk yield. It is important to match carbohydrate and protein sources and to carefully monitor nonfiber carbohydrate levels in the diet to ensure proper fermentation patterns and to maximize milk component content and yield.

Ration Fiber Levels: The level of fiber feeding and the physical size of fiber particles contribute to the effectiveness of a fiber source for stimulating rumination (cud chewing), buffer production (salivation) and maintenance of normal milk fat and protein composition. Feeding of finely ground forages inadequately stimulates rumination and lowers saliva production. This results in a rumen fermentation pattern that produces a higher proportion of propionic acid and, in turn, reduces milk fat percentage. In most situations, forage comprises no less than 40 toZ 50 percent of the total ration dry matter or should be included in the diet at no less than 1.40 percent of body weight. Cows should receive a minimum of 5 pounds of roughage (fiber) that is at least 1.5 inches long per day. Cows require a minimum acid detergent fiber (ADF) level of 19 to 21 percent in the ration dry matter. Maintain total neutral detergent fiber (NDF) intake above 26 percent of the total ration dry matter. Provide 75 percent of the NDF as forage. Below these levels, cows are at an increased risk for acidosis, feed intake fluctuations, laminitis and rapid and extensive body condition loss especially in early lactation. Suggested guidelines for NDF intakes from forages are presented in Table 22.3.

Table 3. Forage and total neutral detergent fiber (NDF) intake guidelines.

Forage NDF (%of Body Weight)	Total NDF Intake (% of Body Weight)
0.75 - 0.80	1.30 - 1.40
0.85	1.10 -1.20
0.90 - 1.20	1.10 - 1.20

Protein Feeding Guidelines: Generally, dietary crude protein level affects milk yield but not milk protein percent, unless the diet is deficient in crude protein. Normal changes in dietary protein ranges do not consistently affect milk fat percentage. Theoretically, insufficient amounts of rumen-degradable protein might result in decreased milk fat percentage if the concentration of ammonia in the rumen does not support the optimal digestion of fiber and microbial growth.

The crude protein requirement for a 1,350-pound cow producing 3.6 percent milk fat ranges from 14.0 percent of total dry matter (TDM) for50 pounds of milk to 18.0 percent TDM for 100 pounds of milk. Depending on the stage and level of production, the recommended level of undegradable protein ranges from 32 to 38 percent of crude protein. Keep soluble protein between 30 to 32 percent of crude protein, or about half of the degradable protein intake level.

It is essential to meet the cow's requirement for both crude protein and rumen undegradable protein to avoid a negative impact on dry matter intake and fiber digestibility. Studies of diets containing no supplemental fat show that each 1 percent increase in dietary protein, within the range of 9 to 17 percent, results in a 0.02 percentage unit increase in milk protein. The additional synthesis of protein by mammary tissue likely is linked to limiting amino acids. Table 22.4 summarizes the various feeding management practices and their potential impact on milk fat and protein concentration.

Table 22.4. Summary of feeding management practices and their potential impact on milk fat and protein concentration.

Management Factor	Milk Fat%	Milk Protein%
Increase feed intake	Increase	Increase
Increase feeding frequency	Increase	Increase slightly
Underfeeding energy	Decrease	Decrease
High NFC (>45 %)	Decrease	Increase
Normal NFC (34 - 40 %)	Increase	No change
Excessive fiber	Increase slightly	Decrease
Low fiber (< 26 %NDF)	Decrease	Increase
Small particle size	Decrease	Increase
High crude protein	No effect	Increase if diet is deficient
Low crude protein	No effect	Decrease if diet is deficient
UIP (34 - 38 %)	No effect	Increase if diet is deficient

23

Managing Milk Compositon: Feed Additives and Production Enhancers

Feed additives and management tools such as bST (bovine somatotropin) play an essential role in enhancing production and yield of milk and milk components. The need for a particular feed additive and its effectiveness depend upon a variety of factors. Producers are encouraged to critically evaluate the cost-to-benefit ratio of each feed additive in their management systems.

Feeding strategies that optimize rumen function result in maximum milk production and milk component percentages and yield. Additionally, producers who use records such as those provided by DHIA (Dairy Herd Improvement Association) can critically evaluate their nutrition and feeding management programs.

Feed Additives

Supplemental Fat: Adding supplemental fat to rations for high producing dairy cows has become a common practice. It is necessary to follow certain guidelines when feeding fat to cattle to avoid a depression of 0.1 to 0.2 units in the milk protein level. When used properly, added fat usually maintains or slightly increases milk fat percent, makes relatively little change in milk protein percent and increases milk production. The net result is increased production of milk protein and nonfat solids. Too much fat in the ration can interfere with fiber digestion, reducing milk fat levels.

Limit total fat to 7.5 percent of the ration dry matter. A good rule of thumb is to provide the same amount of fat in the ration as pounds of milk fat produced. For example: 100 pounds of milk per day x 4.0 percent milk fat = 4 pounds of milk fat or 4 pounds total fat in the ration. Provide one-third of fat in the ration from normal ration ingredients, one-third from oilseeds or natural fats and one-third from rumen inert fat. Recommended guidelines for feeding fat are provided in Table 23.1.

Table 23.1. Fat feeding guidelines.

Recommended Source	Maximum Inclusion
Basal diet	3.0 %
Natural fats	2.0 % - 4.0%
Whole oilseeds	1.0 lb.
Tallow	1.0 lb.
Protected fats	2.0 % (1.0 lb.)
Total	**6.0 - 7.0 %**

Note: When feeding supplemental fats, calcium and magnesium should be provided at 1.0 and 0.35 percent of the ration dry matter, respectively, because these fats can bind with calcium and magnesium and reduce their availability.

Sulfur: Sulfur is necessary for the synthesis of essential amino acids by rumen microbes. Sulfur supplementation is important in rations that contain high levels of non-protein nitrogen (i.e., urea). Low sulfur intake can induce protein deficiency. The likelihood of this problem occurring increases with rations containing corn silage or poor quality grass silage. The recommended level of sulfur is 0.22 to 0.25 percent of the total ration dry matter.

Buffers: Buffers added to the diet help reduce the acid load placed on the rumen when high levels of grain are fed or when hay and grain are fed separately. Sodium bicarbonate, magnesium oxide or a combination are the primary buffers recommended for feeding lactating dairy cows. Supplements of sodium bicarbonate should be 0.6 to 0.8 percent of the total diet dry matter or 1.2 to 1.6 percent of the concentrate mixture. Magnesium oxide should be added as 0.2 to 0.4 percent of the total diet dry matter or 0.4 to 0.6 percent of the concentrate mixture.

When feeding a combination of sodium bicarbonate and magnesium oxide, two to three parts sodium bicarbonate should be mixed with one part magnesium oxide and fed as a supplement at 0.8 to 1.2 percent of the total diet dry matter or 1.6 to 2.2 percent of the concentrate mix. Force-feeding larger amounts of these buffers may depress feed intake. Providing additional sodium bicarbonate free choice, beyond that which is already provided in the base ration, may prove beneficial in some herds when feeding for specific milk component changes. Estimated cost is 6 cents per head per day. The benefit-to-cost ratio is 4-to-1.

Rumen-Protected Amino Acids: Responses to feeding individual amino acids to dairy cattle have not been consistent. Response differences probably occur based on the quantity and proportion of amino acids in the microbial and dietary protein digested and absorbed from the small intestine. Responses are often greater when mixtures of amino acids, rather than individual amino acids, are taken in beyond the rumen. Combinations of rumen-protected methionine and lysine have been shown to increase milk protein yield and concentration in diets low in rumen-degradable protein. Further, supplementing diets that contain added fat with rumen-protected methionine and lysine alleviates the milk protein depression effect of feeding added fat.

Yeast Culture/Fermentation Products: Yeast culture and their fermentation products stabilize the rumen environment and improve fiber digestion. They maintain or increase dry matter intake and milk fat percent. Most benefits are seen in high producing cows or cows in early lactation. Feeding rate is 10 to 120 grams depending on yeast culture concentration. The cost is approximately 4 to 6 cents per cow per day. The estimated benefit-to-cost ratio is 4-to-1.

Niacin: Niacin, a water-soluble vitamin, was assumed to be produced in sufficient quantities by rumen microbes to meet the needs of the host animal. However, bacterial synthesis of niacin may not be adequate for high producing cows. Milk yield and composition responses to niacin feeding are variable, at best.

However, in some situations, niacin fed at 6 to 12 grams per day improves the milk protein depression caused by feeding high levels of fat. The estimated benefit-to-cost ratio is 6-to-1 for the 6-gram feeding level. The approximate cost is 1 cent per gram.

Fig. 23.1

Milk yield, milk components, dry matter intake, growth, health and weight can be impacted when a feed additive is included in the diets of dairy cattle.

Bovine Somatotropin (BST)

The gross composition of milk (fat, protein and lactose) is not affected by treatment with bST. The factors that affect fat and protein content of milk of non-bST-treated cows have the same effects on milk composition of bST-treated cows. For example, certain breeds have a higher milk fat content, and an increase in milk fat typically occurs in late lactation for all breeds. Treatment with bST does not alter these relationships. Likewise, the increase in milk fat content that occurs when the cow is using more energy than it is consuming and the decrease in milk protein content that occurs when the cow has an inadequate protein intake are also observed in bST-treated cows.

Milk from bST-treated cows also does not differ in vitamin content or in concentrations of nutritionally important mineral elements. In addition, proportions of total milk proteins represented by whey proteins and the different casein fractions are not changed substantially. Thus, the manufacturing characteristics are not altered by the use of bST to enhance milk yield in lactating cows.

Evaluating Cost Effectiveness

Consider the following factors in determining if a feed additive should be used:

- anticipated response
- economic return
- available research
- field response.

Anticipated response refers to performance changes such as increased milk yield, increased milk components, improved dry matter intake, improved growth, improved health, and/or minimized weight loss that could be expected when a feed additive is included.

If improvement in milk volume is the measurable response, a breakeven point can be calculated. For example, an additive that raises feed costs 10 cents per day is used. If milk is valued at 12 cents per pound, every cow must produce 0.84 pounds more milk to cover the extra cost associated with the additive. Another consideration is if all the cows receive the additive, but only cows fresh for less than 100 days respond. These responding cows must cover the costs for all cows (responsive and nonresponsive). One guideline is that an additive should return $2 or more for each dollar invested to cover nonresponsive cows and field conditions that could minimize the anticipated response.

Remember, it is difficult to assess management practices that acutely alter milk production. Research is essential to determine if experimentally measured responses can be expected in the field. Rely on research studies conducted under controlled and unbiased conditions that use an experimental protocol similar to field conditions and that have statistically analyzed results.

Results obtained on individual farms are the economic payoff. Managers and consultants must use a database to accurately compare and measure responses. Several tools to measure results include DHIA milk production records, reproduction summaries, somatic cell count data, dry matter intake, heifer growth charts, body condition scores and herd health profiles. These tools will enable managers and consultants to critically evaluate the effectiveness of selected additives.

Economic Evaluation of Dairy Feeds

Feed costs typically represent more than 50% of total costs of producing milk on a dairy farm. Feed cost savings, even a few dollars per ton, add up to significant savings over a year on a large dairy.

For many dairies, a ration-balancing software program that uses linear programming techniques can be used to determine the opportunity cost or price of including a new feed in a ration. However, this requires expertise in using the ration-balancing software, and may not be appropriate when quick decisions need to be made.

The purpose of this guide is to describe alternative methods of pricing various feeds. In particular, four techniques, including the cost/nutrient, index, simultaneous equation, and by-product equation methods are discussed.

What Information is Necessary?

For producers to make proper decisions about purchasing a feed, accurate information is needed about the specific feed. A lab analysis of the feed including dry matter, crude protein (CP), fiber [acid detergent fiber (ADF) or neutral detergent fiber (NDF)], and a prediction of energy is necessary.

It is important to remember that energy [as total digestible nutrients (TDN) or net energy for lactation (NEL)] is not measured in the lab, but is calculated from fiber content. Labs use different equations to predict energy from fiber, particularly for forages. For this reason, if you purchase forages, consider the source of the energy prediction. Also, take caution in using "book" values from published tables such as those in the 1989 Nutrient Requirements of Dairy Cattle. Often, the actual nutrient content in feeds varies considerably from book values.

For dairy feeds, it is critical that feeds are evaluated on a dry basis rather than an as-fed or as-is basis. As-fed basis includes moisture, and dry basis is without water. Many dairy feeds, particularly silages, contain more than 50% water. The water component contains no nutrients, so high-moisture feeds are less valuable per pound on an as-fed basis.

Lab analysis generally provides a nutrient profile on a dry-matter basis. If nutrient concentrations such as crude protein, TDN, NEL, or minerals are given on an as-fed basis, simply divide the percentage of the component by the percent dry matter to obtain concentrations on a dry basis:

% component on as-fed basis / % dry matter

= % component on dry-matter basis

For example, suppose a feed is 40% dry matter and contains 8% crude protein on an as-fed basis. The crude protein on a dry matter basis is:

8.0/0.40 = 20% CP on a dry matter basis.

To convert as-fed pounds to dry-matter pounds, simply multiply the number of as-fed pounds by the percent dry matter:

lb as-fed x % dry matter = lb dry matter.

For example, how many pounds of dry matter are in 1,000 as-fed pounds of corn silage at 35% dry matter?

1,000 x 0.35 = 350 lb of dry matter.

Cost/Nutrient Method

This is a simple, convenient method of calculating cost per unit of protein, energy, fiber, or any other component of a feed. Most feeds are purchased to supply protein or energy, so cost per pound of crude protein and cost per megacalorie (Mcal) of NEL are generally useful.

To calculate cost per pound of each nutrient, two items are necessary: cost, and nutrient content. Since cost is normally expressed as dollars per ton, it is simpler to work on a ton basis. If you know the cost for a ton of feed, the cost per pound of any nutrient can be estimated by determining the number of pounds of the nutrient in a ton of feed, thus

(% of component on dry-matter basis / 100)

x [(% dry matter / 100) x 2,000 lb / ton]

= lb of component / ton on as-fed basis.

Using shelled corn as an example (from table 1), pounds of crude protein in a ton can be calculated from protein content (9% on dry matter basis) and dry matter (89%):

(9.0 / 100) x [(89 / 100) x 2,000] = 160.2 lb CP/ton of as-fed corn.

Thus, a ton of corn contains 160.2 lb of crude protein. If corn costs $150/ton, then cost per pound of protein is

$150/ton / 160.2 lb/ton CP as-fed = $0.936/lb CP as-fed.

The following is the calculation to determine cost per Mcal NEL for corn, assuming corn contains 0.90 Mcal/lb dry matter and 89% dry matter:

Mcal/lb dry matter x [(% dry matter / 100) x 2,000 lb/ton] = Mcal/ton as-fed

0.90 x [(89 / 100) x 2,000 lb/ton] = 1,602 Mcal/ton of as-fed corn

$150/ton / 1,602 Mcal/ton = $0.0936/Mcal

There are three examples of energy sources: corn, barley, and oats. For the prices and nutritive values listed, barley is the least expensive source of energy at $0.090/Mcal NEL, and oats are the least expensive protein source at $0.58/lb crude protein. These feeds would normally be added to a ration to supply energy, and not protein. Thus, cost per pound of protein should not serve as criteria for selecting one of these energy sources.

Among the protein sources listed in table 1, there are differences in cost. Cottonseed meal is the least expensive per unit of energy and protein, and would thus be the better buy. However, another consideration is that cottonseed meal may contain gossypol, and feeding large quantities of both cottonseed meal and whole cottonseed increases the risk of gossypol toxicity. Quality of the feed source and possible interactions with other feeds in the ration are not considered in economic evaluation. Other factors in addition to cost need to be considered.

For the rumen undegradable protein (RUP) sources (table 1), blood meal is the least expensive source of crude protein. For RUP protein sources, cost per unit of RUP may also be of interest.

If we assume that 82% of blood meal protein is undegradable, then the cost per unit of RUP is:

% CP x (percent RUP / 100) = RUP as a % of dry matter

(% RUP of dry matter / 100) x (% dry matter x 2,000 lb/ton) = lb RUP/ton as-fed

$/ton* / lb RUP/ ton as-fed = $/ lb RUP

Example:

90% CP x (82 / 100) = 73.8% RUP of total dry matter

(73.8 / 100) x (0.90 x 2,000) = 1,328.4 lb RUP/ ton of as-fed blood meal

$500 / 1,328.4 = $0.38/ lb RUP.

For fish meal, assuming 65% RUP, the calculation is:

67 x (65 / 100) = 43.6% RUP of total dry matter

(43.6 / 100) x (0.92 x 2,000) = 802.2 lb RUP/ ton as fed fish meal

$550 / 802.2 = $0.69/ lb RUP.

Blood meal is the better buy in terms of cost per pound of crude protein and RUP, but again, quality has not yet been considered. Fish meal has a more desirable amino acid profile than blood meal, which increases its value. This must also be considered before a final purchasing decision is made.

Weaknesses of Cost/Nutrient Method

Although this method is simple and easy to calculate, results should be interpreted with caution. First, feeds should be evaluated based on their most valuable nutrient or what the feed is being purchased for. For example, corn would be purchased to add energy to the ration, so it should be evaluated based on cost per unit of energy. Evaluating corn based on protein would be unwise, as corn contributes little to the total protein in the diet. Likewise, protein sources such as soybean meal and cottonseed meal should be judged mainly on cost per pound of crude protein. Feeds that supply moderate quantities of energy and protein are more difficult to evaluate using this method. For example, distillers' grains typically contain moderate amounts of protein and energy.

A second weakness of the cost/ nutrient method is that it does not consider palatability, digestibility, or quality of the feed source. These factors must also be considered when making purchasing decisions. As an extreme example, consider dried cattle manure and soybean meal. Dried cattle manure typically contains 16% crude protein, and is certainly cheaper per pound of crude protein than soybean meal. Obviously, dried cattle manure is unpalatable and a poor feed source, and is not a good buy as a dairy feed no matter how inexpensive it is.

For cost/nutrient analysis to be useful, feeds of similar nature should be compared. Protein sources should be compared with protein sources, and energy sources with energy sources. In addition, protein sources that supply significant quantities of rumen undegradable or bypass protein such as fish meal and blood meal should not be compared to highly rumen-degradable protein sources such as soybean meal.

Table 23.2. Cost/nutrient for various feedstuffs (dry matter basis).

Feed (%)	DM[1] (%)	CP[2] (Mcal/lb)	NEL[3] ($/ton)	Cost CP	$/lb NEL	$/Mcal
Energy sources						
Shelled corn	89	9.0	0.90	150	0.94	0.094
Barley	88	13.0	0.88	140	0.61	0.090
Oats	89	13.5	0.80	140	0.58	0.098
Protein sources						
Soybean meal	90	55.1	0.91	280	0.28	0.171
Cottonseed meal	93	45.0	0.74	220	0.26	0.160
RUP[4] sources						
Fish meal	92	67.0	0.76	550	0.45	0.393
Blood meal	90	90.0	0.80	500	0.31	0.347

[1]DM: dry matter
[2]CP: crude protein
[3]NEL: net energy for lactation
[4]RUP: rumen undegradable protein

Index Method

The index method is simply an extension of the cost/nutrient method. It accounts for both protein and energy, with weightings of 30% and 70%, respectively. These weightings correspond to their approximate contribution to total feed cost, excluding vitamins and minerals. Table 23.2 provides the index rating for the feeds in table 23.1. The lower the index, the better the buy.

Using the index method, barley and oats are the best buys among the energy sources, cottonseed meal is the best buy among protein sources, and blood meal is the best buy among RUP sources.

Weaknesses for the cost/nutrient and index methods are similar. Specifically, there is no consideration of palatability, digestibility, or quality. Like the cost/nutrient method, only similar feeds should be evaluated using the index method. That is, compare protein sources to protein sources, and so forth. The index method may be most useful for comparing intermediate feeds, such as distillers' grains and brewers' grains, that are not typical protein or energy sources.

Table 23.3. Economic evaluation of feeds using the index method.

	Net energy		Crude protein		
Feed	Cost /Mcal	Weighting	Cost /lb	Weighting	Index
Energy sources					
Shelled corn	0.094 x	0.70 +	0.94 x	0.30 =	0.348
Barley	0.090 x	0.70 +	0.61 x	0.30 =	0.246
Oats	0.098 x	0.70 +	0.58 x	0.30 =	0.243
Protein sources					
Soybean meal	0.171 x	0.70 +	0.28 x	0.30 =	0.204
Cottonseed meal	0.160 x	0.70 +	0.26 x	0.30 =	0.190
RUP sources					
Fish meal	0.393 x	0.70 +	0.45 x	0.30 =	0.410
Blood meal	0.347 x	0.70 +	0.31 x	0.30 =	0.336

Relative Value Compared to Corn and Soybean Meal Using Simultaneous Equations

This method involves solving simultaneous equations to equate the energy and protein value of a feed to the energy and protein in corn and soybean meal. Corn and soybean meal make good comparisons because they are readily available, commonly used dairy concentrates that are widely traded on the open market. By determining a value for a particular feed using this method, a producer can determine a current market value for the product. If the calculated value is less than the current market price, then the feed would not be a good buy. If the value is higher than the current price, then the feed is a good buy. This is an ideal method for valuing forages. However, this method is tedious and prone to error due to the many calculations.

The steps to determine value per ton using simultaneous equations follow. For this example, we will assume the following nutrient profile for corn and soybean meal, on an as-fed basis:

	Crude protein (%)	NEL (Mcal/lb)	Cost/lb
Soybean meal	48.0	0.82	0.14
Corn	8.1	0.80	0.075

Step 1. Simultaneous equations are set up to determine the values of protein (x) and energy (y).

	Protein	NEL		Cost/lb
Eq. 1 (soybean meal)	0.48x +	0.82y	=	0.14
Eq. 2 (corn)	0.081x +	0.80y	=	0.075

Step 2. Solve for the value of protein (x) by dividing Equation 1 by 0.82, and Equation 2 by 0.80.

Eq. 1 (a)

$$\frac{0.48x}{0.82} + \frac{0.82y}{0.82} = \frac{0.14}{0.82}$$

equals: (b)

$$0.585x + y = 0.171$$

Eq. 2 (a)

$$\frac{0.081x}{0.80} + \frac{0.80y}{0.80} = \frac{0.075}{0.80}$$

equals: (b)

$$0.101x + y = 0.094$$

Step 3. From Step 2, subtract Equation 2b from Equation 1b. Then solve for x.

Eq. 1 (b)	0.585x +	y	=	0.171
Eq. 2 (b)	-0.101x +	-y	=	-0.094
	0.484x +	0	=	0.077
		x	=	$0.159/lb of protein

Step 4. Substitute 0.159 for x in either equation in Step 3, and solve for y (value of energy).

Eq. 1 (b)	.585(0.159) +	y	=	0.171
		y	=	$0.078/Mcal of energy

Therefore, the values of protein (x) and energy (y) are \$0.159/lb and \$0.078/Mcal, respectively.

Values per ton for various feeds are calculated in table 3. For the first item, corn silage, value per ton was calculated as follows, assuming corn silage is 35% dry matter, and contains 8% crude protein and 0.70 Mcal/lb on a dry matter basis:

Dry matter lb/ton	=	2,000 lb/ton x (% dry matter / 100)
Crude protein lb/ton	=	(% CP / 100) x dry matter lb/ton
Mcal NEL/ton	=	Mcal/lb x dry matter lb/ton
Value/ton	=	CP lb/ton x cost/lb CP
Dry matter lb/ton	=	2,000 lb/ton x (35 / 100) = 700 lb/ton
Crude protein lb/ton	=	(8 / 100) x 700 = 56 lb/ton
Mcal NEL/ton	=	0.70 x 700 = 490 Mcal/ton
Value/ton	=	[56 lb/ton CP x \$0.159/lb CP] + [490 Mcal/ton x \$0.078/Mcal]
	=	\$8.90 + \$38.22 = \$47.12/ton

For the feeds listed in table 3, all are a good buy, with the exception of blood meal and fish meal. A "good buy" implies that the value per ton is greater than the cost. This illustrates some problems with this method. Like the cost/nutrient and index methods, this method does not consider palatability, quality, or digestibility. In addition, RUP is not considered, hence high RUP prices are not fairly evaluated. This method is most useful for valuing by-product feeds and forages. It is important to note that this method may slightly over-value wet forages. High-moisture forages, such as corn silage and alfalfa haylage, are generally not as marketable as dry feeds due to transportation costs of hauling large quantities of water in the feed.

Table 23.4. Value per ton for various feeds relative to corn (\$150/ton) and soybean meal (\$280/ton).

Feed	DM[1] (%)	CP[2] (%)	NEL3 (Mcal /lb)	lb CP /ton	Mcal/ ton	Value/ ton	Cost/ ton
Forages							
Corn silage	35	8.0	0.70	56	490	\$47.12	\$40.00
Alfalfa hay	85	22.0	0.65	374	1105	\$145.66	\$130.00

(Contd.)

Feed	DM[1] (%)	CP[2] (%)	NEL3 (Mcal /lb)	lb CP /ton	Mcal/ ton	Value/ ton	Cost/ ton
Energy sources							
Barley	88	13.0	0.88	229	1549	$157.19	$140.00
Oats	89	13.5	0.80	240	1424	$149.28	$140.00
Protein sources							
Cottonseed meal	93	45.0	0.74	837	1376	$240.44	$220.00
RUP4 sources							
Fish meal	92	67.0	0.76	1233	1398	$305.09	$550.00
Blood meal	90	90.0	0.80	1620	1440	$369.90	$500.00

[1]DM: dry matter
[2]CP: crude protein
[3]NEL: net energy for lactation
[4]RUP: rumen undegradable protein

Relative Value Compared to Corn and Soybean Meal Using Specific By-product Equations

Specific equations have been developed to determine value per ton for specific feeds relative to corn and soybean meal. Table 23.5 lists these equations, which can be solved simply with the cost per ton of corn and soybean meal. These equations yield similar results as the simultaneous equations method above.

Table 23.5. Specific equations to value feeds based on soybean meal and corn price.

Barley	=	(0.908	x corn $/ton)	+	(0.093 x	soybean mcal $/ton)
Wheat	=	(0.875	x corn $/ton)	+	(0.125 x	soybean meal $/ton)
Hominy feed	=	(1.043	x corn $/ton)	+	(0.012 x	soybean meal $/ton)
Soybean hulls	=	(0.081	x corn $/ton)	+	(0.175 x	soybean meal $/ton)
Alfalfa pellets	=	(0.325	x corn $/ton)	+	(0.241 x	soybean meal $/ton)
Wheat middlings	=	(0.683	x corn $/ton)	+	(0.258 x	soybean meal $/ton)
Whole cottonseed	=	(0.656	x corn $/ton)	+	(0.303 x	soybean meal $/ton)
Dry brewers grains	=	(0.374	x corn $/ton)	+	(0.464 x	soybean meal $/ton)
Wet brewers grains	=	(0.121	x corn $/ton)	+	(0.081 x	soybean meal $/ton)
Dry corn distillers	=	(0.701	x corn $/ton)	+	(0.350 x	soybean meal $/ton)
Cottonseed meal	=	(0.025	x corn $/ton)	+	(0.770 x	soybean meal $/ton)
Peanut meal	=	(0.087	x corn $/ton)	+	(0.996 x	soybean meal $/ton)

Conclusion

There are a number of methods to economically evaluate feeds. Each method has advantages and disadvantages, but provides objective information to aid in making purchasing decisions. It is important to remember that none of the methods described here consider palatability, digestibility, or quality. Considering these criteria in addition to economic analysis should provide ample information to make sound feed purchasing decisions.

24

Process and Quality Control Procedures

Introduction

Chemical and microbiological analyses of cheese milk, finished cheese and cheese whey are required to maintain efficient operations and to ensure food safety and quality. This chapter describes some analytical procedures relevant to cheese making operations, but it is not intended to be a comprehensive process and quality control manual. The following general comments are intended to orient the reader to the general types of analyses required in cheese operations. Subsequent chapters will identify process and quality control requirements in the context of each step in the cheese making process.

Milk Analysis

Milk composition analyses should include both fat and protein, determined by infrared milk analysers. Note that casein content rather than total protein content is the critical parameter with respect to cheese yield. Cheese makers are, therefore, advised to regularly monitor the relative amounts of casein, whey proteins and non-protein nitrogen in their milk. Monthly or bimonthly analysis of protein distribution by Rowland fractionation is sufficient to monitor seasonal trends. Alternatively, an indication of casein and whey protein distribution can be obtained by comparing protein concentration in cheese whey to the protein concentration in the initial milk. This has the advantage that infra red milk analysers can be calibrated to measure protein in cheese whey.

Quality measurements of cheese milk should include total counts (and/or psychrophilic counts), tests for inhibitors and somatic cell counts. Depending on the types of controls in place at the producer level, cheese makers may need to monitor bacteria counts, inhibitors, and somatic cell counts of individual producer milks.

Cheese Analysis

Cheese composition analyses should include fat (by Babcock, Mojonnier, or near infra red procedures), moisture, salt and pH. Cheese pH should be measured at the time of manufacture, 3 - 4 days after manufacture and periodically during curing. Other composition parameters should be determined several days after manufacture to permit time for equilibration of soluble components. Salt in particular, requires time to become evenly distributed throughout the cheese and in the case of brine or surface ripened cheese, uniform salt distribution may never be achieved. For Cheddar cheese and other vat salted cheese, representative samples for accurate determination of salt content can be usually be obtained as early as seven days after manufacture.

With respect to process and quality control, the 'pH profile' during manufacture and curing is vital. 'pH profile is a term I use to describe the set of pH values at critical process control points in the cheese making process. Other critical process control parameters are the ratio of salt to moisture (S/M), the moisture in the nonfat substance (MNFS), and the fat in the dry matter (FDM). These ratios are normally reported as percentages and calculated as in Equations 1a, 1b, 1c, below. Note that percent total solids is 100 minus percent cheese moisture.

$$SIM = \frac{\%\,cheese\,salt \times 100}{\%\,cheese\,moisture}$$

$$MNFS = \frac{\%\,cheese\,moisture \times 100}{100 - \%\,cheese\,fat}$$

$$FDM = \frac{\%\,cheese\,fat \times 100}{\%\,cheese\,total\,solid}$$

Routine cheese microbial analyses should include yeasts and moulds, total coliforms and staphylococci. For raw milk cheese, all vats must be tested for the presence of *Salmonella, Staphylococci, Listeria* and enteropathogenic *E. coli.* Cheese made from heat treated but not pasteurized milk must also be considered higher risk and should be monitored on a regular basis for the presence of common pathogens. Microbial analyses should be performed at the time of manufacture and after curing. Cheese whey should be monitored for the presence of bacteriophage specific for the culture currently in use.

Analytical Quality Control

A simple but vital truism, is that inaccurate analytical results are of less value than no analytical results. The most important causes of poor quality, poor yield efficiency and poor process control are insufficient and inaccurate chemical and microbial analyses. Effective control of quality and plant efficiency requires effective quality control of analytical procedures. Smaller cheese manufacturers generally find it's more economical and reliable to have most analyses performed by an outside laboratory. But, whether the analyses are performed in house or by an outside laboratory, be certain that your laboratory services are accurate and reliable.

Cheese Sampling

Chemical Analysis

Depending on the size and shape, firm to hard cheese should be sampled using a cheese trier (at least 100 g sample) or by taking a sector sample. Soft cheese can be blended for sampling or sector sampled depending on its texture. Cheese samples are stored in opaque air tight containers and fragmented using a grater or other device before analysis. It is important to grind and mix the sample well before subsampling for analysis.

If the analytical procedure requires less than a 1 gm sample it is desirable to prepare a liquid cheese homogenate and a subsample from the homogenate. An homogenate suitable for most purposes can be prepared as follows.

Weigh 40 g cheese into a blender container Add about 100 g of 7% sodium citrate solution. Blend until homogenous (high speed blender such as Polytron is most suitable). Rinse blender shaft into container and make up to final weight of about 200g.

Note that cheese is notorious for inhomogeneous composition. Brine salted cheese have pronounced salt and moisture gradients, namely, higher salt and lower moisture near the surface. Large blocks or wheels of pressed cheese will have moisture and pH gradients, namely, increasing moisture and decreasing pH towards the interior. In addition to moisture and salt gradients, surface ripened cheese also has pH gradients, namely, pH increases at the surface during curing. These difficulties greatly complicate the matter of obtaining accurate composition and mass balance (yield) data. A useful approach to improve yield control of large blocks is to set aside small blocks (eg., 20 kg blocks of Cheddar) for early composition and quality testing, and subsequently, conduct representative sampling of the large blocks (eg., 240 kg blocks of Cheddar) during the cut/wrap process.

Microbial Analysis

Obtain samples as described above for chemical analysis. Triers or knives used for sampling must be flame sterilized. Samples should be stored in sterile bags such as Whirl Pack bags, stored at 0-4C and analysed within 24 hours.

Equipment

1. Balance, 1,000 g capacity
2. Blender
3. Blender container autoclaved or sanitized with 200 ppm chlorine solution for 5 min.

Procedure

1. Break the cheese into small pieces while still in the bag. Use a pestle or similar device if necessary.
2. Heat dilution blanks of sterile aqueous 2% sodium citrate to 40C. Transfer 30 g of cheese to sterile blender container, add

270 ml diluent and mix for 2 min. at speed sufficient to emulsify the cheese properly. If temperature exceeds 40C during blending, use a shorter mixing time or decrease initial temperature of citrate solution. This 1:10 dilution should be plated or further diluted immediately.

3. Further dilutions can be prepared as required. Pipette 11 ml of the 10^{-1} dilution of the homogenate, avoiding foam, into 99 ml dilution blank (0.1% peptone) or 10 ml into 90 ml dilution blank. Shake this and all subsequent dilutions vigorously 25 times in a one foot arc. Prepare 10^{-1}, 10^{-2}, and 10^{-3} dilutions.

Total Solids

Oven Method

1. Pre-dry aluminum dishes (105C, 1 h) and weigh to the nearest 0.1 mg on an analytical balance.
2. Weigh quickly 3-5 g of fragmented cheese into the aluminum dish. The weight of sample is the total weight minus the weight of the dish from Step 1.
3. Dry to constant weight (about 16 h) at 105C. To check for constant weight: weigh at least two samples, return both samples to the oven for an additional 20 minutes, and re-weigh. The difference between the weights before and after the additional drying period should be less than 1 mg.
4. Cool in desiccator and determine total dry weight. Sample dry weight is the total dry weight less the weight of the dish determined in Step 1.

Report total solids and moisture contents on weight percent basis as follows:

Note: Several rapid moisture tests based on infrared or microwave drying are available. Check with your laboratory equipment supplier.

Application

Accurate cheese moisture analysis is critical to composition and yield control. Rapid moisture tests (e.g., microwave moisture oven) can be used to obtain early feed back (e.g., cheese moisture immediately after pressing) information to help with process control.

Titratable Acidity

Apparatus and Reagents

1. An acidimeter equipped with a burette graduated in tenths of a ml up to 10 ml, and some means of filling the same without undue exposure of the solution to the carbon dioxide of the atmosphere.
2. N/10 sodium hydroxide solution.
3. A dropping bottle containing a 1% alcoholic phenolphthalein solution.
4. White cup, glass stirring rod, 17.6 ml pipette (or 8.8 or 9.0 ml pipette)
5. For cream, Torsion balance and 9 g weight.

Method

1. Mix sample thoroughly by pouring it from one container to another. The temperature of the sample should be near 20C.
2. Pipette 17.6 ml of milk or cream into a white cup. Note: 8.8 ml pipettes may also be used but are no longer as readily available as 17.6 ml pipettes. Readily available 9 ml pipettes are also used but require application of a correction factor to the final result.
3. Add six drops of phenolphthalein indicator solution to milk, 10 drops if the product is cream.
4. Titrate the sample with the N/10 sodium hydroxide solution (0.1 Normal NaOH) while stirring the sample with the glass rod. Look for the appearance of a faint pink colour which signals the endpoint. Add another drop or half a drop of NaOH if the pink colour does not persist for 30 s.
5. Record the number of ml of NaOH used to reach the endpoint. This value is called the 'titre'. Titratable acidity reported as percent lactic acid is dependent on the volume of sample.

For the 8.8 ml pipette, % Lactic acid = titre

For the 17.6 ml pipette, % Lactic acid = 0.5 x titre

For the 9.0 ml pipette, % Lactic acid = 0.98 x titre.

Note that there is practically no lactic acid in fresh milk, but it is a North American convention to report TA in terms of % lactic acid.

Application

As described in the next section, both titratable acidity (TA) and pH are measures of acidity. However, for most process control purposes, pH is a more useful measurement. Many cheese makers, however, still use TA to monitor initial acid development (that is to check for culture activity) during the first hour after adding the culture. For this purpose, TA is a more reliable indicator because relative to pH measurement, it is more sensitive to small changes in milk acidity.

When using TA to monitor initial culture activity note that:

1. You are looking for a measurable increase in TA to confirm that the culture is active. For example, if the initial TA taken immediately after the culture was added is 0.183% lactic acid, and the TA after one hour of ripening is 0.194 % lactic acid, the change in TA is 0.194 - 0.183 which is 0.011%.
2. Different people will interpret the coloured endpoint differently, so it is important that the same person takes both the initial and final TA measurements.
3. Carefully performed, it is possible to reliably measure a change in TA of 0.05% lactic acid, so if the TA increase is greater than 0.05% you can conclude that the culture is active. In most cases TA increases in the range of 0.05% to 0.10% are obtained after about 30 minutes of ripening (that is, 30 minutes after adding the culture).
4. It is critical to take the initial TA reading after the culture is added, because the culture (especially the bulk culture) is acidic.

pH

Concepts of Acidity and pH: All aqueous systems (including the water in you and in cheese) obey the following relationship (Equation 3) between the concentration of hydrogen ions (H^+) and hydroxyl ions (OH^-). Note, the square brackets indicate concentration in moles per litre. A mole is 6 x 10^{23} molecules, that is, the numeral six with 23 zeros after it.

[H+] x [OH-] = 10-14

Because the actual concentrations in moles per litre are small, it is customary to express the values as exponents. For example, if we know that the concentration of hydrogen ions [H^+] in a sample of milk is 0.000001 moles/l which is equivalent to 10^{-6} moles/l, we can calculate the concentration of hydroxyl ions as $10^{-14}/10^{-6} = 10^{-8}$ moles/l which is the same as 0.00000001 moles/l.

If [H^+] = [OH^-] the solution is neutral with respect to acidity.

If [H^+] > [OH^-] the solution is acidic.

If [H^+] < [OH^-] the solution is basic or alkaline.

Chemicals which contribute H^+ or absorb OH^- are acids, while bases contribute OH^- or absorb H^+.

The concept of pH evolved as a short hand method to express acidity. We have already seen that a hydrogen ion concentration of 0.000001 moles/l can be expressed as [10^{-6}], an expression which defines both the unit of measurement and the numerical value. The concept of pH is a further abbreviation which expresses the concentration of hydrogen ions as the negative log of the hydrogen ion concentration in units of moles/l. This sounds complex but is quite easy to apply. For example, the $\log_{10}$ of hydrogen ion concentration of [10^{-6}] is equal to -6. The final step is to take the negative of the log, that is -1 x -6 which is 6. So, 0.0000001 moles/l = [10^{-6}] = pH 6. From the relationship expressed in Equation 3, if the concentration of one of OH^- and H^+ is known, it is always possible to calculate the concentration of the other. So, if the pH of a solution is 6, the pOH is 14 - 6 = 8. Because this relationship is understood, the convention is to only report pH. Note, that because the negative sign was dropped by convention, decreasing pH values mean increasing acidity, that is, increasing concentration of H^+ ions. So, although both TA and pH are measures of acidity, pH decreases with increasing acidity.

All of this can be summarized by a description of the pH scale. The pH scale for most practical purposes is from 1 to 14, although a pH of less than one is theoretically and practically possible.

pH 7.0 is neutral acidity $[H^+] = [OH^-]$
pH < 7.0 = acid condition $[H^+] > [OH^-]$
pH > 7.0 = alkaline condition $[H^+] < [OH^-]$

pH *vs.* Titratable Acidity

TA and pH are both measures of acidity but, for most purposes, pH is a better process control tool, because the pH probe measures only those H^+ which are free in solution and undissociated with salts or proteins. This is important because it is free H^+ which modifies protein functionality and contributes sour taste. It is also the pH rather than titratable acidity which is the best indicator of the preservation and safety effects of acidity. It must be emphasized, that the most important factor available to the cheese maker to control spoilage and pathogenic organisms is pH control. The pH history during and after cheese manufacture is the most important trouble shooting information. Cheese moisture, mineral content, texture and flavour are all influenced directly by the activity of free hydrogen ions (i.e. pH).

Titratable acidity (TA) measures all titratable H^+ ions up to the phenolphthalein end point (pH 8.5) and, therefore, varies with changes in milk composition and properties. During cheese manufacture, the pH gives a true indication of acid development during the entire process so that the optimum pH at each step is independent of other variables such as milk protein content. However, the optimum TA at each step in cheese making will vary with initial milk composition and the type of standardization procedure used.

A good practical illustration of the difference between TA and pH is the effect of cutting. Up to the time of cutting, TA of the milk increases with the development of acidity by the culture. After cutting the TA of the whey is much lower. This does not mean that acid development stopped. It simply means that titratable H^+ ions associated with the milk proteins are no longer present in the whey. This leads to the concept of buffer capacity, which is an important principle in cheese making. The effect of protein removal on the TA of whey, is related to the ability of protein to 'buffer' the milk against changes in pH. That same buffer property is the reason it helps to take acidic medication, like aspirin, with milk.

Buffer capacity can be described as the ability of an aqueous system, such as milk, to resist changes in pH with addition of acids (added H^+) or bases (added OH^-). Specifically, buffer capacity is the amount of acid or base required to induce a unit change in pH. For example, a small addition of acid to distilled water will cause a large reduction in pH. The same amount of acid would have a small effect on the pH of milk because milk proteins and salts neutralize the acidity.

The two most important buffer components of milk are caseins (buffer maximum near pH 4.6) and phosphate (buffer maxima near pH 7.0). The buffer maximum near pH 5.0 is extremely important to cheese manufacture because the optimum pH for most cheese is in the range of 5.0 - 5.2. As the pH of cheese is reduced towards pH 5.0 by lactic acid fermentation, the buffer capacity is increasing (i.e., each incremental decrease in pH requires more lactic acid). The effect is to give the cheese maker considerable room for variation in the rate and amount of acid production. Without milk's built in buffers it would be impossible to produce cheese in the optimum pH range.

Another way to illustrate the difference between TA and pH is to consider typical ranges of pH and TA for normal milk. TA is a measure of the total buffer capacity of milk for the pH range between the pH of milk and the phenolphthalein end point (about pH 8.3). The pH of milk at 25C, normally varies within a relatively narrow range of 6.5 to 6.7. The normal range for titratable acidity of herd milks is 0.12 to 0.18% lactic acid In other words, pH is a good indicator of initial milk quality, while the traditional measurement of TA to indicate bacterial growth in milk is less precise.

pH Measurement

The pH of cheese milk, whey and soft cheese can be measured directly. Firm and hard cheese must be fragmented before analysis. Always measure cheese pH in duplicate and use extreme care in handling the electrode. Place the fragmented cheese in a 30 ml vial or small beaker and gently push the electrode into the cheese. To ensure good contact, press the cheese around the electrode with your fingers. There is no need to rinse the electrode between cheese samples. However, if the electrode is stored in buffer it should be rinsed with distilled water before measuring cheese pH. Always store the electrode in pH 4 buffer or as directed by the manufacturer. Do not rub the electrode. The electrode should be washed with detergent and rinsed with acetone occasionally to remove fat and protein deposits.

Babcock Methods for Milk Fat

Apparatus and Materials

1. Babcock centrifuge.
2. Water bath at 55C.
3. Torsion balance, 9 and 18 g weights.
4. Babcock shaker.
5. Glassware: 8% milk bottles, 50% cream bottles, 50% Paley bottles, 17.5 ml cylinders, 17.6 ml pipette, .
6. Reagents: - Babcock sulphuric acid (Sp. Gr. 1.82-1.83)
   - N-butyl alcohol
   - Glymol.

Milk

1. Temper sample to 20C and mix by pouring gently from original container to a beaker of similar capacity 4-5 times.
2. Transfer 17.6 ml (18.0g) of milk to 8% bottle with 17.6 ml pipette. Allow pipette to drain then blow out the remaining drop into the bottle.
3. Add 17.5 ml sulphuric acid (Sp. Gr. 1.82-1.83) in at least three increments using special cylinder. Rotate bottle between thumb and fingers while adding acid to wash milk from neck. Mix thoroughly 2 min. after each addition of acid by moving the bulb of the bottle in rapid circular motion. Final colour of mixture should be chocolate brown.
4. Centrifuge 5 min.
5. Add distilled water at 60C to bring contents to within one-quarter inch of base of neck. Do not mix.
6. Centrifuge 2 min.
7. Add water at 60C to float fat into neck of bottle. Top meniscus should be about even with the top of the graduated portion. Do not mix.

8. Centrifuge 1 min.
9. Temper bottles in water bath at 55C for 5 min.
10. Measure length of fat column with dividers from top of upper meniscus to bottom of lower meniscus. Place one divider point at zero mark and read percentage fat by weight directly where other point touches the scale.

Cream and Cheese

1. Temper cream sample to 20C and mix. Grind cheese to small particles.
2. Weigh 9 g of cream into 50% cream bottle and add 9 ml of distilled water at 20°C. Weigh 9 g of cheese into a 50% Paley bottle and add 10 ml of distilled water at 60C.
3. Add 17.5 ml sulphuric acid in at least three increments. Mix until colour is uniform chocolate brown and all cheese particles are dissolved.
4. Centrifuge 5 min.
5. Add distilled water at 60C to bring contents to within one-quarter inch of base of neck. Do not mix.
6. Centrifuge 2 min.
7. Add water at 60C to float fat into neck of bottle. Do not mix.
8. Centrifuge 1 min.
9. Temper bottles in water bat at 55C, for 5 min.
10. Place 4-5 drops glymol on the fat column letting these run down the side of the neck. Measure the length of the fat column from the demarcation between fat and glymol to the bottom of the lower meniscus.
11. Report fat in percent by weight.

Skim milk, Buttermilk, Whey

1. Temper sample to 20C and mix gently.
2. Transfer 2 ml N-butyl alcohol and then a 9 ml sample to an 18 g double neck bottle. Mix thoroughly with a circular motion.
3. Add 9 ml of Babcock sulphuric acid for skim milk or buttermilk, 7 ml for whey.
4. Centrifuge 6 min. Place bottles in the centrifuge cup with the small neck facing the outside.

5. Add water at 60C to bring contents 1 cm from the base of the neck. Do not mix. Centrifuge 2 min.
6. Temper bottles in water bath at 55C for 5 min.
7. Place a finger over the large neck and press down until the lower meniscus of fat in the small neck corresponds to a major division.

Cheese Salt

Cheese salt determination using the Volhard procedure is described below. Other methods which have proven to give accurate results are:

1. Automatic Chloride Titraters operate on the principle of coulometric silver ion generation to titrate chloride ions in the sample. When all chloride ions are titrated free silver ions cause a conductivity change which signals the end of titration.
2. Quantab Chloride Titrater depends on the reaction of chloride ions with silver dichromate, which is brown, to form silver chloride chromate ion and silver chloride which is white. The reaction takes place on a calibrated strip which permits direct estimation of chloride content.

Volhard Procedure for Salt Determination

Apparatus and Materials

1. A torsion moisture balance
2. 250 ml erlenmeyer flask and a 500 ml beaker
3. Two graduated cylinders, one 50 ml and the other 100 ml
4. A 10 ml pipette and a 5 ml graduated pipette
5. Burette graduated in ml and 1/10 ml, and burette stand
6. An electric or gas hot plate
7. Chemically pure concentrated nitric acid
8. Saturated potassium permanganate solution
9. 0.1711 N potassium thiocyanate solution (contains 16.63 g per litre) in a brown glass bottle
10. 0.1711 N silver nitrate solution (contains 29.07 g per litre) in a brown glass bottle

11. A saturated solution of ferric ammonium sulphate
12. Sucrose
13. Boiling chips such as carborundum granules or glass beads.
14. Fume hood

Method

1. Prepare cheese sample as for cheese moisture test.
2. Weigh about 3 g cheese into a clean dry 250 ml erlenmeyer flask.
3. Add 10 ml of 0.1711 N silver nitrate solution as accurately as possible to the flask. If cheese contains more than 3% salt, add more silver nitrate.
4. Add 15 ml of the chemically pure nitric acid.
5. Add 50 ml of distilled water.
6. Add a few boiling stones.
7. Place flask on hot plate in fume hood and boil.
8. When contents of flask are boiling uniformly, carefully add 5 ml of saturated potassium permanganate. Continue boiling until purple colour disappears, then add a second charge of 5 ml of potassium permanganate. When purple colour again disappears, add another 5 ml of potassium permanganate. Continue boiling until all cheese particles are digested. To ascertain when digestion is complete, remove flask from hot plate and allow to stand quietly for a few moments. Undigested cheese particles will float upon the surface, while the white precipitate of silver chloride will sink to the bottom of the clear liquid. When no more white particles are seen upon the surface, digestion is complete.
9. Add sufficient distilled water to bring the volume up to approximately 100 ml. Allow precipitate to settle and very carefully pour off the liquid into a beaker. Be careful not to pour off any of the white precipitate of silver chloride.
10. Add 100 ml of distilled water to flask and swirl contents to wash precipitate.
11. Add 3 ml of saturated ferric ammonium sulphate as an indicator and titrate the excess silver nitrate with 0.1711 N potassium thiocyanate. A reddish colour denotes the end point.

12. The number of ml of 0.1711 N silver nitrate originally added minus the titration value found in step 11, divided by the weight of the cheese in the sample equals the percentage of salt in the cheese.

Example

3.00 g of cheese to which 10.00 ml of 0.1711 N silver nitrate had been added gave a reading of 4.00 ml in Step 11.

4.00 ml 0.1711 N potassium thiocyanate required to combine with excess silver nitrate.

6.00 ml 0.1711 N silver nitrate combined with salt in cheese.

Therefore per cent salt by weight = 6.00/3.00 = 2.00

Because the salt in the cheese is measured by its chloride content, it is necessary to test the reagents used for chloride, or related substances content. This is done by carrying out a test using sucrose instead of cheese. The titration value subtracted from the original amount of silver nitrate added is subtracted from the value found in Step 12 before dividing by weight to find the percentage salt in the cheese.

To check the strength of the 0.1711 N silver nitrate solution, dissolve 10 g chemically pure dry sodium chloride in sufficient water to make up one litre of solution. Each ml of this solution is equivalent to one ml of 0.1711 N silver nitrate. When the silver nitrate has been standardized, each ml of silver nitrate is equivalent to one ml 0.1711 N potassium thiocyanate.

Culture Activity Test

Purpose: This simple test is useful to ensure that cheese cultures have adequate activity before inoculating the cheese vat. For most cheese a general rule of thumb is that the activity and amount of inoculum should be sufficient to produce a titratable acidity of about .34% lactic acid, in 10% reconstituted skim milk, after 4 h of incubation at 37C. The test is also useful to compare types of cultures or bulk cultures prepared under different conditions. For these purposes a pH versus time chart is quite useful. A further application is to check sensitivity of the culture to bacteriophage in the plant.

Procedure:

1. Mix 10 g of low-heat, antibiotic-free skim milk powder in 90 ml of distilled water in a 100 ml Erlenmeyer flask.
2. Sterilize at 15 lb pressure (1.05 kPa.) for 10 min.
3. Cool to 37C.
4. Inoculate with 3.0 ml starter or other amount as appropriate. Rinse pipette twice by drawing the sterile milk into it.
5. Incubate at 37C for at least 4 h. Longer if desired for pH versus time profile.
6. Check pH at 30 min. intervals.
7. Titrate 17.6 ml with N/10 sodium hydroxide (NaOH) using 1 ml phenolphthalein. Divide the required ml of NaOH by 2 the obtain titratable acidity in units of percent lactic acid.
8. Record starter activity as follows:

   Active, over 0.34%

   Slow 0.26 to 0.30%

Detection of Bacteriophage

The following tests are based on the principle that bacteriophage specific to the culture in use will be present in high numbers in the cheese whey. Therefore, by monitoring whey for the presence of phage "a dead vat" on subsequent days can be avoided.

Culture Activity Test: The culture activity test described above can be used to detect the presence of phage in cheese whey. Prepare 300 ml of reconstituted skim milk and place 99 ml in each of three beakers. Add 1 ml of whey to Beaker 1 (100 x dilution), then transfer 1 ml from Beaker 1 to Beaker 2 (10,000 x dilution) and finally, transfer 1 ml from Beaker 3 to Beaker 4 to make a 1 million times dilution. Add culture and monitor pH as described in section 3.8.

Bromocresol Purple (BCP) Phage Inhibition Test: This test is quite simple to perform, and produces more accurate results than the culture activity test.

1. Prepare Materials
   - BCP stock solution (1 g/100 ml water)
   - Test tubes containing 9.9 ml sterile BCP-milk (5 ml BCP stock solution/litre milk)

- 30-32C water bath or heating block
- 1 ml graduated pipettes
- Membrane filter (0.45 u) – optional
- Disposable syringe – optional
- Clinical centrifuge – optional
- Whey sample for phage testing
- Freshly grown culture, frozen syringe, or frozen can of each strain

2. Add Whey to BCP Milk and Make Dilutions: Transfer 0.1 ml of fresh (or filter-sterilized) whey to the first dilution tube (10^{-2}) and mix well. Transfer 0.1 ml from the first to the second dilution tube and mix well. Repeat process for the third dilution tube. (If unfiltered whey is used, a control tube containing BCP milk and whey only, must be prepared. This control tube tests for the presence of active culture in the whey that could mask phage inhibition of a strain.) Whey samples should be refrigerated immediately after collection and held cold until tested for phage.
3. Add Culture to Control and Whey Dilution Tubes: Cheese culture (0.2 ml) is added to whey dilution tubes and to a control tube for each strain. If you are using direct-to-the-vat culture, dilute 1 ml of culture in 9 ml of milk and then add 0.2 ml of the mixture to the dilution tubes. The control tube contains only BCP milk and culture—NO whey. The control tube serves to show starter strain inhibition by colour comparison with the other tubes.

Incubate Tubes and Interpret Results. Incubate both control and dilution tubes for 6 hours at 30-32C. Compare the colour of the whey dilution tubes to that of the control tube. Ignore coagulation. An uninhibited culture will produce sufficient acid to turn the BCP dye from blue to yellow. Strains should be removed from the culture blend when full inhibition persists at the 10^{-6} dilution level. The following system should be used to record phage inhibition:

0 = No inhibition at any dilution

1 = Partial inhibition at 10^{-2} dilution

2 = Full inhibition at 10^{-2} dilution

3 = Partial inhibition at 10^{-4} dilution

4 = Full inhibition at 10^{-4} dilution
5 = Partial inhibition at 10^{-6} dilution
6 = Full inhibition at 10^{-6} dilution

Inhibitory Substances

Regulations: Most jurisdictions have regulations concerning the testing methods and limits of certain antibiotics in raw milk. *The Milk Act of Ontario*, Regulation 761, Section 52, Subsection, states:

"The milk of every producer shall be tested at least once a month for the presence of an inhibitor by an official method."

An official method is described in a separate inhibitor policy document which states:

The minimum sensitivity of an official method to test for the presence of an inhibitor under section 52 of Regulation 761 shall be:

1. 0.01 international units of penicillin per millilitre of milk by the Standard Disc Assay (*Bacillus stearothermophilus*) procedure.
2. 10 parts per billion sulfamethazine by the High Performance Liquid Chromatography (modified Smedley and Weber) procedure.

A concentration of .01 international units of penicillin per millilitre of milk is equivalent to 6 parts per billion (ppb). Note: 1 ppb is equivalent to a single penny in $10 million or one second in 32 years.

Detection Methods: It is beyond the scope of this manual to discuss any specific methods in detail. What follows is are brief descriptions of five types of inhibitor tests which are currently used in the dairy industry. For each category one or more brand name tests are listed to indicate possible choices. For cheese manufactures seeking assistance with inhibitor testing, there are many private labs which provide suitable services. In Ontario, a wide range of expertise and methodologies are available from Laboratory Services Division, University of Guelph.

Growth Inhibition Assays

Examples: Delvotest P, Delvotest SP, BR test, BR-AS test, Charm Farm, and the Disk Assay

This test format involves a standard culture of a test organism in an agar growth media, usually *Bacillus stearothermophilus*, that is inoculated with a milk sample and incubated for periods of up to several hours. If the milk contains sufficient concentrations of inhibitory substances the growth of the organism will be reduced or eliminated. The presence of an inhibitory substance is indicated by zones of inhibition or a change in colour of the media (pH and redox indicators).

The major disadvantages of these tests are that they are not very specific for identification purposes, have limited sensitivities to many antibiotics and take a long time before results are available. Growth inhibition tests are only able to classify residues into either the ß-lactam (penicillin like antibiotics) or other than ß-lactam antibiotic families. A further concern is that growth inhibition tests are subject to the effects of natural inhibitors (eg. lysozyme, lactoferrin, complement and defensins) which can be found in high levels in mastitic milk and may give false positive test results, particularly when used at the cow level. These effects can be minimized by heating individual cow samples at 82C for 2-3 minutes in a microwave oven or water bath before testing to destroy natural inhibitors and allow antibiotics which are more heat stable to remain.

The advantages of these tests are that they are cheap, easy to perform and have a very broad detection range.

Enzymatic Colorimetric Assays

Example: *Penzyme Test for ß-lactams*

The penzyme test is based on the inactivation of an enzyme by ß-lactam antibiotics. The enzyme (DD-carboxypeptidase or penicillin binding protein) is present in all bacteria and is involved in the synthesis of the bacterial cell wall. ß-lactam antibiotics will bind specifically with this enzyme and block it's activity, thus preventing the formation of the bacterial cell wall. This enzyme has been freeze dried and placed in sealed vials to which the milk sample is added. After addition of 0.2 ml (200 µl) of milk sample to the vial the sample is incubated for 5 minutes at 47C. During this time any ß-lactams present in the milk bind to the enzyme and inactivate a certain amount depending on the concentration present.

Reagent tablets specific for the enzyme (D-alanine peptide and D-amino acid oxidase) are then added to the milk sample and the sample is incubated at 47C for 15 minutes. During incubation any remaining active enzyme will react with the reagent added. The end product of the substrate and enzyme reaction (pyruvic acid and hydrogen peroxide) is measured by a redox colour indicator and the final colour is compared to a colour chart provided with the kit.

An orange colour (reduced) indicates a negative test result.

A yellow colour (oxidized) indicates a positive test result.

Microbial Receptor Assays:

Example: *Charm II*

This test uses bacterial cells (*Bacillus stearothermophilus*), which contain natural receptor sites on or within the cells for antibiotics, and radio labelled (C^{14} or H^3) antibiotics. Milk sample is added to a freeze dried pellet of bacterial cells (binding reagent) in a test tube and the sample is mixed and incubated. During incubation any antibiotic present in the milk will bind to it's specific receptor site. Radio labelled antibiotic (tracer reagent) is then added and the sample is mixed and incubated. Unbound receptor sites on the bacterial cell will be bound by the radio labelled antibiotic. The sample is then centrifuged to collect the bacterial cells in the bottom of the test tube and the supernatant and butterfat is discarded. The bacterial cells are then resuspended and mixed in scintillation fluid. Binding is measured with a scintillation counter and compared to a positive and negative control. The more antibiotic present in the sample the lower the scintillation counts determined by the equipment.

Charm currently has test kits in this format for ß-lactams, macrolides, aminoglycosides and sulfonamides.

Immunoassays: Unlike other residue testing methods immunoassays are fast, sensitive, inexpensive, reproducible, reliable and simple to perform. The technique depends upon the measurement of the highly specific binding between antibodies (Ab) and antigens (Ag). Antigens are substances which are foreign to the body (eg. bacteria, viruses, toxins, pollens, drugs, hormones and pesticides) and that when introduced into the body give rise to the production of antibodies. Antibodies are proteins produced in the body by white blood cells (lymphocytes) as a result of exposure to antigens (destroy invading pathogens). The extreme sensitivity of the immunoassay is due to the development of certain labelling techniques for molecules (conjugates), enabling the measurement of very small masses (picogram or parts per trillion) of substances.

Immunoassays are classified according to the label which is attached to either the antigen (the anolyte being measured) or the antibody. The label may be a radioactive atom as in radio immunoassays (RIA), or an enzyme as in enzyme immunoassays (EIA or ELISA (Enzyme- linked immunosorbant assay)) or a fluorescent substance as in fluorescence immunoassays (FIA).

There are 3 major types of immunoassays used commonly for the detection of antibiotics in milk:

1) Enzyme-Linked Immunoassay (eg. LacTek tests, SNAP for Tetracyclines, Single Step Block for SMZ)
2) Enzyme-Linked Receptor Binding Assay (eg. SNAP for ß-lactams, Delvo-X-Press)
3) Radio immunoassay (CHARM II for tetracyclines and chloramphenicol)

Rennet Activity

Coagulation Time versus Setting Time: Rennet is generally described in the industry as single, double or triple strength. Single strength is considered to be that concentration where 200 ml is sufficient to set 1,000 kg of milk in 30 - 40 min. at 30 - 32C. Setting time is the point where the curd will break cleanly and exude clear whey. Coagulation time is the point where flecks of curd first appear on a spatula or slide dipped into the milk. Coagulation time is about half of setting time, so typically, coagulation using single strength rennet requires 15-20 minutes followed by setting at 30-40 minutes. The following simple test can be used to check coagulation time which can be measured much more accurately than setting time. The test uses skim milk because the presence of fat globules makes it difficult to see the first sign of coagulation.

Measurement of Coagulation Time

1. Prepare 200 ml samples of 10% reconstituted low heat skim milk powder in 250 ml beakers. Add 0.02% calcium chloride dihydrate (40 mg per 200 ml).
2. Temper to 32C in a water bath.
3. Add 1.0 ml of 5% rennet solution to each sample.

4. Determine the clotting time by dipping a clean spatula or glass slide into the milk. When coagulation has occurred flecks of curd will appear in the milk film on the slide.

Relative Milk-Clotting Activity Test: A more rigorous test of coagulant activity is the "Relative Milk-Clotting Activity Test" (RMCAT) which measures the activity of rennet and other coagulants in "International Milk-Clotting Units" (IMCU). The method is described in International Dairy Federation standard 157:1992.

Yeasts and Moulds

Selective media for yeasts and moulds include acidified media and antibiotic media. The method described below uses acidified potato dextrose agar.

Equipment and Material

- Potato dextrose agar
- Equipment for plating
- Tartaric acid solution (10 aqueous)
- Incubator set at 22-25C

Procedure:

1. Prepare cheese homogenates and serial dilutions as described in Section A.
2. Predetermine the quantity of sterile 10% tartaric acid solution necessary to obtain a pH of 3.5 + 0.1. Put a portion of the medium in a small beaker and titrate to pH 3.5 at 45C. Check the accuracy of the titration by allowing the agar to cool to incubation temperature, place electrodes directly into the solidified medium, and read the pH. It should be 3.5 + 0.1. Calculate the amount of sterile 10% tartaric acid solution necessary for the volume of tempered agar to be used for pouring plates.
3. Place 5 ml of the 0.1 dilution and 1 ml of additional dilutions as required into each of duplicate petri dishes.
4. Add the tartaric acid solution to the tempered agar immediately before pouring 15 - 20 ml into each of the plates containing the sample dilutions.
5. Mix well and let solidify before inverting the plates. Incubate at 22 - 25C.

6. Count the plates at 3 and 5 days of incubation. Yeast cells will appear as cream coloured shiny colonies.

Presumptive Coliforms

1. Prepare cheese homogenates and serial dilutions as described in Section A.
2. Place 5 ml of the 0.1 dilution (= 0.5 g of original sample or Omega dilution) and 1 ml of additional dilutions as required into each of duplicate petri dishes and add molten VRB agar. (Note: Do not sterilize VRB agar.) When solidified, pour over layer (5 ml VRB).
3. Incubate at 35C + 1^{0}C for 18 - 24 hrs.
4. Count the dark red colonies, at least 0.5 mm in diameter, and record results as coliforms per g of sample.

Samples of cottage cheese and other acid milk products should be plated within 24 hrs. after manufacture because coliform counts decline under acid conditions. Coliforms also decrease in number during aging of ripened cheese varieties.

It must be emphasized that this method provides a presumptive count only. If presumptive counts are consistently high, colonies should be confirmed (see Standard Methods). The Canadian Food And Drug Act and Regulations permit 500 coliforms/g of cheese made from pasteurized milk and 5,000 coliforms/g of cheese made from unpasteurized milk. Permitted counts of *Eshericia coli* are 100 and 500/g respectively.

Staphylococci

Procedure A: The method described here enumerates total Staphylococci by surface plating on Baird-Parker media. A coagulase test can be used to determine if individual colonies are *S. aureus.* Canadian Food And Drug Act and Regulations permit up to 100 coagulase positive *S. aureus* in pasteurized milk cheese and up to 1,000/g in cheese made from unpasteurized milk.

Equipment and Materials

- Plating equipment
- Glass spreaders (hockey stick-shaped glass rods)

- Incubator set at 37C
- Baird-Parker Agar

Procedure:

1. Pour plates of B.P. agar (15 ml/plate) and dry surfaces (using sterile laminar airflow cabinet — 2 hrs).
2. Pipette 0.1 ml of homogenate and of subsequent dilutions onto surface of agar and spread evenly with a sterile bent glass rod until surface appears dry. Prepare duplicate plates. Use 10^{-1}, 1-^{-2}, and 1-^{-3} dilutions.
3. Incubate at 37C for 48 hrs.
4. Count the number of colonies in each of the following groups:
   (i) convex, shiny, black, with or without narrow gray-white margin, surrounded by clear zone extending into opaque medium.
   (ii) convex, shiny, black, with or without narrow gray-white margin, surrounded by clear zone extending into the opaque medium with an inner opaque zone.
   (iii) convex, shiny, black, with or without narrow gray-white margin, $\geq$1 mm in diameter.

Procedure B: Pipette 1 ml or 0.1 ml of homogenate and of subsequent dilutions into petri dish.

Add approximately 10 ml Baird-Parker medium. Mix well. Let stand on bench.

When solidified, invert and put in incubator at 37C (for 48 hours).

Read the same as Procedure A.

Note: Add 5 ml of well mixed Ey Tellurite, enrichment, at 5C to Baird-Parker agar prior to pouring plates.

Temperature 37 C

Inoculum 2% of mother culture prepared with 10% reconstituted skim milk powder.

Test media 1 10% skim milk powder, low heat, antibiotic free.

Test media 2 Same as one with 1% cheese whey.

Results

Titratable acidity after 4 hours:

Treatment 1 0.34%

Treatment 2 0.25%

pH versus time

Time	0	1	2	3	4	5	6	7	8	9
Skim powder	6.62	6.59	6.5	6.4	6.15	5.74	5.39	5.08	4.92	4.87
Skim with whey	6.61	6.57	6.5	6.42	6.35	6.31	6.3	6.3	6.29	6.29

Interpretation

1. Test media 1 shows normal growth. 0.34% acidity after 4 h with a 2% inoculum is adequate for most types of cheese. pH versus time plot is typical, reaching pH 5.2 between 6 and 7 hours.
2. Test media 2, containing cheese whey, shows inadequate acid development, indicating the probable presence of bacteriophage in the cheese plant.

Bibliography

Allen, R. H., Gottlieb, M., Clute, E., Pongsiri, M. J., Sherman, J., and Obrams, G. I. (1997). Breast Cancer and Pesticides in Hawaii: The Need for Further Study. Environmental Health Perspectives *105*, 679-683.

Anzano, M. A., Smith, J. M., Uskokovic, M. R., Peer, C. W., Mullen, L. T., Letterio, J. J., Welsh, M. C., Shrader, M. W., Logsdon, D. L., Driver, C. L., et al. (1994). 1-alpha, 25-dihydroxy-16-ene- 23-yne-26, 27-hexafluorocholecalciferol, a new deltanoid for prevention of breast cancer in the rat. Cancer Research *54*, 1653-1656.

Armstrong, B. (1975). Environmental Factors and Cancer Incidence and Mortality in Different Countries, with Special Reference to Dietary Practices. International Journal of Cancer *15*, 617-631.

Banni, S., Angioini, E., Casu, V., Melis, M. P., Scrugli, S., Carta, G., Corongiu, F. P., and Ip, C. (1999b). An Increase in Vitamin A Status by the Feeding of Conjugated Linoleic Acid. Nutrition and Cancer *33*, 53-57.

Banni, S., Angioni, E., Casu, V., Melis, M., Carta, G., Corongiu, P., Thompson, H., and Ip, C. (1999a). Decrease in linoleic acid metabolites as a potential mechanism in cancer risk reduction by conjugated linoleic acid. Carcinogenesis *20*, 1019-1024.

Barger-Lux, M. J., and Heaney, R. P. (1994). The role of calcium intake in preventing bone fragility, hypertension, and certain cancers. Journal of Nutrition *124*, 1406S-1411S.

Campbell, C., Luedecke, L. O., and Shultz, T. D. (1999). Yogurt consumption and estrogen metabolism in healthy premenopausal women. Nutrition Research *19*, 531-543.

Carroll, K. K., Jacobson, E. A., Eckel, L. A., and Newmark, H. L. (1991). Calcium and carcinogenesis in the mammary gland. American Journal of Clinical Nutrition *54*, 206S-208S.

Chin, S. F., Liu, W., Storkson, J. M., Ha, Y. L., and Pariza, M. W. (1992). Dietary sources of conjugated dienoic isomers of linoleic acid, a newly recognized class on anticarcinogenes. Journal of Food Composition and Analysis *5*, 185-197.

D'Avanzo, B., Negri, E., Gramenzi, A., Franceschi, S., Parazzini, F., Boyle, P., and La Vecchia, C. (1991). Fats in seasoning and breast cancer risk: an Italian case-control study. European journal of Cancer *27*, 420-423.

Epstein, S. S. (1996). Unlabeled milk from cows treated with biosynthetic growth hormones: a case of regulatory abdication. International Journal of Health Services *26*, 173-185.

Esther, M. J., Schwartz, G. G., Dreon, D. M., and Koo, J. (1999). Vitamin D and Breast Cancer Risk: The NHANES I Epidemiologic Follow-up Study, 1971-1975 to 1992. Cancer Epidemiology, Biomarkers & Prevention *8*, 399-406.

Fischer, S. M., Leyton, J., Lee, M. L., Locniskar, M., Belury, M. A., Maldve, R. E., Slaga, T. J., and Bechtel, D. H. (1992). Differential effects of dietary linoleic acid on mouse skin-tumor promotion and mammary carcinogenesis. Cancer Research *52*, 2049s-2054s.

Frodin, M., and Gammeltoft, S. (1994). Insulin-like growth factors act synergistically with basic fibroblast growth factor and nerve growth factor to promote chromaffin cell proliferation. Proceedings of the National Academy of Science *q* 1771-1775.

Gaskill, S. P. (1979). Breast cancer mortality and diet in the United States. Cancer Research *39*, 3628-3637.

Giovannucci, E., Stampfer, M. J., Colditz, G. A., Manson, J. E., Rosner, B. A., Longnecker, M., Speizer, F. E., and Willet, W. C. (1993). A comparison of prospective and retrospective assessments of diet in the study of breast cancer. American Journal of Epidemiology *137*, 502- 511.

Herbert, J. R., and Rosen, A. (1996). Nutritional, socioeconomic, and reproductive factors in relation to female breast cancer mortality: findings from a cross-national study. Cancer Detection and Prevention *20*, 234-244.

Hirayama, T. (1978). Epidemiology of Breast Cancer with Special Reference to the Role of Diet. Preventive Medicine *7*, 173-195.

Ip, C. (1997). Review of the effects of trans fatty acids, oleic acid, n-3 polyunsaturated fatty acids, and conjugated linoleic acid on mammary carcinogenesis in animals. American Journal of Clinical Nutrition *66*, 1523S-1529S.

Jacobson, E. A., James, K. A., Newmark, H. L., and Carroll, K. K. (1989). Effects of dietary fat, calcium, and vitamin D on growth and mammary tumorigenesis induced by 7,12-dimethylbenz(a)anthracene in female Sprague-Dawley rats. Cancer Research *49*, 6300-6303.

Jain, M. (1998). Dairy foods, dairy fats and cancer: a review of epidemiological evidence. Nutrition Research *18*, 905-937.

Kato, I., and al., a. e. (1987). Relationship between westernization of dietary habits and mortality from breast and ovarian cancers in Japan. Japanese Journal of Cancer Research *78*, 349-357.

Kelly, M. L., Kolver, E. S., Bauman, D. E., Van Amburgh, M. E., and Muller, L. D. (1998). Effect of intake of pasture on concentrations of conjugated linoleic acid in milk of lactating cows. Journal of Dairy Science *81*, 1630-1636.

Khan, N., Yang, K., Newmark, H., Wong, G., Telang, N., Rivlin, R., and Lipkin, M. (1994). Mammary ductal epithelial cell hyperproliferation and hyperplasia induced by a nutritional stress diet containing four components of a western-style diet. Carcinogenesis *15*, 2645-2648.

Klurfeld, D. M., Weber, M. M., and Kritchevsky, D. (1984). Comparison of dietary carbohydrates for promotion of DMBA-Induced mammary tumorigensis in rats. Carcinogenesis *5*, 423-425.

Knekt, P., Albanes, D., Seppanen, R., Aromaa, A., Jarvinen, R., Hyvonen, L., Teppo, L., and Pukkala, E. (1990). Dietary fat and risk of breast cancer. American Journal of Clinical Nutrition *52*, 903-908.

Knekt, P., Jarvinen, R., Seppanen, R., Pukkala, E., and Aromaa, A. (1996). Intake of dairy products and the risk of breast cancer. British Journal of Cancer *73*, 687-691.

Kolar, Z., Negrin, R., and Lisato, L. (1989). Effect of some sugars on the growth and differentiation of MCF-7 cells: I. Detection of glycosylative changes using lectin histochemistry. Acta Universitatis Palackianae Olomucensis Facultatis Medicae *122*, 113-120.

La Vecchia, C., and Pampallona, S. (1986). Age at First Birth, Dietary Practices and Breast Cancer Mortality in Various Italian Regions. Oncology *43*, 1-6.

La Vecchia, C., Decarli, A., Parazzini, G., Gentile, A., Negri, E., Cecchetti, G., and Franceschi, S. (1987). General epidemiology of breast cancer in northern italy. International Journal of Epidemiology *16*, 347-355.

Lipkin, M., and Newmark, H. L. (1999). Vitamin D, calcium, and prevention of breast cancer: a review. Journal of the American College of Nutrition *18*, 392S-397S.

Malven, P. V., Head, H. H., Collier, R. J., and Buonomo, F. C. (1987). Periparturient changes in secretion and mammary uptake of insulin and in concentrations of insulin and insulin-like growth factors in milk of dairy cows. Journal of Dairy Science *70*, 2254-2265.

Moon, R., and Constantinou, A. I. (1997). Dietary retinoids and carotenoids in rodent models of mammary tumorigenesis. Breast Cancer Research and Treatment *46*, 181-189.

Newmark, H. L. (1994). Vitamin D adequacy: a possible relationship to breast cancer. Advances in Experimental Medicine and Biology *364*, 109-114.

Outwater, J. L., Nicholson, A., and Barnard, N. (1997). Dairy products and breast cancer: the IGF-I, estrogen, and bGH hypothesis. Medical Hypotheses *48*, 453-461.

Parodi, P. W. (1994). Conjugated linoleic acid: An anticarcinogenic fatty acid present in milk fat. Australian Journal of Dairy Technology *49*, 93-97.

Parodi, P. W. (1997a). Milk fat conjugated linoleic acid: Can it help prevent breast cancer? Proceedings of the Nutrition Society of New Zealand *22*, 137-149.

Reddy, B. S., and Rivenson, A. (1993). Inhibitory effect of bifidobacterium longum on colon, mammary, and liver carcinogenesis induced by 2-amino-3-methylimidazo[4,5-f]quinoline, a food mutagen. Cancer Research *53*, 3914-3918.

Rice, L. J., Chai, Y.-J., Conti, C. J., Willis, R. A., and Locniskar, M. F. (1995). The effect of dietary fermented milk products and lactic acid bacteria on the initiation and promotion stages of mammary carcinogenesis. Nutrition and Cancer *24*, 99-109.

Ritskes-Hoitinga, J., Meijers, M., Timmer, W. G., Wiersma, A., Meijer, G. W., and Weststrate, J. A. (1996). Effects of two dietary fat levels and four dietary linoleic acid levels on mammary tumor development in Balb/c-MMTV mice under ad libitum feeding conditions. Nutrition and Cancer *25*, 161-172.

Rohan, T. E., McMichael, A. J., and Baghurst, P. A. (1988). A population-based case-control study of diet and breast cancer in australia. American Journal of Epidemiology *128*, 478-489.

Rose, D. P., Boyar, A. P., and Wynder, E. L. (1986). International comparisons of mortality rates for cancer of the breast, ovary, prostate, and colon, and per capita food consumption. Cancer *58*, 2363-2371.

Rosfjord, E. C., and Dickson, R. B. (1999). Growth factors, apoptosis, and survival of mammary epithelial cells. Journal of Mammary Gland Biology and Neoplasia *4*, 229-237.

Serra-Majem, L., La Vecchia, C., Ribas-Barba, L., Prieto-Ramos, F., Lucchini, F., Ramon, J. M., and Salleras, L. (1993). Changes in diet and mortality from selected cancers in southern Mediterranean countries. European Journal of Clinical Nutrition *47*, S25-S34.

Shultz, T. D., Chew, B. P., and Seaman, W. R. (1992b). Differential stimulatory and inhibitory responses of human MCF-7 breast cancer cells to linoleic acid and conjugated linoleic acid in culture. Anticancer Research *12*, 2143-2145.

Shultz, T. D., Chew, B. P., Seaman, W. R., and Luedecke, L. O. (1992a). Inhibitory effect of conjugated dienoic derivatives of linoleic acid and beta-carotene on the in vitro growth of human cancer cells. Cancer Letters *63*, 125-133.

Simard, A., Vobecky, J., and Vobecky, J. S. (1991). Vitamin D deficiency and cancer of the breast: an unprovocative ecological hypothesis. Canadian Journal of Public Health *82*, 300-303.

Smith, R. J. (1982). Hawaiian Milk Contamination Creates Alarm. Science *217*, 136-140.

Trichopoulou, A., Katsouyanni, K., Stuver, S., Tzala, L., Gnardellis, C., Rimm, E., and Trichopoulos, D. (1995). Consumption of olive oil and specific food groups in relation to breast cancer risk in Greece. Journal of the National Cancer Institute *87*, 110-116.

Ursin, G., Bjelke, E., Heuch, I., and Vollset, S. E. (1990). Milk consumption and cancer incidence: a Norwegian prospective study. British Journal of Cancer *61*, 454-459.

Weisburger, J. H., Rivenson, A., Garr, K., and Cesar, A. (1997). Tea, or tea and milk, inhibit mammary gland and colon carcinogenesis in rats. Cancer Letters *114*, 323-327.

Westin, J. B. (1993). Carcinogens in Israeli milk: a study in regulatory failure. International Journal of Health Services *23*, 497-517.

Xue, L., Lipkin, M., Newmark, H., and Wang, J. (1999). Influence of dietary calcium and vitamin D on diet-induced epithelial cell hyperproliferation in mice. Journal of the National Cancer Institute *91*, 176-181.

Yanagi, S., Yamashita, M., and Imai, S. (1993). Sodium butyrate inhibits the enhancing effect of high fat diet on mammary tumorigenesis. Oncology *50*, 201-204.

Yuan, J. M., Wang, Q. S., Ross, R. K., Henderson, B. E., and Yu, M. C. (1995). Diet and breast cancer in Shanghai and Tianjin, China. British Journal of Cancer *71*, 1353-1358.

Zhang, S., Hunter, D. J., Forman, M. R., Rosner, B. A., Speizer, F. E., Colditz, G. A., Manson, J. E., Hankinson, S. E., and Willett, W. C. (1999). Dietary carotenoids and vitamins A, C, and E and risk of breast cancer. Journal of the National Cancer Institute *91*, 547-556.

Index